DRAMATISTS
AND THE
BOMB

Recent Titles in
Contributions in Drama and Theatre Studies

DRAMATISTS
AND THE
BOMB

American and British Playwrights
Confront the Nuclear Age, 1945–1964

Charles A. Carpenter

Contributions in Drama and Theatre Studies, Number 91

GREENWOOD PRESS
Westport, Connecticut • London

Library of Congress Cataloging-in-Publication Data

Carpenter, Charles A.
    Dramatists and the bomb : American and British playwrights
confront the nuclear age, 1945–1964 / Charles A. Carpenter.
        p.   cm.—(Contributions in drama and theatre studies, ISSN
    0163–3821 ; no. 91)
    Includes bibliographical references (p.   ) and index.
    ISBN 0–313–30713–X (alk. paper)
    1. American drama—20th century—History and criticism.
2. Nuclear warfare and literature—United States—History—20th
century.   3. Nuclear warfare and literature—Great Britain—
History—20th century.   4. English drama—20th century—History and
criticism.   5. Apocalyptic literature—History and criticism.
6. Antinuclear movement in literature.   7. Atomic bomb victims in
literature.   8. Atomic bomb in literature.   9. War in literature.
I. Title.   II. Series.
PS338.N83C37   1999
812'.5409358—dc21   98–37715

British Library Cataloguing in Publication Data is available.

Library of Congress Catalog Card Number: 98–37715
ISBN: 0–313–30713–X
ISSN: 0163–3821

First published in 1999

Greenwood Press, 88 Post Road West, Westport, CT 06881
An imprint of Greenwood Publishing Group, Inc.
www.greenwood.com

Printed in the United States of America

The paper used in this book complies with the
Permanent Paper Standard issued by the National
Information Standards Organization (Z39.48–1984).

10 9 8 7 6 5 4 3 2 1

Copyright Acknowledgments

The author and publisher gratefully acknowledge permission for use of the following material:

A revised version of Charles A. Carpenter, "A 'Dramatic Extravaganza' of the Projected Atomic Age: *Wings Over Europe* (1928)," originally published in *Modern Drama* 35 (1992): 552–61, is printed by permission of *Modern Drama*.

A revised version of Charles A. Carpenter, "American Dramatic Reactions to the Birth of the Atomic Age," originally published in *The Journal of American Drama and Theatre* 7, no. 3 (Fall 1995): 13–29, is printed by permission of *The Journal of American Drama and Theatre*—CASTA.

A revised version of Charles A. Carpenter, "Shaw's Dramatic Reactions to the Birth of the Atomic Age," originally published in *SHAW: The Annual of Bernard Shaw Studies* 18 (1998): 173–79, is reprinted by permission of SHAW.

Excerpts from Upton Sinclair, *A Giant's Strength* (Girard, KA: Haldeman-Julius, 1948) are reprinted by permission of The Bertha Klausner International Literary Agency.

Excerpts from Herman Wouk, *The Traitor: A Play in Two Acts* (New York: French, 1949) are reprinted by permission of BSW Literary Agency.

Excerpts from Cornel Lengyel, *The Atom Clock* as revised in *Poet Lore* 64 (1969): 435–57, are reprinted by permission of Cornel Lengyel.

Excerpts from Bernard Shaw, *Buoyant Billions, Farfetched Fables*, and newspaper articles, are reprinted by permission of The Society of Authors on behalf of the Bernard Shaw Estate.

Excerpts from Marghanita Laski, *The Offshore Island: A Play in Three Acts* (London: Cresset Press, 1959) [Laski/2.4.98], are reprinted by permission of David Higham Associates Limited.

Excerpts from Doris Lessing, *Each His Own Wilderness* in *New English Dramatists*, edited by E. Martin Browne (Harmondsworth: Penguin, 1959), 11–95; reprinted in Lessing, *Play with a Tiger and Other Plays* (London: Flamingo, 1996). Copyright © 1959 Doris Lessing. Reprinted by kind permission of Jonathan Clowes Ltd., London, on behalf of Doris Lessing.

Excerpts from Robert Bolt, *The Tiger and the Horse* in his *Three Plays* (London: Heinemann, 1963), 209–307. Copyright © Robert Bolt 1961. Reprinted by permission of Casarotto Ramsay Ltd. All rights whatsoever in this play are strictly reserved and application for performance etc., must be made before rehearsal to Casarotto Ramsay Ltd., National House, 60–66 Wardour Street, London W1V 4ND. No performance may be given unless a license has been obtained.

Excerpts from David Campton, *Laughter and Fear: Nine One-Act Plays* (London: Blackie, 1969) are reprinted by permission of David Campton.

Excerpts from Samuel Beckett, *Endgame* (New York: Grove Press, 1958) are reprinted by permission of Grove Press.

Excerpts from "Edward Albee Interviewed by Digby Diehl," *Transatlantic Review* 13 (Summer 1963): 72, are reprinted by permission of Digby Diehl.

Excerpts from "The State of the Theater: Interview by Henry Brandon [with Arthur Miller]," *Harper's Magazine* 221 (November 1960): 69, are reprinted by permission of Arthur Miller.

Excerpts from *Dramatists in America: Letters of Maxwell Anderson, 1912–1958*, edited by Laurence G. Avery. Copyright © 1977 by the University of North Carolina Press. Excerpts from *A Southern Life: Letters of Paul Green, 1916–1981*, edited by Laurence G. Avery. Copyright © 1994 by the University of North Carolina Press. Used by permission of the publisher.

Dedicated to my four cherished daughters, Carol, Linda, Janet, and Diane. Born and raised in the years of escalating nuclear terror, they are now free of the atomic sword of Damocles that was poised above all of our heads.

Contents

Personal Prologue

This might be called a brief subconscious history of a book about the Nuclear Age. So many people asked me how I could spend years studying, teaching, and writing about such a thing that I tried to figure it out. My daughters, to whom this book is dedicated, were certainly big factors. But the underground activity of my imagination was the biggest.

When the first atomic bomb dropped, I was a sports-obsessed teenager. After an appalled shake of the head I forgot the event. A movie newsreel of the elegant white mushroom cloud and the gray debris that had been downtown Hiroshima reawakened my awareness, but as far as I knew these images had little impact on me. In college, despite the presence of many veterans who might have had to invade Japan but for the Bomb and the spate of interminable bull sessions (in which world affairs did occasionally intrude upon religion and sex), I don't believe the Bomb was ever the topic of discussion, much less the new age that it begot. As a budding journalist I was vaguely aware of the Baruch plan, the Bikini tests, and the Berlin airlift, but I don't recall noticing the Soviets' proof that they too could blow up a city with a single explosion. Before beginning graduate work for my first career, I missed by an eyelash being drafted for the Korean War. All I did was sigh with mild relief, never realizing that I had escaped a conflict which in time threatened to become global and perhaps nuclear. As a full-time librarian (not a journalist after all) with a growing family during the mid-1950s, taking graduate courses at Cornell on the side, I had only glimmers of consciousness that the Thermonuclear Era was in full swing. H-bomb tests in the Pacific and over Siberia, Khrushchev's boast that "we will bury you," the film of *On the Beach*, even the warnings that my children might be ingesting strontium 90 through their milk had little apparent effect on me. I seemed to be surviving the worst years of the early Nuclear Age in relative obliviousness, a prime guinea pig for Robert Jay Lifton.

Then my first nuclear nightmare hit me. I was standing at the edge of the Morse Chain parking lot on South Hill in Ithaca looking down into the back yard of my house where my four daughters were playing. An atomic bomb exploded, and I watched my children gradually dissolve into black dust. That ghastly surreal dream recurred about once a week for a couple of months. Around that time a pleasant, low-keyed professor from whom I had taken a course gassed himself to death in his garage and left a note saying that he could not endure knowing that he had brought four children into this kind of a world. That's enough of an answer for people who say, Why would anyone write about *that*?

But the truth for me, as for most Americans, was that I still paid little attention to the nuclear situation. I recall Sputnik and the Cuban missile crisis quite distinctly, but I have no memory at all of my older children doing "duck and cover" drills in school (*they* remember them). By the mid-1960s the atmospheric test-ban treaty offered an excuse for nuclear lethargy and the Vietnam War an occasion for redirected political activism. The killing of four students at my first graduate school, Kent State University, aroused my anti-Establishment energies more than any nuclear event ever had. Watergate, Agnew's ouster, and Nixon's subsequent resignation became a cathartic process of getting even. Whatever happened on the nuclear front in the seventies didn't dent my consciousness.

Then along came the great communicator of nuclear terror, Ronald Reagan. The frantic escalation of the arms race that his administration brought, his characterization of the U.S.S.R. as an "evil empire," the loose talk about winnable and limited nuclear war, shook me as much as the Russians. I found myself starting courses in contemporary drama with the off-the-wall observation that at this very moment an H-bomb was targeted for our classroom (or at least for IBM across town, which added up to the same thing). Jonathan Schell's passionate, revelatory 1982 book, *The Fate of the Earth*, clinched the grip of my imagination on the current nuclear scene.

Actually launching a search for all the plays that dealt with the Nuclear Age, then writing about them, required lots of additional prompting. Arthur Kopit's *End of the World* was a major nudge. This ingeniously witty and incisive drama made it clear that the challenge of tackling the issue of nuclear terror honestly, yet in viable theatrical terms (the precise challenge Kopit received from financier Leonard Davis), could be met triumphantly. As I discovered one relevant play after another, most of them mediocre, I realized that few approached his success; Edward Bond's *War Plays* and Steven Dietz's *Foolin' Around with Infinity* were notable exceptions. But luckily, research is self-generating. I recall telling a mid-1980s seminar on the literature of the Nuclear Age that I had discovered *thirty* plays that fit into the bounds of the course, at least ten more than anyone else had listed. In the ensuing decade I came across fifty more.

By 1995 I had a huge sheaf of notes and two articles on nuclear dramas, but only nebulous plans for a book. Then it dawned on me that the methodology applied in Spencer Weart's *Nuclear Fear: A History of Images* might be adapted to a study of playwrights: move between the realities of nuclear events, the perceptions of them in the public mind (often a warped version), and the ways they are projected in dramatic works. Among other things, this made the wealth of playwrights' comments on various aspects of the nuclear situation in memoirs, letters, interviews and the like that I had uncovered just as integral as the plays some of them wrote (or began writing). Both reveal in their own ways the attempts of sensitive literary artists to express the effects of nuclear stimuli on their intellects and imaginations. My subject was not just "Dramas of the Nuclear Age" but "Dramatists and the Bomb." The book would be two-thirds dramatic criticism but one-third investigative journalism. To keep it within bounds, I had to treat only English-language dramatists and (for now) only the first major phase of the nuclear era. All I needed was time, and I had retirement for that. Later I learned that I also needed incredible expertise at securing permissions to quote without ruining chapters, bankrupting myself, or spoiling my retirement. But that intrusion of sordid reality is not integral to this psychic autobiography of a book in process. It did not affect my imagination.

Acknowledgments

I owe my greatest debt of gratitude to four people whose comments and leads actually contributed valuable substance to this book. The first two are playwrights whose work I discuss, Cornel Lengyel and David Campton; both were disarmingly gracious and forthcoming. The others are scholars who went out of their way to assist me: John Ahouse, the Upton Sinclair bibliographer, and James Knowlson, perhaps the world's leading authority on Samuel Beckett. Footnotes spell out the specific contributions of these four. I also wish to acknowledge the following people for significant small favors: Arthur Miller, Fred D. Crawford, Digby Diehl, David Greenebaum, John Vernon, and Irmgard Wolfe. My wife Martha read parts of the manuscript and served incessantly as my sounding board, but I am most thankful simply for her presence and patience during long hours of working on this project.

Three sections of this book contain material which has been published in somewhat different form: Chapter 2, "A 'Dramatic Extravaganza' of the Projected Atomic Age: *Wings Over Europe* (1928)," appeared in *Modern Drama* 35 (1992): 552–61; much of Chapter 3 appeared as "American Dramatic Reactions to the Birth of the Atomic Age" in *Journal of American Drama and Theatre* 7 (Fall 1995): 13–29; and the Shaw section in Chapter 4 appeared as "Shaw's Dramatic Reactions to the Birth of the Atomic Age" in *SHAW: The Annual of Bernard Shaw Studies* 18 (1998): 173–79. I am grateful to the journals' editors for permission to reprint these articles.

Introduction

Dramatists and the Bomb: American and British Playwrights Confront the Nuclear Age, 1945–1964 treats a hitherto unexamined dimension of cultural history: the responses of a particular group of American and British writers, the playwrights, to the provocations of new nuclear weapons and the Cold War. The book deals with the measured, clear-cut reactions of these playwrights, whether in a theatrical or discursive context. From the standpoint of its reactive content the book serves as a modest supplement to such invaluable studies as Spencer R. Weart's *Nuclear Fear: A History of Images* and Paul Boyer's *By the Bomb's Early Light: American Thought and Culture at the Dawn of the Atomic Age.*[1] But the primary focus is interactive: in discussing plays, the book spells out relationships between elements of the literary work and elements in the current nuclear situation, thus illuminating obscurities in plot, theme, and dialogue and identifying qualities that are derivative or innovative. No book (or series of articles) that covers the same ground as this one exists. The relevant fiction of the period has been classified and described, and a recent volume examines the poetry written by Americans.[2] But no study of America's or Britain's nuclear-age drama which is anywhere near comprehensive has been published—not even a checklist of relevant plays.[3]

None of the dramatic works of the early period is a neglected masterpiece. Those I have discovered, roughly a dozen each from the United States and Great Britain, often deal tentatively or awkwardly with their intimi-

dating subjects, and there are no stunning exemplars comparable to Max
Frisch's *The Chinese Wall* (1955) or Friedrich Dürrenmatt's *The Physicist*
(1962). The most impressive English-language dramas come much later,
notably Arthur Kopit's *End of the World* (1984) and Edward Bond's *The
War Plays* (1985). Taken as a group, however, these plays reflect the prevailing climate of thoughtful response to the early Nuclear Age in the re-
spective countries of the dramatists. Each play also exemplifies the groping
for artistic means to project images of human beings acting and reacting
in a world newly dominated by the reality of atomic power. The means,
in this case, are dramatic and theatrical—not simply to be experienced
privately, as with poetry and fiction, but also publicly, as only in the per-
forming arts. Though few of these plays were performed enough to have
much impact in the theatre, nearly all were written with the contingencies
of performance in mind. Their dramatic materials and strategies are interesting and revealing enough to warrant resurrecting them from the almost
total neglect they have received so far.

Generally speaking, the American plays tend to be inferior to the British.
For one thing, few American dramatists of this period who could be called
prominent (and thus promising) wrote plays that tackle nuclear concerns.
The nonliterary reactions of these dramatists are interesting in their own
right, however, and that is one reason why this book also embraces nondramatic responses. Several major American playwrights made significant
statements about atomic or hydrogen bombs, the arms race, the threat of
nuclear war or some related issue, and at least three reached the planning
stage of a nuclear drama. The only important American playwright to finish
a drama of the early Nuclear Age before 1964 was Lorraine Hansberry—
a short play that was not published or performed until 1972. However,
Thornton Wilder, Clifford Odets, and Arthur Miller all left accounts of
abortive attempts to write one; and Wilder, Miller, and Hansberry, along
with Edward Albee, Maxwell Anderson, and Paul Green, made revealing
comments on the nuclear situation. (Green even telegraphed President Truman protesting the decision to withhold atomic information from Soviet
scientists.[4]) Moreover, the works that lesser playwrights completed are by
no means negligible in interest or quality, whether the conventional dramas
of such recognizable names as Upton Sinclair, Herman Wouk, and Dore
Schary or the theatrical experiments of Hallie Flanagan, Cornel Lengyel,
Arch Oboler, and Ruth Angell Purkey. Lengyel's *The Atom Clock* (1950),
for instance, is a surprisingly effective poetic drama.

Four fairly prominent British dramatists completed full-length stage plays
on nuclear themes, and one wrote a drama for television which has been
published. Not coincidentally, all five were outspoken antinuclear activists:
J. B. Priestley, Doris Lessing, Robert Bolt, Bernard Kops, and David Mercer. But the most daring and impressive play of the period, *The Offshore
Island*, was written by a semi-popular novelist (and early feminist), Mar-

ghanita Laski; and the most fascinating theatrical experiments were created by a little-known admirer of Ionesco, David Campton. (Laski and Campton were also activists.) The most engrossing reflections on nuclear issues were written by two elderly Irish expatriates, Bernard Shaw and Sean O'Casey, and two new-wave dramatists, Arnold Wesker and John Osborne. Parts of two Shaw plays, *Buoyant Billions* and *Farfetched Fables*, directly reflect his public statements on the pros and cons of atomic discoveries, showing how close the link can be between dramatic and rhetorical expression.

The Nuclear Age has two distinct crescendoes, each followed by a diminuendo. The second crescendo is close to us all: the Reagan-Weinberger nuclear saber-rattling 1980s; we all welcomed the incredible dénouement, the end of the Cold War with the dissolution of the Soviet Union. The present study treats the period of the first crescendo. This commenced, of course, with the dropping of the atomic bombs on Hiroshima and Nagasaki by U.S. aircraft on August 6 and 9, 1945. It encompasses Russia's unexpectedly early demonstration of an atomic capability in 1949, the emergence in both countries of the hydrogen bomb during the early 1950s (and in Great Britain in 1957), and the development of missiles armed with nuclear warheads in the later 1950s. The period culminated with two "on the brink" incidents: the conflict over German unification in 1961 which led to the construction of the Berlin wall, and the Cuban missile crisis in 1962. The diminuendo began after the Cuban crisis was resolved, and it settled on a plateau when the three nuclear powers agreed to ban atmospheric testing in late 1963. A "worldwide collapse of interest in nuclear war" ensued, according to Weart (262). This is no doubt true of openly expressed interest, but psychologists such as Robert Jay Lifton would say that nuclear fear, like bomb-testing, remained pervasive and simply moved underground.[5] Not surprisingly, a clear correlation exists between the active presence of nuclear anxiety and the writing of plays that reflect it. The production of American and British dramas related to the nuclear situation experienced the same two crescendoes and diminuendoes outlined above: about twenty-five plays were written from 1946 to 1964, only ten from 1965 to 1980, and about thirty from 1981 to 1989. I know of only one produced since the Cold War ended, and that remains unpublished.

From the standpoint of its impact on imaginative writers, the early Nuclear Age differs from the later one in two important respects. First, a sense of newness or immediacy accompanied the advent of one startling nuclear development after another, provoking the wide range of imaginative stimulants distinctive to it, from horror and despair to elation and desperate hope. Second, a sense of concreteness or substantiality accompanied the graphic images of wasted Hiroshima, A-bomb explosions in Nevada and H-bomb tests in Bikini and Siberia, Sputnik cruising overhead, schoolchildren learning to "duck and cover," and President Kennedy talking firmly on television about the missiles in "Cuber." These events and their effects dwindled into memory for those who had experienced them (and often relived them in nightmares) and became mere historical data for those who had not. The contrast is compactly expressed by the narrator in Steven Dietz's 1988 play *Foolin' Around with Infinity*: "This was, after all, the 'if-it-happens-it-happens-80's' and not the 'prepare-for-the-worst-50's.' "[6] The attitude that evolved emerges comically in two other plays of the 1980s: a character in Michael Snelgrove's *Sleep Tight Tonight* is called "An Englishman to the last—facing Armageddon with a joke on his stiff upper lip"[7]; and a Hollywood starlet anticipating a nuclear attack in Jean-Claude van Itallie's *Sunset Freeway* manages to say, "It could drop right now. What if it did? I'd be eating doritos."[8] The period this book deals with is the one recalled from his childhood by William Cowling, the protagonist of Tim O'Brien's novel *The Nuclear Age*:

> I was a frightened child. At night I'd toss around in bed for hours, battling the snagged sheets, and then when sleep finally came, sometimes close to dawn, my dreams would be clotted with sirens and melting ice caps and radioactive gleamings and ICBMs whining in the dark.
>
> I was a witness. I saw it happen. In dreams, in imagination, I watched the world end.[9]

In a much broader perspective, the period 1946 to about 1965 was the heyday of the Literature of the Absurd. The gradual evolution of World War II into the most widespread and indiscriminately destructive war in history, the beastly atrocities of the Holocaust, and the invention and questionable use of atomic weapons with unlimited potential for extinction-enhancement added up to a kind of can-you-top-this game of man's inhumanity to man. The shock of recognition from glaring, undeniable evidence of these wartime revelations drained life of significance and possibility for many thinkers. Samuel Beckett reiterated Democritus's "Nothing is more real than nothing" both literally and metaphorically throughout his work. Events seemed to confirm Albert Camus's thumbnail sketch of the human condition as Absurd Man, irresistibly craving purpose and meaning (waiting for Godot) in a universe which, if it had any purpose or meaning, kept it inaccessible. In 1963 Edward Albee communicated this feeling in an informal but cogent comparison of writers' states of mind before and after the 1940s:

> Maybe there were easier answers [then] than there are now in the sixties, even indeed than there were in the fifties. . . . We were gullible, naive, and we also did not have at that point, potential for destroying ourselves quite so efficiently as we have now. The existentialist and

post-existentialist revaluation of the nature of reality and what everything is about in man's position to it came shortly after the 2nd World
War. I don't think that it is an accident that it gained the importance
in writers' minds that it has now as a result of the bomb at Hiroshima.
We developed the possibility of destroying ourselves totally and completely in a second. The ideals, the totems, the panaceas don't work
much anymore and the whole concept of absurdity is a great deal less
absurd now than it was before about 1945.[10]

The decline of the fiction and drama of the Absurd as distinct forms
began not with the evaporation of this consciousness, but with its gradual
transmutation from a new and intense feeling to a tacit assumption, a *donée*
to which attention no longer had to be called. Like nuclear fear and bomb-
testing, it went underground. The esteemed chronicler of the Theatre of the
Absurd, Martin Esslin, locates its decline in the mid-1960s. As a "genuine
contribution to the permanent vocabulary of dramatic expression," he
states, the form became "part of the everyday vocabulary of playwriting in
general."[11] But its wasted landscapes, dead-end and cyclical actions, grotesque and maimed beings engaged in halting or nonsensical dialogue—in
short its most flagrant reflections of the doom-ridden worldview during the
early Nuclear Age—became "yesterday's fashion" (430). Interestingly, as
early as 1960 Arthur Miller prophesied this decline with direct reference
to the nuclear situation:

One thing the theater will not stand for too long . . . is boredom. The
blue play is now becoming predictable in mood. We expect a pathetic
defeat in the play and the documentation of alienated loneliness. I
think they're quite suddenly going to become old hat.
   Perhaps it is only my feeling; but I think life is now perhaps less
impossible than it was, say, even two years ago. And this is as much
a political and social fact as it is a theatrical fact. I mean to say that
the possibility of the survival of the human race now appears to be
a reasonable hope for a person to take hold of. Certain steps have
been taken that would indicate that a rapprochement of some sort
can be made between two civilizations.
   . . . I think there are indications that we may have a right to state
once again that all is not lost. And as soon as that really happens,
the black air surrounding many plays may appear unjustified; it will
not long seem the way things are; and the style itself will seem willful
and self-conscious.[12]

Miller of course is not simply referring to the more dismal plays of the
Theatre of the Absurd in this interview, but to all of the "blue" or "black"
plays of the period.

Few dramas that are discussed in this book have much in common artistically with the works described by Esslin. Chapter 7 treats a thoroughly Absurd work, Samuel Beckett's *Endgame,* but only because an exploration of its subtle Nuclear Age analogies and metaphors was overdue and, I think, proves illuminating. The relevant plays of David Campton are the only ones whose affinities with the Theatre of the Absurd are noteworthy. Nevertheless, underlying many of the plays I discuss is the same sense of futility and rootlessness that inflicts Absurd literature. Writing not long after the first atomic bombs were dropped, and referring just as much to other horrors of the war as to that one, Maxwell Anderson attributed "the present impotence of the theatre" to one basic cause:

> For the first time in our history the majority of thinking people have come up against a crippling lack of faith. . . . Now a good play cannot be written except out of conviction—for or against—and when convictions wobble the theatre wobbles. . . . [W]e are beginning to wonder whether there are standards based on anything firmer than a desire to survive. . . . The fission of the atom adds to our confusion, of course. With unlimited power in a few hands it grows doubtful that democracy can operate much longer, and democracy . . . was about all we had left to cling to. Only the insensitive and the fanatics remain unconfused at present—and they don't write good plays.[13]

Bernard Shaw might have said exactly the same thing (about everything but democracy).

In later years "fanatics" did emerge who wrote quite good plays, notably the British antinuclear protestants mentioned above. However, even the most positive of them, Bernard Kops, went no further than to summon humanity to "Sing over the abyss." Their heroes and heroines consistently manifest a deep sense of helplessness or chaos in the face of the Bomb; they protest in the spirit of Robert Bolt's Stella in *The Tiger and the Horse* who, after agreeing with her thoroughly pessimistic father that "nothing will stop humanity from using that thing" (a sentiment Bolt himself expressed), insists that protesting "is something we can do. When we've done what we can do, then's the time to worry about what we can't do."[14] On the other side of the coin, no playwright of this period seems to have been able (or willing) to write a simple, unqualified Protest Play, sub-genre Antinuclear. The distinguished drama critic Kenneth Tynan issued an eloquent call for this kind of drama in 1957:

> Dramatists who want to change the world seldom write very subtly, and there is no reason why they should. Subtlety operates best in a *status quo,* just as ripples are best seen in a standing pool. In a stormy sea only waves are visible; and we, who live in imminent danger of

the hydrogen tempest, need plays that are waves, and big, crashing ones at that. . . . If all art is a gesture against death, it must not stand by while Cypriots are hanged and Hungarians machine-gunned, and the greater holocaust prepares.[15]

As far as I have been able to determine, no protest play in print meets his agitprop standards (though Upton Sinclair's comes close). Most of the playwrights, to their credit, chose to present both sides of issues and to focus on the personal complexities that accompany antinuclear activism.

The scope of this book should be clear if readers bear in mind that its subtitle says "playwrights *confront* the Nuclear Age." I describe at least briefly every original American or British dramatic work I could find which comes to grips with a major aspect of the nuclear situation, and I selectively quote or paraphrase statements that fill the same bill. Plays are ruled out of consideration if their connections are too fragmentary and unserious or their analogies too remote. For example, the "Civil War" section in the collaborative satire *Beyond the Fringe* is not only brief but trivial; in Charles Morgan's *The Burning Glass*, the intercontinental super-flamethrower controlled by an isolated scientist-inventor bears little resemblance to atomic weapons in the hands of superpowers. One not-far-under-the-borderline case should clarify the level of exclusion (and lighten up the proceedings): a successful three-act play by Spike Milligan and John Antrobus, *The Bedsitting Room*.[16] It takes place during the "first anniversary of the Nuclear Misunderstanding which led to World War Three" and killed forty-eight million Britishers in two and a half minutes, and is gradually killing everyone else with radiation sickness (10). The play begins with a silent film of an H-bomb test and has a few grim moments, some involving mutant babies. But the predominant mode of the play is madcap farce, as one might expect from authors who were involved in the popular Goon Show. Lunatic improbabilities prevail: the new queen turns into a chest of drawers; Prime Minister Wilson becomes a parrot; the bedsitting room is Lord Fortnum, transformed, until he re-transforms into God. The degree of seriousness about nuclear war is conveyed by the play's best joke: during the war Captain Pontius Kak sent the £500 million "British deterrent" to Russia, but it was returned to sender because the postage was nine pence short. Captain Kak pleads, "We had to economise somewhere" (58–59).

All the plays were written or fully conceived before 1964, but not necessarily performed or published by that year. Adaptations of others' works, such as two that tried to capitalize on the popularity of Pat Frank's novels, were excluded—although I would have broken this rule if the new version had attained original qualities worth noting. Another basic criterion was availability in published form, since otherwise I would have to rely on others' descriptions. This eliminated most plays written for television. However, I characterize a few of the most noteworthy unpublished stage and television plays in footnotes (such as Donald Ogden Stewart's fantasy *How I Wonder* and Peter Shaffer's TV melodrama *Balance of Terror*), and I describe a full-length drama that Upton Sinclair left unpublished, "Doctor Fist," not only because no other description seems to exist but also because it revises the history of J. Robert Oppenheimer as if he were a latter-day Dr. Faustus.

The most notable exclusions are of course plays from countries other than the United States and Great Britain. I have only discovered one of these that was written originally in English: *Pacific Paradise* by the Australian Dymphna Cusack. Inspired by the film "Children of Hiroshima" and first performed in 1955, this earnest but hokey antinuclear propaganda play became a staple of protest meetings in Australia and socialist countries during the 1950s and 1960s. It features a conflict between the strongminded natives of a South Pacific island called Tinika and a monolithic International Atomic Control Board which is intent on carrying out a hydrogen bomb test in that area. The Tinikans not only resist heroically, but expose the evil means that "Inter-Atom" uses to achieve its ends. They manage to spread their story around the world by amateur radio transmission, and in the nick of time incite enough indignation to cause the enemy to cancel the test.[17] As for foreign-language plays, in addition to those by Frisch and Dürrenmatt mentioned above, I have come across the following:

1948:   Oskar Wessel, *Hiroshima* (radio play published in 1962)

1950:   Eduardo De Filippo, *La paura numero uno*

1952:   Henri Pichette, *Nucléa*

1955:   Carl Zuckmayer, *Das kalte Licht*

1955:   Hotta Kiyomi, *The Island* (translated from Japanese)

1955:   Wolfgang Weyrauch, *Die japanischen Fischer* (radio play)

1956:   George Soria, *L'Orgueil et la nuée*

1958:   Günther Weisenborn, *Die Familie von Nevada* (later entitled *Die Familie von Makabah*)

1958:   Weisenborn, *Göttinger Kantate*

1958:   Tanaka Chikao, *The Head of Mary* (translated from Japanese)

1959:   Hans Henny Jahnn, *Die Trümmer des Gewissens* (posthumously staged in 1961 as *Der staubige Regenbogen*)

1960:   Alberto Mechoulam, *Bombe atomiche*

1962:   Ana Inés Bonnín, *La difícil esperanza*

1962:   Betsuyaku Minoru, *The Elephant* (translated from Japanese)

1963:   Gabriel Cousin, *Le Drame du Fukuryu-Maru*

1963:   Edmundo Rivera Álvarez, *El cielo se rindió al amanecer*

1964:   Alfred Fabre-Luce, *La Bombe*[18]

The first chapter of this book presents a selective account of key nuclear-related events and issues in the early period as a "context of provocations" for the varied responses of playwrights. Further details of a given aspect are offered when they promise to throw light on particular dramas or statements. Thus, for example, the main reasons for the rise of antinuclear protest in the late 1950s are noted in Chapter 1, but the specific provocations for the extensive involvement of English playwrights in such protest are saved for the chapter that treats these writers. Chapter 2 discusses the only genuine precursor of nuclear-age drama, *Wings Over Europe*, written in 1928 by Robert Nichols and Maurice Browne. This is a flawed but fascinating drama of ideas about a projected Atomic Age, complete with a Shellyan scientific genius and a doomsday weapon which he almost sets off. Chapters 3 and 4 of the book take up, successively, American and British playwrights' reactions to the birth of the Atomic Age; Chapters 5 and 6, the various ways they confronted the early Thermonuclear Era. The final chapter isolates three plays that deal with the dilemma of fallout-shelter owners who face non-family members clamoring to enter: an American television play and an English courtroom drama, where the issue is overt and explicit, and Beckett's *Endgame*, where it is one dimension of an ambiguous metaphorical and analogical structure. Some time in the future I hope to explore the dramatic developments of the later Thermonuclear Era.

The terms I have employed in discussing facets of the nuclear situation need to be clarified at the start. All nuclear weapons are atomic weapons, but in common usage the term "atomic bomb" (or "atom bomb") refers to fission bombs, the kind used on Japan, and the terms "hydrogen bomb" and "thermonuclear bomb" denote the much more powerful fusion bombs.[19] I have adopted this somewhat illogical but convenient distinction, and have extended it to calling the immediate post-Hiroshima period the Atomic Age and the post-H-bomb period the Thermonuclear Era. The Nuclear Age through 1964, then, comprises the Atomic Age and the early Thermonuclear Era. Again following common practice, I have used "the Bomb" to designate a generic nuclear threat (as in my title), but "the bomb" for a particular kind the text has referred to. Obviously some of the playwrights and authorities I quote have not followed this practice, but the hobgoblin consistency seems worth pursuing in my own exposition.

A few forewarnings about quotations and citations are necessary. Quoting from plays, I remain faithful to the distinctive formats of the printed texts in giving characters' names and stage directions. However, I rarely follow the hyper-punctilious practice of italicizing stage directions when no dialogue accompanies them; *"She looks skyward toward the roar"* should be muted, not emphatic. Unspaced ellipses within quotations are the original author's; spaced ellipses indicate omissions from the text. In footnotes, for the convenience of readers I give full bibliographical data the first time a source is quoted in *each chapter*. Later citations of the same source within a chapter are given in the text. In citing the *Bulletin of the Atomic Scientists*, I use *BAS* after the first reference.

CHAPTER 1

A Context of Provocations: The Early Nuclear Age

THE BIRTH OF THE ATOMIC AGE

The atomic bomb that decimated Hiroshima on August 6, 1945, was not remarkable mainly for its effects on the war or even on the people it vaporized, maimed, traumatized, or poisoned. It was remarkable mainly for its impact on the human imagination. Two days after the event, a *New York Times* columnist said that the bomb caused "an explosion in men's minds as shattering as the obliteration of Hiroshima."[1] The bomb single-handedly stamped ghastly imprints on the human consciousness, starkly etched with images of a flash "brighter than a thousand suns," buildings disintegrating, human flesh melting, a burgeoning mushroom cloud, and eerie "black rain." For many it was a vision of apocalypse, prefiguring the extermination of mankind by man's own hand. The destruction of Dresden and Tokyo by incendiary bombs took a similar toll, but did not provoke such an extravagant, almost surreal reaction.[2] President Truman's initial announcement specified the crucial difference: "It is an atomic bomb. It is a harnessing of the basic power of the universe."[3]

In a famous editorial published only twelve days after Hiroshima, "Modern Man Is Obsolete," Norman Cousins announced the birth of the Atomic Age. He foresaw that it would have a "saturating effect . . . , permeating every aspect of man's activities, from machines to morals, from physics to philosophy, from politics to poetry."[4] By mid-1946 the most renowned scientist in the world, Albert Einstein, could declare: "Today the atomic bomb has altered profoundly the nature of the world as we knew it, and the human race consequently finds itself in a new habitat to which it must adapt its thinking."[5] In his rich retrospective study, *By the Bomb's Early Light: American Thought and Culture at the Dawn of the Atomic Age*, Paul Boyer describes the bomb as "a profoundly unsettling new cultural factor" which "transformed not only military strategy and international relations, but the fundamental ground of culture and consciousness."[6] Just as strategists now had to "think the unthinkable," writers were now compelled to imagine the unimaginable. For most people, atomic weapons meant first and foremost the possibility of atomic warfare and the dreaded consequences that might ensue. But for others, the foreshadowing of apocalypse bred its own counteracting agents: phoenix-like, dreams emerged of a world in which peace was now mandatory because war was out of the question and atomic energy would bring a great boon to mankind rather than just a great boom. In whatever ways the new reality impinged on fantasy, the potentialities of atomic power remained a central preoccupation of imaginative life in the aftermath of Hiroshima. Since then, as two American poets have expressed it, we have all been "on the road from Hiroshima"; Hiroshima "flows through us."[7]

The Bomb exerted a pervasive political influence for a time. It spurred immediate interest in creating an international agency to control atomic power, and beyond that a world government with a structure far more cohesive than the current one of the United Nations. Cousins said that "the greatest obsolescence of all in the Atomic Age is national sovereignty" (20). Einstein put it more forcefully: "In the light of new knowledge, a world authority and an eventual world state are not just *desirable* in the name of brotherhood, they are *necessary* for survival" (7). Even the subsequent arch-promoter of the H-bomb, Edward Teller, thought that one of the "clear-cut duties" of scientists was "to work for a world government which alone can give us freedom and peace."[8] However, American proposals for an international control agency, such as the Baruch plan, did not attract wide approval in the United States and were firmly rejected by the Soviet Union. This knocked the crucial prop out from under the world-government movement. Continued expansionism by the Soviets, their blockade of Berlin in 1948 (circumvented by the amazingly successful airlift), and finally their explosion of an atomic device in September 1949, established the Cold War as a going concern. The "clock of doom" on the cover of the *Bulletin of the Atomic Scientists* sums up the story symbolically. The editors had put it there in mid-1947 and set it at eight minutes to midnight because of "the slow progress of negotiations for the international control of atomic energy, on which all their hopes have centered since 1945."[9] After the Russian atomic explosion, they moved the hands to three minutes before doomsday. Gravely and accurately, they predicted the onset of "an open atomic arms race" which might well lead to "the abyss of an atomic war."[10]

Genuine prospects of war bred the first surge of interest in civil defense. In 1950 Communist North Korea invaded South Korea, a United Nations affair but largely an American war. In the same year Truman created the Federal Civil Defense Administration, which immediately "flooded the country with sixteen million copies of a booklet called *Survival Under Atomic Attack*; distributed a movie of the same title narrated by Edward R. Murrow; [and] prepared a civil-defense exhibit called Alert America that was hauled around the country by a convoy of ten tractor-trailer trucks" (Boyer, 322). According to Weart, sporadic talk about bomb shelters in the American press, spurred by Russia's 1949 explosion, "rose to a clamor" after the Korean war broke out (129). As would also happen in the early 1960s, the clamor soon subsided. Many public buildings were marked with black and yellow signs for use as shelters, but few were stocked with provisions, and comparatively few private shelters were built.

THE EVOLUTION OF THE THERMONUCLEAR ERA

The arms race took a giant leap forward early in the next decade. Against the advice of such luminaries as J. Robert Oppenheimer and Enrico Fermi, in January 1950 President Truman ordered the construction of the first thermonuclear weapon, dubbed the superbomb. Again Einstein was prescient as he defined the futile and perhaps fatal nature of the quest for nuclear superiority: "The ghostlike character of this development lies in its apparently compulsory trend. Every step appears as the unavoidable consequence of the preceding one. In the end there beckons more and more clearly general annihilation."[11] As early as November 1952 the world's first nuclear-fusion or hydrogen device, 700 times more powerful than the Hiroshima bomb, was exploded at Eniwetok. It was re-dubbed the Hell Bomb.[12] Spencer Weart observes, "From the outset everyone saw fusion as something that went farther even than fission bombs into the realm of apocalypse" (155). When the Soviets exploded their own fusion device a year later the clock of doom was changed again, giving Elmer Davis a title for his journalistic sum-up of the nuclear situation of the time, *Two Minutes to Midnight*. Davis called the period "Year One, Thermonuclear Era."[13] The year was capped, and the world stunned, by the American test at Bikini on March 1, 1954. The fifteen-megaton explosion was so stupendous that an experienced observer thought for a moment that its fireball might "swallow up the whole world."[14] Fallout sickened Marshall Islanders 100 miles away and mortally inflicted a crewman of the Japanese fishing vessel Lucky Dragon. From Weart's perspective, images of H-bomb tests gave rise to the idea that "releasing nuclear energy was a blasphemous and guilty horror, a violation of the entire planet" (184).

By the mid-1950s, the Cold War had evolved to the point where two superpowers who sharply opposed and mistrusted each other ideologically had also developed the capacity to inflict such profound damage that war between them should have been out of the question. Unfortunately it was still far from inconceivable. The full-blown Korean War, marked by the intervention of the new People's Republic of China, put America "in a full-dress shooting war with Communist soldiers" and "began a new phase of the Cold War."[15] McCarthyism fed on this tangible evidence of a "red peril" abroad to sanction its campaign to root out Communist sympathizers at home. Statesmen such as John Foster Dulles began to speak of "a global conflict between Good and Evil" in which "every nation must choose its side" (paraphrased in Moss, 106–7). NATO, formed in 1949, was matched by the Warsaw Pact in 1955. The concept of ultimate deterrence based on a "balance of terror," later called "Mutual Assured Destruction" or MAD, was tenuously installed as a foundation block of foreign policy in the United States and the Soviet Union. Great Britain soon joined the two superpowers. After developing and testing its own fission bomb by 1952, it began a program to develop an H-bomb (brought to fruition in 1957). Winston Churchill forecast the effect of his country's strategy by pointing out a "sublime irony" that applied to all three nuclear powers: a stage will be reached "where safety will be the sturdy child of terror, and survival the twin brother of annihilation."[16] Air Force generals at American nuclear bases reduced MAD to a simple paradox: "These weapons are useful only if they're never used" (Moss, 123).

The Cold War had a chance to thaw for a while after the end of the Korean War and the death of Stalin in 1953. The subsequent exposé/denunciation of the Stalinist regime's purges and other repressive policies was at once terribly disillusioning for long-term English and American leftists and at the same time an encouraging sign that the new regime would be more tractable. The Kremlin, Weisberger notes, was now "willing to talk of 'many roads to socialism' and of 'peaceful competition' with capitalism" (188). Meanwhile the public imagination was struck by revelations about the probable effects of radioactive fallout from atmospheric H-bomb tests, including such bugaboos as leukemia and genetic mutations. Everyone heard about traces of strontium-90 found in milk. This "fallout scare" provided momentum for antinuclear protest groups which had sprung up in 1957–58, to the extent that demonstrations by the National Committee for a Sane Nuclear Policy in the United States and the Campaign for Nuclear Disarmament in Great Britain became front-page news. (SANE used the catchy slogan, "No Contamination Without Representation.") In November 1958 the three nuclear powers agreed to suspend all bomb-testing as a prelude to negotiating disarmament, a moratorium that lasted until September 1961.

This hopeful trend in the later 1950s was periodically blighted. During the Suez crisis in 1956, the Soviet Union's thinly veiled nuclear threat frustrated the British and French, whose armies had to abandon their so-far successful attempt to regain control of the canal. In the same year the brutal Soviet suppression of the Hungarian revolt frustrated the American leadership, who had proclaimed that they would help satellite countries break from their iron bonds, but in reality could do little but urge the "freedom fighters" to keep resisting the Russian tanks. The arms race featured a competition among the nuclear powers to develop delivery systems for nuclear warheads. Polaris missiles to go on American nuclear submarines were in the planning stage when in October 1957 the Soviet Union's Sputnik I, propelled by the world's first intercontinental ballistic missile, gloated through its historic orbit. Weart describes the slightly irrational American reaction: "Unstoppable missiles had seemed like something for a remote science fiction future; suddenly they seemed like something that could drop on the United States next year. The American press erupted in almost hysterical alarm" (216). The more impressive Sputnik II followed closely, and panic arose that Russia could quickly build hundreds of missiles and tilt the balance of power severely. This embarrassment to a Republican administration helped John F. Kennedy win the 1960 election and gain a considerable increase in the defense budget. However, no "missile gap" materialized: by 1961 both the Soviet Union and the United States had about thirty ICBMs (Moss, 212). And the United States was far ahead in the production of nuclear warheads.

CLOSEST TO THE EDGE—AND BEYOND

In spite of the mixed results of Cold War activities in the late 1950s, the *Bulletin of the Atomic Scientists* saw fit to move its clock of doom back an encouraging five minutes at the start of the new decade. The editors chose to trust their sense that a positive drift in relations between America and the Soviet Union had occurred and boded well for the future. Eugene Rabinowitch wrote: "A new world of international cooperation is beginning to take shape under the frozen crust of the old world of self-centered nations deadlocked in power conflicts. . . . In our time, the survival and prosperity of any individual or group is becoming more and more obviously tied up with the well-being and security of mankind as a whole."[17] Unfortunately, just three years later the editor was compelled to report, "In 1962, mankind came as close as never before to the abyss of a nuclear war."[18] He was of course referring to the Cuban missile crisis of October 1962, but that was only the culminating incident in a series of disturbing events that brought the United States and their Soviet antagonists, in Weisberger's phrase, "Closest to the Edge."[19]

Fidel Castro had taken over Cuba in February 1959, a people's revolutionary triumphing over an exploitative dictatorship. But he soon emerged as an intolerable enemy of capitalism by seizing American properties. Forceful retaliation on the part of the U.S. government, from closing markets to severing diplomatic relations, led him into the open arms of Russian communists. Cuba soon became an "unthinkable Soviet foothold, ten minutes from Miami by jet plane" (Weisberger, 204). This new situation led inexorably to the disastrous Bay of Pigs invasion in April 1961, to Chairman Khrushchev sparring with President Kennedy over American complicity (much as he had sparred with President Eisenhower in 1960 over the U-2 incident), and to the Soviets secretly equipping Cuba with the best self-defense available, nuclear missiles.

Four months after the Bay of Pigs fiasco (as it is called even in retrospect), a crisis arose in divided Berlin. The West-German zone, isolated armed camp though it was, had become much more prosperous over the years than that of the East Germans, who lived under conditions of austerity and suppression. As a result, East Germans were abandoning their area by the thousands. A Soviet proposal to make Berlin a single independent city was flatly refused by the allied countries, who knew that their "island of freedom in a Communist sea" had to be shielded.[20] Khrushchev's vow in Kennedy's presence that he would grab Berlin within seven months and "fight anyone who tried to stop him" prompted Kennedy to reply, "It will be a cold winter."[21] The President then told the American people that he would request more funds for military expenditures, including an extensive civil defense program, and quietly advised building private fallout shelters as "insurance" against nuclear attack.[22] "Nothing could more clearly underline that the President was thinking the unthinkable," Weisberger says (212). Suddenly, starting on August 13, the Soviets erected a crude wall banked with barbed wire on the twenty-five-mile demarcation line through Berlin. The Kennedy government chose to do nothing provocative in response, and one of the prime symbols of the Nuclear Age was firmly established: a nearly literal "iron curtain." Two weeks later the Soviets resumed atmospheric bomb-testing, and on October 30 created another sharp stimulant for the imagination by exploding a fifty-eight-megaton H-bomb—three thousand times more powerful than the bomb dropped on Hiroshima. Speaking before the United Nations for the first time, Kennedy summed up the world situation graphically: "Every man, woman and child lives under a nuclear sword of Damocles, hanging by the slenderest of threads, capable of being cut at any moment by accident or miscalculation or by madness" (quoted in Fuller, 278). He went on to call for international nuclear disarmament.

This series of events incited great interest in private fallout shelters. In a special issue of *Life* magazine, President Kennedy personally urged Americans to consider building them.[23] London's *Economist* summed up the development in an editorial: "Since the barriers went up in Berlin and radioactive particles came down from the Russian nuclear tests the 'revival for survival' called for by the American civil defence authorities has generated its own mushroom cloud. Fall-out shelters make a daily appearance on the front pages of newspapers and in the advertisement columns."[24] Construction companies that suddenly specialized in building home shelters enjoyed a brief boom, but the chief result was widespread public debate.[25] Despite the general awareness, especially in England, that it would be futile to rely on public shelters which were largely situated in "ground zero" areas downtown, few private shelters were actually built.[26] Eugene Rabinowitch explained the feeling that evolved: "The only kind of shelter program which could have any effect on the outcome of a nuclear conflict would be a systematic effort directed from Washington. . . . Haphazard construction of shelters by individual citizens hoping to assure their own and their families' survival in a general holocaust will neither protect them, nor help their country as a whole."[27] Put in terms of the contemporary joke, "If going in one *did* save you, who would want to come out?"

After the passive resolution of the Berlin crisis, nearly a year passed without a nerve-wracking nuclear event. Russian-manned spaceships orbited the earth, but the Americans replied in kind. The Soviets were distracted by discord with Communist China, which was fast becoming a nuclear power. Few objected to underground nuclear tests carried out by the United States; the Soviet atmospheric explosions met some protest, but were found to be relatively "clean" of radioactive fallout. Then the United States discovered the Russian missiles in Cuba.

The complex twists and turns behind the scenes of this critical military and diplomatic crisis were largely kept hidden from public view, and in fact were not fully disclosed even after the Cold War was over.[28] What struck the public consciousness first was President Kennedy's grave announcement on October 22, 1962, that Russia had placed "offensive" missiles in Cuba, that this could not be tolerated, and that any missiles fired from Cuba would provoke "a full retaliatory response upon the Soviet Union" (Weisberger, 221). Norman Moss records the impression he received from his vantage point in England: "To millions of people all over the world, the crisis made thermonuclear war, with giant fireballs burning up the cities, possible for the first time. It seemed suddenly that it could *really happen*" (307). In Britain especially, he adds, "there was a widespread sense that the end might be at hand." Next came the suspenseful story of the Soviet reaction to the American blockade of their ships, the gratifying culmination of which evoked Secretary of State Dean Rusk's graphic one-liner: "We're eyeball to eyeball, and I think the other fellow just blinked." Few grasped the full import of the news five days later that an American spy plane had been shot down over Cuba and the pilot killed.[29] However, everyone welcomed the report on Sunday, October 28, that Russia had agreed to dismantle its missiles and take them back home, along with bombers and military personnel. The brink had been reached, and sanity had prevailed.

What followed was "a sudden rush of unaccustomed warmth in Soviet-American relations" (Weisberger, 226). Both sides worked earnestly for a comprehensive test-ban treaty as a genuine first step toward disarmament. Khrushchev called such a treaty a "noble and humane goal"; Kennedy summoned the two countries to put their differences aside and "help make the world safe for diversity" (226–27). Unfortunately, habitual distrust from advisers on both sides kept a necessary element in the treaty, on-site inspections at frequent intervals, from materializing. A severely reduced Partial Test Ban Treaty was finally signed on July 23, 1963: the Soviet Union, United States, and Great Britain agreed not to conduct nuclear tests in the atmosphere, outer space, or under water. Thus it permitted testing underground—and the United States actually increased its rate of testing in the ensuing years. But its double effect of reducing environmental damage from radioactive fallout and bringing an end to the stream of much-publicized *images* of nuclear explosions greatly pacified the general public.[30] The establishment of a "hot line" between Washington and Moscow to reduce the risk of accidental war was a welcome fringe benefit.

By moving its "clock of doom" back five more minutes in the immediate aftermath of the test-ban treaty, the *Bulletin of the Atomic Scientists* renewed its conviction, first stated in 1960 but quickly thrown into doubt, that "a new cohesive force has entered the interplay of forces shaping the fate of mankind, and is making the future of man a little less foreboding."[31] The journal's editor summed up in the New Year's issue: "The general— if largely unexpressed—reaction of people everywhere to the outcome of the Cuban crisis was that the big powers had looked into the medusa's face of nuclear war, and had shrunk before it. They were not likely soon again to engage in brinkmanship."[32] The series of favorable events also considerably muted public interest in nuclear concerns. Rabinowitch noted: "The abatement of the Cuban conflict, the test-ban treaty, and vague signs of rapprochement between the Soviet Union and the United States encouraged the public attention to turn in other directions. Recent polls and reports showed that war had been displaced as the paramount concern of Americans by more familiar domestic worries" (2). This change in emphasis was not confined to America: the whole world breathed an enormous sigh of relief. It was self-deluding, since the arms race continued and was poised to escalate in the 1980s, and it played into the hands of those interested in keeping the Western world divided into two excessively armed camps. But it was an understandable and well-deserved release of tension after eighteen years on a nuclear roller coaster, the last two calculated to singe the nerves of the hardiest souls.

CHAPTER 2

A "Dramatic Extravaganza" of the Projected Atomic Age: *Wings Over Europe* (1928)

The scientific seeds of the Nuclear Age had been planted long before they sprouted on August 6, 1945, as that ever-burgeoning mushroom cloud. In fact, as soon as the concepts of radioactivity, atom-splitting, and chain reactions reached the public eye, the vision of a world profoundly affected by atomic power began to grow in the minds of imaginative writers. From their fantasies emerged a projected Atomic Age (the banner-headline term they preferred). Not surprisingly, it featured the same dichotomy of atomic disaster and utopian transformation that marked the immediate post–A-bomb consciousness.

Most of these representations of a projected Atomic Age appeared in science fiction magazines, which welcomed the new reality-based genre. About fifteen full-length novels written before 1946 deal directly or obliquely with the theme.[1] Oddly, this quite copious literature includes only one work in dramatic form. Almost wholly neglected by scholars,[2] it is an interesting and highly symptomatic play which possesses distinctions well beyond its mere uniqueness. These stand out clearly by viewing the work in relation to earlier treatments of the same hypothesis, and by examining it as an unusual example of "Extravaganza," a dramatic genre that proved especially compatible for depicting the possibilities of a new Atomic Age.

The first and only work of drama to attempt this feat before 1946 is *Wings Over Europe: A Dramatic Extravaganza on a Pressing Theme*.[3] It was conceived by the little-known poet Robert Nichols (1893–1944), who then collaborated with an active man-of-the-theatre, Maurice Browne (1881–1955).[4] The play, although the work of Englishmen and set entirely at No. 10 Downing Street, was first produced by the New York Theatre Guild in 1928 and not in London until 1932.[5] It is a peculiar mixture of realism, fantasy, satire, and prophecy. The main character is Francis Light-foot, a twenty-five-year-old scientific genius (acclaimed by Einstein and Sir Ernest Rutherford, we hear). He confronts the Prime Minister and his Cab-inet with the astounding news that he has learned how to control the energy in the atom. The double-edged consequence, he proclaims, is that human beings are now capable of wiping out the civilized world, or—with suffi-cient will and organization—of transforming it into a utopia. Lightfoot is rapturously confident that his discovery can bring about a "New World, the Summer of Mankind, the Golden Age" (518)—and he is willing to use the destructive power that he controls to force that outcome, if necessary. The Cabinet members, skeptical and resistant to change, seem destined to make it necessary.

In the context of earlier speculations about the results of harnessing the atom, the basic situation in *Wings Over Europe* is typical rather than ex-ceptional. The dichotomy between hopes and terrors is a focal point of writings that grapple with the unfolding revelations of nuclear physics. The alternatives of destruction and transformation are most often pictured in apocalyptic terms, as virtual Armageddon or Millenium.[6] These alternatives are rarely viewed as mutually exclusive: Man *is* free to choose, and the fulcrum of choice is the awareness and beneficence of the men (always men) in control. The direct fictional ancestor of *Wings Over Europe* is H. G. Wells's *The World Set Free* (1913).[7] In this work as in the play, the threat of total destruction is a necessary prelude to the cooperative transformation of society. Wells's novel postulates the invention of atomic bombs as well as the exploitation of limitless atomic energy for peaceful purposes. These two developments interact to "set the world free." A devastating atomic war breaks out, and finally provokes world leaders to form a government that will promote "permanent and universal pacification" (185). Atomic energy eventually brings enrichment to everyone. "The atomic bombs burnt our way to freedom," a character states (228); a new Eden is the result. Wells's dedication notes his indebtedness to *The Interpretation of Radium* (1908) by Frederick Soddy, a brash but brilliant physicist to whom Francis Lightfoot bears some affinities. As early as 1903, Soddy ventured that con-trolling the atom might lead to a technology potent enough to destroy the planet, but might also produce a heaven on earth: "A race which could transmute matter . . . could transform a desert continent, thaw the frozen poles, and make the whole world one smiling Garden of Eden."[8] In Wells's humbling application of this dichotomy, terror of continued world destruc-tion becomes the propellant for short-sighted leaders to change their ways and make Utopia feasible, now that it is conceivable.

"To-day, for the first time in history, Man is free!" trumpets Francis Lightfoot to the Prime Minister of England in *Wings Over Europe* (510). The vision of a "world set free" that he projects is later scorned by the Secretary of War as a "sort o' Shaw-Wells Utopia" (531). Whereas Wells's novel patiently spells out a reasoned hypothesis of an ultimate welfare-state world (the "Shaw" connection) to a now-receptive audience, the play develops its vision in a series of idea-grenades hurled at a group predisposed to resist radical change.[9] Lightfoot is a "type of artist-scientist" (508) given to oracular rhapsodizing rather than sensible discourse. At the invitation of the Prime Minister (who also happens to be his uncle), he announces to an unprepared Cabinet: "To-day I put into your hands . . . ultimate power over matter; the power of—of a god, to slay and to make alive." Without a trace of reflexive irony he adds, "Incidentally it means food, shelter, abundance, for everyone" (518). Responding to questions from representatives of the law, the army, colonial interests, and the financial system, he declares that they are all in effect passé. Echoing Wells (and anticipating the concept of Mutual Assured Destruction), he envisions a world in which "all displays of force are equally criminal," simply because "either party is equally able to destroy the other." Thus all military forces plus the backbone of the present system of law, the police, "cease to exist" (519). If this aspect of his vision smacks of prophecy, others are tinged with alchemy. "If I want to change this table into gold, I can," Lightfoot says. The upshot is that the financial system, "which is founded on gold, has ceased to exist." Similarly the colonies, chiefly sources of much-needed raw materials, "cease to exist" as such. These staggering novelties so abruptly revealed (to paraphrase a minister) elicit such shocked and incredulous reactions that Lightfoot's response is a crescendo of arrogance: "Behave like adults; stop babbling like children about your departments. Wake up. All that stuff is totally and for ever scrapped. Put it out of your minds" (520). It is little wonder that someone dubs him "an infant gas-bag" (521).

The electrifying figure of Francis Lightfoot is an amalgam of the poet Shelley and the character Eugene Marchbanks in Shaw's *Candida* (with touches of Frederick Soddy—and Sophocles' Prometheus). A Cabinet member notes that he bears "a remarkable likeness to Shelley" (512). The basic premise of the authors' characterization emerges when Lightfoot says that one of his professors, Alfred North Whitehead, told him that if Shelley had lived today, "he would have been a great chemist."[10] Shelley's poems, he continues, "seem almost like my own voice talking to me" (512). The total impression Lightfoot is designed to convey certainly reflects Matthew Arnold's oft-repeated image of the poet as "a beautiful and ineffectual angel, beating in the void his luminous wings in vain." The stage direction describing his nature shows, however, that Nichols and Browne have secretly borrowed prominent elements of Shaw's Marchbanks: "[Lightfoot's] face is very beautiful and rather unearthly. To prosaic people there is something rather noxious in his unearthliness, just as to poetic people there is something angelic in it. He has fine eyes which, in repose, alternate between dreaminess and daring; in action they betray, as do his brows, nostrils, and mouth, a fiercely petulant wilfulness and an extreme pride" (509). The second sentence of this passage (minus the non-Shavian word "rather") is cribbed straight from the stage direction describing Marchbanks in *Candida*, and what follows is close to Shaw: "his nostrils, mouth, and eyes betray a fiercely petulant wilfulness."[11]

The added ingredient of "extreme pride" is independent of these two models, however, and it is this quality that sparks such adamant resistance. The wisest member of the Cabinet, Evelyn Arthur, warns his colleagues that Lightfoot is "actuated . . . pre-eminently, by pride" (524). The young scientist confirms this later not only by calling Arthur "Antichrist" but by deeming himself "the Lord of the Atom" and "the greatest benefactor Mankind has ever known" (532). Arthur admonishes, "You are not Prometheus, after all." Lightfoot's pride is keenly rankled in a series of developments that incite him first to nuclear blackmail against England, then to an actual attempt to blow up the planet. In Act I he gives the Cabinet a week to plan how "a House for Man" can be built (521). On deadline day in Act II, the Cabinet entreats him to reveal his discovery to no one else and to destroy its secret. Lightfoot has prepared for this eventuality, and threatens to turn their island into "a whirlpool of disintegrating atoms" unless by noon tomorrow they begin to formulate "a constructive program satisfactory to *me*" (533). At the first-act curtain Evelyn Arthur had said solemnly to his colleagues, "It would be better for that poor young man and for the world had he never been born" (521); at the close of Act II he exhorts Lightfoot, "Then you will crucify Man on the cross of your impossible hopes?"

By now the rash genius resembles mankind's greatest benefactor much less than he does the latest version of a traditional literary stereotype, "the dangerous scientist-inventor," familiar in medieval wizard legends, *Frankenstein*, and more currently Anatole France's *Penguin Island* (1908).[12] In effect, Lightfoot is the projected atomic-power dichotomy in capsule form: he has both Armageddon and Millenium at his fingertips (or thinks so). He can be viewed as a test case of people in control of limitless power. If the world is to survive and bloom, he must curb his personal pride—an action analogous to governments subordinating their self-interest for the common good. He must also abjure threats of destruction—renounce the use of atomic weapons—and cooperate with experienced people to work for mutually desired goals—align with an international governing and planning organization. Even though Lightfoot claims Humanity is his religion (512), his subsequent actions are diametrically opposed to this pro-humanistic formula. In Act III the Prime Minister tells him that the Cabinet has decided it must capitulate to his demands, so that he would now have its help in rebuilding the House of Man. Extraordinarily, Lightfoot announces that the previous behavior of the Cabinet, and more importantly his own, has convinced him that "Man has not yet sufficiently evolved" to be able to manage its new powers to great advantage. Trusting that Nature will engender a more successful process of evolution somewhere else in the universe, he will therefore "assist Nature" by dematerializing the earth in fifteen minutes.[13] In a clanking series of eleventh-hour plot turns, Nichols and Browne save humanity from Lightfoot. As one would expect, he has no allies to help carry out his apocalyptic plan; he alone can squeeze the atomic trigger. Moments before doomtime, a lorry runs over him.[14] He has just enough strength left to utter, "Hail, new dimensions! . . . We go to the Eternal Mind!" and to move a pointer on his remote-control world-destruction device, a watch. But he has strength only to move it from the off position to safety—not to on. A Cabinet member sums up this ironic drama: "his great final gesture—death froze his fingers in mid-journey—where? at safety" (543–44).

Stretching brink-of-disaster credibility beyond the breaking point, the playwrights resort to even more improbable means in order to rekindle the suspense of nuclear oneupmanship. The Cabinet barely has time to sigh with relief when a letter arrives from "the Guild of United Brain-Workers of the World" (544).[15] An elaborate hidden conspiracy of benevolence unfolds: the Guild, "owing to the co-ordination of immense labors," has learned how to control the atom, *and* has worked out a program for the new era of infinite power. Since a non-member (Lightfoot) has discovered the secret independently, immediate steps have been taken: world leaders must assemble in Geneva at once and begin complying with the Guild's program. In case anyone thinks of resisting, "Six aeroplanes are over you as you read this. They contain atomic bombs. Such bombs hang over the capitals of every civilized country" (544).

The recycling of Lightfoot's second-act nuclear blackmail moves the play closer to the mode of Wells's *The World Set Free*, in which a similar "sword of Damocles" effect spurs leaders to form a world government. Nichols and Browne are not done with their eccentric departures from this mode, however: the planet will be threatened with annihilation once more. Astonishingly, a character with "the charm of Puck, the wisdom of Prospero, the coolest . . . temperament in Europe," Evelyn Arthur, becomes the threatener. Somewhat bafflingly termed "the play's protagonist" (511), Arthur has to this point proved to be Lightfoot's most formidable antagonist. But when the young man unequivocally becomes the arch-antagonist of mankind, Arthur does an about-face. The prospect of oblivion apparently strikes a responsive chord in his incipiently nihilistic nature. He actually comes to welcome the prospect—and feels cheated, to a degree, when it is erased. Faced with his last moments of life he reads Benedetto Croce. "Philosophy!" a minister exclaims; "in the face of the futility of everything."

Arthur replies: "And what is philosophy for, if not to reconcile us to that futility?" (536). Moments later, he stuns his colleagues by saying: "I must testify to the truth before I go ... This boy is right. Nature, not he, has put Humanity on trial; and, because we have failed to evolve a faith adequate to our opportunities she rejects us for new experiments. That is the truth, and I am glad to have come to it" (540). When Lightfoot is prevented from carrying out his plot, his new apostle manifests his conversion even more blatantly. Instead of attending to the letter from the Guild, which has just arrived, he says "dreamily": "The clock, to the great scandal of all hopeful souls, having been set back, the tortoise humanity will now cover its inch during the ensuing century" (544). Clarity is not the authors' strong point, but this seems to mean that he deplores the fact that humanity will have to continue at its own snail-like pace of evolution, contrary to what he, Lightfoot, and other "hopeful souls" wished. After finally hearing the Guild's demands, accentuated by the drone of the planes carrying atomic bombs, Arthur addresses the corpse of Lightfoot: "Five minutes past twelve. The clock cannot be set back. If not you, Francis ... another. . . . Nature doesn't often give us a second chance" (544–45). Again the text is hazy; has he decided to complete what Lightfoot set out to do (at precisely twelve)? The instrument of a "second chance," the world-destruction device, is intact and poised an eighth of an inch from the on position. When Arthur seizes it, the action perversely echoes something the Prime Minister said in Act I about his most-valued colleague: he has "immense courage" because "he doesn't give a damn, not the remotest fraction of a damn" (511). After kissing Lightfoot and thanking him, Arthur brandishes the remote-control watch before his colleagues—and the audience—like an anarchist with a hissing bomb. This turns out to be only a prank ("a last flicker of Puck," the stage direction says), but he does tell the men that he alone is going to Geneva, and he locks them in. In Geneva, we presume, he will oppose the Guild's limited nuclear blackmail with his own omnicidal brand—to what specific purpose is left unsaid. The finale of the play is deliberately ambiguous, with hopes and terrors balanced. One minister bewails, "Between them [Lightfoot and Arthur], the end!" Another retorts, "No, gentlemen, between them, if Man can find faith, the Beginning!" About half the ministers end up "scowling . . . as if expectant of calamity"; the others stand "with hands raised as if to welcome a supreme hope." The essential dichotomy of the nuclear situation is ritualized. The dominant theatrical effect of the finale, however, stresses the strong possibility of nuclear devastation from one source or another. By now "the roar of aeroplanes fills the entire theater," drumming consciousness of the atomic sword of Damocles into the audience, and Evelyn Arthur is spotted heading for the airport. "If not you, Francis ... another."

The play as a whole, then, is in one important respect a mirror of early speculations about a projected Atomic Age. Because the miraculous potentialities of atomic power have been harnessed, the prospect of a Millenium for mankind exists (incidentally, no hazards are foreseen). Hand in hand with this, unfortunately, is the possibility of a nuclear Armageddon. Since world leaders tend to lack "a faith adequate to [these] opportunities," they may have to be subjected to the threat of Armageddon in order to be prodded toward Millenium. The play shares this idea-complex with the more or less sober scientific and quasi-scientific earlier writings of Frederick Soddy, Ernest Rutherford, Gustave Le Bon, and H. G. Wells, among others. But no one would accuse the play of sobriety.

The subtitle of *Wings Over Europe* is *A Dramatic Extravaganza on a Pressing Theme*. Its treatment of this pressing theme is, to say the least, extravagant. The potentialities of atomic power are depicted at almost absurd extremes, and are wielded by an addict of such extremes. Lightfoot demonstrates his ability to effect the "sudden redistribution of atoms" by having an assistant (offstage) detonate a lump of sugar so that "a crater as big as St. Paul's" is left, then transmute a latchkey into gold and then India rubber. But to observers these were "nothing" compared to "that last thing—" which they describe only as "Appalling!" and "Blasphemous!" (522). The young physicist's decision to vaporize the planet and thus help Nature "correct one of her casual blunders" (535) is the utmost possible exaggeration of what might happen if leaders prove incapable of handling limitless power. Although two doctors who have examined Lightfoot assure the Cabinet that he is not touched with megalomania, the self-styled Lord of the Atom, who also says he represents "the furtherest reach of Man's Mind" (534), is nothing short of a mega-megalomaniac. His apparent success in converting the once-wise statesman Evelyn Arthur to his farfetched views on evolution also makes him something of a Mesmer, if not a Mephistopheles.

In 1928 the term "Dramatic Extravaganza" would have evoked the kind of play in which a fanciful or downright irrational situation is carried to its logical extremes, and this throws light (usually satirical) upon contemporary behavior and values.[16] In the hands of J. R. Planché or W. S. Gilbert, an Extravaganza was a popular entertainment full of ingenious spectacle and farcical high jinks, although in such examples as Gilbert's *Iolanthe* and *Utopia, Limited* "topsy-turvydom" yields a keen edge of political satire. That the genre can accommodate serious critical and philosophical ends, however, is evidenced by Bernard Shaw's late-period plays, several of which he called Extravaganzas. The first labeled as such is *The Apple Cart*, performed the year after *Wings Over Europe*, but a previous play incorporates the mode to a marked degree: *Back to Methuselah*, published in 1921. In that huge five-part drama, the "irrational proposition rationally pursued" which Martin Meisel designates as the key element of Extravaganza (381) is that people can will themselves to live for 300 years. The effects of anticipating a much-prolonged life and the benefits for society in living one are explored in depth. Nichols and Browne, Cambridge graduates, would surely have read *Back to Methuselah*, and in applying a popular, imaginative mode of drama to exalted themes may have consciously followed its lead. One of the most striking ideas in their play is a variation of one of Shaw's: if humans cannot will themselves much longer lives and thus achieve much more efficient organization, Nature may supersede them with "a new form of life, better adapted to high civilization."[17] Part of Lightfoot's rationale for hastening this process clearly echoes both Don Juan in the dream scene of *Man and Superman* and Lilith in the finale of *Back to Methuselah*. Claiming to speak as Nature's "Sibyl," he says:

> Gentlemen, there was a planet called the Earth. After inconceivable millenia, sentience emerged from that planet's slime. Again aeons passed, and unimaginable agonies, and at last that sentience, which was now none other than the Mind of Man—of you, gentlemen, and of me—earned the right to such an intensity of apprehension that it seemed on the brink of unriddling the profoundest enigma of the universe; with that unriddling, the universe would have become conscious of itself. Suddenly, every dream was shattered, not by a sidereal accident, but by the very constitution of Man himself. But the genius of Nature is inexhaustible: on another star that consciousness will be accomplished. (535)

Wings Over Europe is of course far more arbitrary and improbable than a Shavian Extravaganza, as well as a good deal less logical.[18] But its fantasy does embody a degree of prophecy sufficient for it to qualify as the first dramatic harbinger of the Atomic Age, just as *The World Set Free* did for fiction. We can excuse Browne for ignoring Wells when he proclaimed in 1955: "*Wings Over Europe* foretold nuclear fission—and its consequences—when the fact was a phrase unknown except to a handful of scientists: seventeen years before that monstrous crime over Hiroshima, twenty-six before the explosion which ended an atoll [Bikini] and a world" (*Too Late to Lament*, 300). Nichols, whose imagination yielded the prophecy, put the emphasis elsewhere: "To me the theatre does not exist to discuss problems, or take sides, or ventilate grievances," and he called the play "a ballet of ideas."[19] Nevertheless, as a dramatized hypothesis (however extravagant) of political and ethical problems that might arise at the onset of a nuclear age, the play not only adopts the Shavian principle of making drama "a means of foreseeing and being prepared for realities as yet unexperienced,"[20] it also incorporates a notable degree of his thoughtfulness and earnest concern. At the same time, it remains a dazzling and diverting theatrical exhibition, as charming as it is fascinating for its semi-absurd fantasy.

CHAPTER 3

American Playwrights and the Birth of the Atomic Age

The first atomic bombs were created in America and dropped by Americans. As a double-barreled event, the atomic destruction of Hiroshima and Nagasaki was simultaneously the final crescendo in an increasingly brutal, inhuman war and the first tumultuous cacophony of the newborn Atomic Age. British, Canadian, French, Italian, German, Danish, and Hungarian scientists helped develop the bombs, but not even Britain had a say in the final decision to drop them. The successful program, the decision, and the triumphant missions were at once America's pride and America's shame.

The day after Nagasaki was attacked, President Truman declared in a radio address, "It is an awful responsibility which has come to us." He added: "We thank God that it has come to us instead of to our enemies; and we pray that He may guide us to use it in His ways and for His purposes."[1] An editorial in the popular photo magazine *Life* expressed gratitude that "Prometheus, the subtle artificer and friend of man, is still an American citizen." But it went on to remind the reader that "Power in society has never been controlled by anything but morality. . . . No limits are set to our Promethean ingenuity, provided we remember that we are not Jove."[2] In his invaluable book *By the Bomb's Early Light: American Thought and Culture at the Dawn of the Atomic Age*, Paul Boyer points out the irony in these reactions: "The American Prometheus who had assumed Jove's mantle and obliterated two cities with his newly discovered atomic thunderbolts was now being sternly told that he must resist the temptation ever again to play god."[3] Writing at about the same time, the conservative columnist David Lawrence posed the new debacle of America's self-image in unvarnished terms: "We—the great, idealistic, humane democracies, on the so-called civilized side—began bombing men, women and children in Germany. Last week we reached the climax—we destroyed hundreds of thousands of civilians in Japanese cities with the new atomic bomb." Though we may rejoice in victory, he continued,

> ... we shall not soon purge ourselves of the feeling of guilt which prevails among us. Military necessity will be our consistent cry in answer to criticism, but it will never erase from our minds the simple truth that we, of all civilized nations, though hesitating to use poison gas, did not hesitate to employ the most destructive weapon of all times indiscriminately against men, women and children. What a precedent for the future we have furnished to other nations even less concerned than we with scruples or ideals![4]

A whole gamut of responses to these electrifying events could be garnered from the memories and statements of American literary figures. Kurt Vonnegut was able to contrast the "tower of smoke and flame" which he had survived at Dresden with the "twin towers" at Hiroshima and Nagasaki, recalling that he had become "crazy" enough to regard the latter as "works of art. Beautiful!"[5] William Styron, a Marine officer headed for the impending invasion of Japan, remembered feeling "ecstatic" to have "an almost tactile burden of insecurity and dread" removed, while John Ciardi, a bomber pilot in the Pacific who characterized his duties as a near-daily lottery with life or death as the prize, said that "when news of that atom bomb came ... we won the lottery. Hey, we're gonna get out of here!"[6] Writers not involved in combat tended to accent the negative, however. Editorializing in *Time* magazine, James Agee echoed David Lawrence: "the sudden achievement of victory was a mercy, to the Japanese no less than to the United Nations [i.e. the Allies], but mercy born of a ruthless force beyond anything in human chronicle. ... [T]he demonstration of power against living creatures instead of dead matter created a bottomless wound in the living conscience of the race."[7] Ernest Hemingway issued a warning that must have irked many celebrants of American victory:

> For the moment we are the strongest power in the world. It is very important that we do not become the most hated. ...
>
> It would be easy for us, if we do not learn to understand the world and appreciate the rights, privileges and duties of all other countries and peoples, to represent in our power the same danger to the world that Fascism did. ...
>
> This is no time for any nation to have any trace of the mentality

of the bully. It is no time for any nation to become hated. . . . It is no
time for any nation to be anything but just.[8]

Perhaps the most memorable reflection was William Faulkner's in his 1950
Nobel Prize address: "Our tragedy today is a general and universal fear so
long sustained by now that we can even bear it. There are no longer problems of the spirit. There is only the question: When will I be blown up?"[9]
In more distant retrospect, during a visit to Tokyo in 1957 (with John
Hersey, among others) John Steinbeck ruminated about the subtle emotional residue of the atomic bomb attacks: "the feeling about the bomb is
something. It is strange and submerged and always present. It isn't quite
anger and not quite sorrow—it is mixed up with a curious shame but not
directed shame. It is an uncanny thing—in the air all the time."[10] An in-
terviewer on the trip said that Steinbeck "kept dwelling on the subject with
me. The very idea of the existence of the atomic bomb upset him. . . . He
was particularly upset that Americans had so quickly and easily shrugged
off those attacks."[11]

American playwrights who recorded their reactions to Hiroshima (disappointingly few, unless we count writers who tried their hand at drama
only a few times, such as most of the figures mentioned above) cover the
same broad spectrum. Maxwell Anderson, regarded by most at the time as
America's leading active dramatist, told a reporter for *PM*: "My first reaction was an obvious one. I have two sons in service, and I hoped the
bomb would help shorten the war. But . . . at the same time I felt a great
apprehensiveness. This new bomb, you know, is a very dangerous plaything
for civilization."[12] Arthur Miller recalls feeling awe and pride as well as
relief in response to the news of Hiroshima, but he was later appalled at
his reactions.[13] Robert E. Sherwood looked back in 1950 to the event and,
while declaring "problematical" the argument that a million allied lives
were saved because no invasion was necessary, asserted: "I believe that the
bomb should have been dropped for the information and warning of the
whole human race. The tragedies of Hiroshima and Nagasaki were necessary to tell the rest of us what we are up against." By "the rest of us" he
clearly meant the Soviet Union, whose expansionist moves of the last five
years he deplored. Stalin, he said, "has already displayed a capacity for
abysmal stupidity" and might start another world war.[14] Paul Green, in
contrast, could find no positive side to the dropping of the bomb. In a mid-
1946 letter to a friend he confided, "For the first time in my life I find
myself ashamed of being an American." He even predicted (wrongly) that
a fellow North Carolinian, the bombardier on the Enola Gay, "will come
to the realization that perhaps he has the awful precedent honor of being
the greatest mass murderer of all time—considering the amount of time it
took to do the killing."[15]

American reactions in dramatic form to the first atomic bombs do not

include works by any of these playwrights, nor by Maxwell Anderson,
Thornton Wilder, Clifford Odets, Lillian Hellman, Tennessee Williams, Arthur Miller, or William Inge, all of whom were actively writing in the late
1940s and early 1950s (Eugene O'Neill was not). In January 1947 the
novelist John Steinbeck, whose playwriting was restricted to dramatizing
his fiction, was invited by the actor Burgess Meredith to develop a scenario
with a nuclear theme into an effective play; a premier at the Abbey Theatre
in Dublin would result. Meredith explains: "The title was 'The Last Joan.'
The idea was that there are always Joan of Arcs who hear voices. . . . And
that in a modern sense we better heed what the present Joan tells us of the
atom bomb, because it's the last time that we'll have a Joan to tell us what
to do."[16] Steinbeck was excited by the prospect and worked on a script for
over three months, finishing "a rather poor draft of it" by late winter and
other versions thereafter (Parini, 367). But he finally decided, "The play is
no good . . . It just didn't come off and I would rather destroy it than to
have it destroyed by others."[17] It is more tantalizing to learn that around
1960 Arthur Miller tried to compose a play about remorseful atomic physicists. He recalls in his autobiography, *Timebends*: "Ever since Hiroshima
I had been thinking about a play that would deal with the atom bomb.
Now, fifteen years later, it was less a feeling of guilt than of wonder at my
having approved the catastrophe[18] that moved me to investigate firsthand
how the scientists themselves felt about what they had created" (516). After
visiting Hans Bethe at Cornell and J. Robert Oppenheimer at Princeton,
Miller says, he wrote "page after page of a play in blank verse about an
Oppenheimer-like character preparing to signal the fateful test explosion
of Fat Man, the first experimental bomb. The scenes had a certain elegance
but would not bleed—I was too remote from the character's daily life."
Even though he thought the play "might well illuminate the dilemma of
science," it was turning out to be "interesting when it should have been
horrifying." He abandoned the attempt (520).[19]

Several American plays of the immediate postwar period by more or less
obscure playwrights do treat the nuclear situation involving Hiroshima and
its aftermath. The first is perhaps the most overtly symptomatic: a brief
skit written by a nuclear physicist, Louis N. Ridenour, and published (in
Fortune!) within six months of the Hiroshima blast. A grim warning in
non-serious terms, "Pilot Lights of the Apocalypse" depicts a partly farcical
scenario for all-out atomic war evolving from American over-confidence in
its nuclear technology. Theatre hacks turned it into a performable but tur-
gid one-act, *Open Secret*, in late 1946. The second play, better termed a
stage spectacle, is well characterized by its full title: *E=mc²: A Living
Newspaper About the Atomic Age*. Hallie Flanagan (Davis) concocted the
script, with research help, in late 1947 to convey the Jekyll-Hyde nature
of the newly harnessed atom in an appealing theatrical context. The script
concludes with a slightly doctored version of "Pilot Lights of the Apoca-

lypse." The first full-fledged American drama of the Atomic Age is Upton Sinclair's *A Giant's Strength* (1948). This much more conventional play portrays reactions on the domestic plane to both Hiroshima and an atomic war, while presenting an array of disturbing information and ideas about the real and imagined nuclear situations. However, Sinclair awkwardly skews its naturalism to bolster the recurring contemporary thesis that atomic power must be controlled by a world government if civilization is to endure. The next full-length play, Herman Wouk's *The Traitor* (1949), exploits Cold War anxieties in depicting a highminded nuclear physicist who intends to pass vital secrets to Russia. The play is three-fourths spy melodrama and, surprisingly, one-fourth discussion. In 1950, Cornel Lengyel used an atomic weapons plant as the setting in his one-act allegorical fantasy *The Atom Clock*. A young employee becomes a kind of Everyman figure as he hears the pros and cons of the plant's ultimate mission, winning the arms race. At least three other American plays of the period touch on nuclear themes, but do not represent highly significant dramatic reactions to the new era.[20]

RIDENOUR'S APOCALYPTIC PLAYLET AND ITS ADAPTATION

Louis N. Ridenour's imaginative and witty playlet, "Pilot Lights of the Apocalypse," must have been conceived in the immediate aftermath of the atomic assaults on Hiroshima and Nagasaki.[21] Yet it projects a world situation roughly equivalent to our own in the early 1980s, when the superpowers seemed to be considering "limited" nuclear war a viable option and several countries with lesser arsenals were poised for defense or attack. Ridenour pushes his hypothetical scenario to the limits of absurdity: *all* the industrialized nations "have mastered the production and use of atomic power"; the United States is "ahead in the armaments race," but its 2,000 radio-controlled bombs in outer space are overmatched by 3,400 belonging to other nations, and no one knows how many atomic mines have been planted in the world's major cities, or by whom. The only deterrent to war is America's superior ability to retaliate. Moreover, the technology of detection lags far behind that of waging nuclear war: meteors have been mistaken for missiles, and the aggressor in a presumed attack must be determined by political scientists on the basis of "the highest negative rating" at the moment.

The skit is set in a Defense Command center in the San Francisco area. After a pep-talk visit by the President (during which he gloats, "Who'd dare attack us when we're set up like this?"), the "pilot light" for San Francisco goes red. What is later revealed to be an earthquake is mistaken for a nuclear attack, and the search for an "enemy" comes up with an unlikely leading candidate: Denmark. (Statues presented to its King by the United States have met "widespread disapproval," and the sculptor lives in

San Francisco.) Cautious military officials want Security Council approval before retaliating, but an apoplectic Colonel—shouting "What have we got this stuff for if we don't use it?"—rushes to the control board and pushes a key that will bring a bomb down on Copenhagen. A logically chaotic chain reaction ensues: Stockholm goes red after Copenhagen (Colonel Peabody explains, "Sure. The Danes thought it was the Swedes. That export-duties row"), then four British cities (the Swedes were also arguing with England), then Russian cities, then our own. "Dark Ages, here I come," Peabody utters.

Ridenour's playlet is a farce with an implicit moral. According to an editor's headnote doubtless approved by the scientist, the moral is that "we should do all that decently can be done to avoid an atomic-armaments race."[22] In the play, American over-confidence in its atomic superiority, falsely insured by its apparent monopoly on the latest technology, leads to the destructive attitude expressed comically by the person who later starts the bombardment, Colonel Sparks: "I'm glad I was born an American. We've got the know-how. I'm glad I'm on the side that's ahead in the race." The latest technology is also shown to be woefully inadequate not only to detect a genuine attack and identify its source, but also to stop a war started inadvertently. The play concludes with the Brigadier sending a futile message: "THERE IS NO REPEAT NO WAR," to which Colonel Peabody can only respond, "The hell there isn't. New York's gone red, and Chicago, and. ..." The room rocks and crumbles, and the apocalyptic pilot lights go out.

One reason why Ridenour's tiny futuristic parable is effective is that its moral remains implicit, emerging only from the dynamic interaction of dialogue and events. Dangerous premises are exposed by being stated in a manner that casts ridicule upon them; their logical consequences are dramatized at extremes that evoke both absurdity and horror. This is the mode of many successful fictional treatments of nuclear disaster, perhaps most notably the film "Dr. Strangelove." Unfortunately, it is far from the mode of the skit's semi-commercial adaptation, Open Secret.[23] The work of two musical comedy and filmscript writers, George Bellak and Robert Adler (ostensibly with Ridenour's help), Open Secret begins with a didactic prologue in which a physics professor addresses the audience, a stand-in for his class, at some length. Professor Shulman directly voices Ridenour's argument for international control of nuclear power, which becomes the overt moral of the play: America's great superiority in atomic weapons and futile policy of atomic secrecy will "lead inevitably toward this country's becoming the focal point of world hatred and suspicion" (182). When the accident that prompts the war occurs, the countries that had developed nuclear technology despite American secrecy turn on the United States as "the only known possessor of the bomb" and thus the only "logical enemy" to destroy (202).

In the play proper, the professor has served for some time as an army general supervising the technology of atomic defense in the eastern sector. Incongruously, he has devised "a perfect engine of destruction" (189), the panoply of radio-controlled space missiles from "Pilot Lights of the Apocalypse," which has been kept "top secret" even though he still deplores the idea of "leaving the entire thing in military custody" (184). Two main elements are added to the plot to expand Ridenour's playlet: the array of space missiles from other countries is detected for the first time, and Shulman suddenly realizes that there is "an immediate danger of collision" (198). He wants to retrieve the American space arsenal at once, but the Colonel Sparks of this play, Major General Harris, stops him just before San Francisco goes on the red. The search for an enemy is de-farcicalized by invoking the growing Red Scare and having the U.S.S.R. chosen as the most probable aggressor; the American government refused to recognize their claim to Arctic uranium deposits. General Harris rushes to pull the Moscow lever, and the chain reaction in this case is much less chaotic: the Russians react by bombing (fascist) Madrid, and someone bombs Paris, Buenos Aires, and London, but from then on American cities are the focus of everyone's wrath. Harris himself screams, "Tell them it was a mistake. THERE IS NO WAR!" as "the terrible sound of destruction rises" until "the sound fades to an eternity of silence" (202).

Professor/General Shulman is able to end the play as he begins it, spelling out its moral at the same time that the action demonstrates it. When the full import of the thousands of orbiting missiles in space dawns on him, he is given the chance to explain the crisis of conscience that has plagued him since submitting himself to government control: "All the time I was designing this wonderful piece of machinery, I had a thought in back of my mind. One day, I said, someone will press a button, and because of my machine a few million of the world's inhabitants will be blown to dust. Then I'd reassure myself. No. This is purely a defensive measure, to strike back at anyone who strikes at us" (194). But when he proposes bringing down the satellite bombs as a gesture of good will to prospective enemies, the harsh reaction from Harris leads him to deplore having "created this thing for you. . . . So you could be there first with the most" (198). The vengeful apocalypse ensues. *Open Secret* certainly contains more intellectual substance, and a higher degree of probability, than its miniscule predecessor. But its attempt to fuse a set of logical cause-effect relations to a basically farcical scenario (not only the inciting event, the misconstrued earthquake, but also the flocks of murderous missiles circling the earth, ready to pounce) creates a disconcerting disparity in effect. Its "set pieces" of doctrine and rarely relieved grimness water down whatever dramatic excitement might have arisen from the depiction of a human catastrophe.

FLANAGAN'S "LIVING NEWSPAPER," $E=mc^2$

Unlike *Open Secret*, the version of "Pilot Lights of the Apocalypse" that concludes $E=mc^2$ is only slightly altered from the original. The skit is one of a variety of sources tapped in this theatrical montage, or "Living Newspaper," which was first performed in December 1947.[24] Its guiding spirit, if not only begetter, was the originator of the Living Newspaper in America, Hallie Flanagan (Davis). As director of the Federal Theatre Project in 1935–39, she developed stage productions whose aim was to treat "the most poignant problems of individual and collective judgment ever faced by mankind" (Flanagan quoted by Bigsby, 232) and to show "their historic development and their effect on people."[25] Strategically designed to dispense vital information in a digestible and entertaining format, these scripts were worked up in collaboration with researchers and reporters as well as theatre practitioners. They were supposed to be "carefully documented" and their facts "handled with judicious restraint" (Flanagan, 72). Accordingly, in $E=mc^2$ sources include the authoritative (and best-selling) 1946 volume *One World or None: A Report to the Public on the Full Meaning of the Atomic Bomb*, with contributions by Einstein and Ridenour, among others[26]; government reports on the effects of atomic explosions; articles from such journals as the *Review of Modern Physics* and the *Bulletin of the Atomic Scientists*; hearings, interviews, news reports, and similar materials. The attempt at balanced presentation of facts is conveyed by one of the many footnotes in the playscript: "The following sub-scene has been adapted for theatrical purposes from the Hearings before the Senate Section of the Joint Committee on Atomic Energy, February 4, 1947, p. 121. Dialogue is verbatim. The testimony has been substantially cut, but the intent of the questioning has been in no way altered" (57). The prominent critic George Freedley surely gratified the play's creators when he called it "a highly effective lecture in dramatic form" (quoted in Hostetter, 96).

The overall composition of $E=mc^2$ accomplishes its didactic task quite satisfactorily. Act I (of two) first dramatically recreates the impact of the birth of the Atomic Age at Hiroshima, then presents the essential scientific and historic background, culminating in the decision to use the bomb. Act II focuses on questions for the present and future: who shall control atomic power and how shall it be used? The act begins by showing its "great boon" potentialities and ends with the "great boom" in Ridenour's skit; in between, the conflict over administering this enormous source of power is dramatized in staged hearings pitting advocates of military/government control against spokesmen for civilian/international control. Invented characters ranging from ordinary citizens to Clio, muse of history, alternate with "real" people played by actors, viewed in films, or quoted by the emcee of this episodic pageant, the Stage Manager.

Early in the play the Stage Manager says pointedly, "There's more than *one* way of releasing atomic energy—and this is the *theatre* way" (26). Robert Hostetter has treated the script at length from the theatrical point of view in his dissertation; I will examine some of the dramaturgic problems that arise in its attempt to disseminate information and ideas about the nuclear crisis in "the *theatre* way." As Hallie Flanagan recognized, this mode requires not only arousing theatrical excitement but also synchronizing widely disparate elements of content and form. Like most plays that tackle the nuclear crisis, $E = mc^2$ intermixes extremes of fact and fiction, stark realities and engrossing fantasies. When the impact sought is that of "a highly effective lecture," the imaginative elements must not call too much attention to their fantastic and improbable qualities; they must adhere to their primary function of making facts and ideas intelligible and interesting, and above all not jar incongruously with these realities. The most problematic element in $E = mc^2$, from this standpoint, is one of its most prominent fictions, the Atom.

Conceived as "the clothes line on which the Living Newspaper would be fashioned" (Sylvia Gassel, quoted in Hostetter, 91), the character of Atom conceptually embodies limitless potentialities for improving or blighting the lot of mankind, depending on how it is used by those who control it. The concept itself is made explicit at various times in the play, for instance by a professor who states: "atomic energy can cure disease—or cause it—create food—or poison it—provide heat for the whole world—or blow it sky-high—you see, it's going to be up to you and me" (50). Atom contributes by expressing in personal, emotional terms the main point of the play:

> You people have got to get together with people all over the world and take control! *(Starts to grow wild)* Because I can't wait forever, see?—I have my hypomanic moments and when I'm in that state I may go into fission any minute, see? . . . I'm gettin' so wrought up I'm goin' to have a nuclear breakdown, see? But you won't *believe* it till you're in it. . . . You won't believe a thing till you see it for yourself! (74–75)

The problem of characterization arises from the very nature of real atoms. As Atom herself notes, her real-life counterparts are not only invisible but static if not set in motion: sheer potential. Yet she is given a "hypomanic" character to demonstrate her latent energy. The first time she appears on stage, "She springs to her feet, vital and dynamic," and "turns several cartwheels" (26). At one point she proclaims: "there's so *many* things in me I want to *express*"; then, after "insane gyrations, beating [her] breast violently," she continues: "I've got so much—in *here*!—that I want to get out— . . . I've got so much—*energy*!" (31–32). Moreover, within this established norm of explosive (though ostensibly unreleased) energy, Atom must somehow reflect the "dual personality" that the two-sided potential of atomic power implies. Her manner is supposed to be "docile and meek" at times, "hard and manic" at others, as if the *nature* of atomic energy itself differed when used benevolently or destructively. Quite apart from the general lack of appeal of this frenetic, comic-book figure, its striking lack of congruity with the concept it represents would disturb discriminating spectators and hamper the teaching function of the play.

Other fantastic elements that have mixed success in this respect are those in the category of prophetic or futuristic. The play begins with a striking theatrical rendering of a precise historical event: a man's grotesque shadow being etched on a wall in Hiroshima when the bomb exploded. The ensuing sequence depicts a fictional but convincingly realistic cross-section of ordinary Americans' reactions to the news of Hiroshima. Then the Stage Manager introduces the valid but hardly necessary reminder that certain people had foreseen the approach of the Atomic Age. This serves as a pretext to stage a brief scene from the only play that prefigured atomic power, *Wings Over Europe*. The trouble is that the excerpt is introduced as if it contains highly serious prophecy, whereas it must come across to post-A-bomb spectators as wildly extravagant and far removed from scientific projections. The brash young scientific genius, Lightfoot, announces to Parliament that he has learned to control the energy in the atom. What this means, he proclaims, is that civilization as it exists "is relegated at last to its proper place as the confused remembrance of an evil dream. Yesterday, man was a slave; today, he's free!" (21). Following the excerpt, the sober predictions of living scientists (mostly culled from *One World or None*) only accentuate the incongruity. In the same general vein, when Ridenour's "Pilot Lights of the Apocalypse" is staged as the play's finale, Atom introduces it as if it were a grim enough bombshell to stir people to action: "All right, all right!—You won't control me?—Then here goes— here *goes!*—If you *don't* control me, *this* is the way it's going to be!" (75). After the half-farcical skit, the Stage Manager comments that it was not written by a dramatist or a dreamer but by a physicist. "He is allowing us to use it because he wants as many people as possible to *know*—that it *could* happen that way" (82). It is difficult to imagine sensing "a terrifying prophetic reality" in the playlet, although I am quoting a reviewer who said he did (Richard Watts, quoted in Hostetter, 96). As an experiment in treating the nuclear situation through theatrical means, then, $E=mc^2$ is surely unique and fascinating, and in its time it would have been reasonably successful in promoting an awareness of one of the "most poignant problems of mankind." Apart from its unavoidable dated quality, however, it is not deeply coherent or integrated enough to impress—or endure—as a work of theatrical art.

SINCLAIR'S NATURALISTIC THESIS DRAMA,
A GIANT'S STRENGTH

The extremely prolific and well-informed socialist writer Upton Sinclair had a long career of treating topical issues in essays and novels behind him when he chose the medium of drama to address the atomic threat in 1948. He interrupted the writing of his popular Lanny Budd series of novels, he reminisced, "to do a play about the atomic bomb, which everybody was speculating about at the end of the 1940's. . . . Is our world going to be ended with a bang—or will it take several? I put my speculations into a play called *A Giant's Strength*."[27] He had tried the dramatic form many times, but most of his plays remained unproduced. *A Giant's Strength: A Three-Act Drama of the Atomic Bomb*[28] depicts the political conditions that lead to an atomic war, the war itself, and the aftermath for a group of survivors. The play teems with concrete knowledge and ideas about the nuclear situation as well as Sinclair's speculations on it, most of them echoes of the current liberal *Zeitgeist*. Its topical interest was surely what gave this play, unexceptional as drama, a fleeting theatrical life. After its amateur premiere in 1948, it was performed briefly in both London and New York.[29]

The play is an earnest, if somewhat clumsy, attempt at naturalistic thesis drama. Sinclair aims to suspend disbelief and arouse empathy in spectators to lure them into experiencing vicariously how disastrous a nuclear war would be—a vital preliminary to the play's pitch for world-government control of atomic power. He brings the dramatized situation close to the audience by showing its effects on two thirtyish sisters, their husbands and father, and a ten-year-old son (who grows to early maturity by Act III). In Act I this group reenacts spectators' reactions to President Truman's electrifying press release about the Hiroshima bombing and General MacArthur's address when Japan surrendered—with its (forgotten?) admonition that since the "utter destructiveness" of atomic weapons has made war no longer feasible, "Armageddon will be at our door" unless a "spiritual recrudescence and improvement of human character" occurs (16). The boy, and through him the audience, is subjected to a grim vision of the consciousness that will prevail under the atomic sword of Damocles: "You, my little man, are going to live the rest of your life with one of those dreadful bombs hanging just over your head. You will never have it entirely out of your thoughts; and you're going to have to make the world all over—or else have the bomb wipe you out in the millionth part of a second, you and everybody and everything you know" (17). Act II, which takes place six or seven years later, adds the (fictionalized) testimony of an atomic physicist before the House Committee on Un-American Activities, focusing on the probability that other countries have secretly developed atomic bombs and supplied their ideological allies with them.

This array of documentary and quasi-documentary particulars provides a firm basis of verisimilitude for Sinclair's hypothetical but acceptably "historic" international crisis that unfolds and finally results in atomic war. France, which has become "Red" since World War II, suddenly invades "fascist" Spain to help the insurgents in their campaign to depose Franco (21)—a venture they wouldn't undergo unless the Russians had supplied them with atomic bombs, since Peron's Argentina had almost surely equipped Spain. The United States, uncomfortably siding with Spain, demands that France withdraw within twenty-four hours and turn "the problem of Franco" over to the United Nations (22). France makes no move to meet the deadline; the United States indicates its readiness to act when the ultimatum expires; and one or more countries initiates a massive preemptive strike on the major cities and nuclear facilities of the United States and its allies. American (and presumably British) retaliation leads to near-global devastation, though the characters (and audience) are assured that the United States will prevail because it has by far the largest store of bombs. The attacks on cities are carried out by the "most deadly method of all" deduced from the second Bikini test in 1946: setting off bombs planted in harbors, thus creating immense tidal waves and spreading "radioactive mist" (27). Small enemy planes and helicopters from hidden bases in the United States finish off uranium and plutonium plants. The domestic group, staying in Princeton at the time, is spared from the immediate dangers, and their ensuing frantic preparations for flight (presented in survival-handbook detail) foreground the grimly realistic panorama of horror that emerges from radio reports and their own informed speculations. We hear, for example, that in the harbor of New York City, "close below the Battery," a single bomb has produced a huge tidal wave which has "overwhelmed the downtown district of Manhattan Island" (26–27). The attempts of survivors to flee, pursued by a spreading "atomic cloud," are concretely visualized: "hundreds of thousands of people will be massed at the entrances" to the few bridges in lower Manhattan, "crushing each other to death and climbing over the bodies of the dead and dying"; other thousands will be trying to crowd into the subways, "but the trains block the tubes, and when the crowd comes to a train, thousands will be crushed and suffocated, until the tubes are packed solid with bodies" (32). Most of those who succeed in escaping will suffer the cumulative effects of radiation poisoning, we are reminded. "And don't forget, if you beget children, they may turn out to be freaks of some sort, pinhead idiots, or without eyes" (33–34). To Sinclair's credit, he does not overdo injecting the audience with such grisly images of the probable consequences of nuclear war.

Unfortunately, key ingredients in the play's naturalistic mix strain our sense of credulity and render empathy difficult. The household is far from a representative one. It includes the prominent atomic scientist heard testifying before HUAC, Barry Harding, who made major contributions to the atomic bomb's development and is able to describe its appalling effects. He also serves as a partial spokesman for Sinclair, expressing his fears that in the hands of the military the Bomb will become "another toy" in "the game of power politics" and tendentiously calling for "democratic world government and control of atomic power at every stage of its production." Only then can a "new civilization" be built such as "no H. G. Wells ever dared to dream" (17). He once pompously declares, "We physicists know best, and it's our duty to inform the public" (18). Another character, "Gramp" Ferguson, is a retired history professor who, not coincidentally, is writing an account of the rise and fall of civilizations. A cynical doom-sayer throughout, his only desire after the war begins is to record the final fall. The long-term view that he expresses reflects the cosmic optimism of Shaw (a favorite of Sinclair's): "Nature never gives up, and . . . even if civilized man renders himself extinct, she will try again and again, and may succeed in creating some form of life with better brains, and even . . . better moral sense" (38–39). However, whatever uplift may derive from such an idea is undercut by the cynical cast of its delivery. The biggest sacrifice in the interests of ideological fullness lies in the character of "Bub" Chester, a "kids are like that" character in Act I and a know-it-all late adolescent in Act II. The family's four-month stay in a cave-home in the Black Hills of South Dakota is presumed to have transformed him into an authoritative figure, an admirable pacifist determined to leave his isolated existence, "go back where there are people," learn what they are thinking, and "find a way to bring this war to an end" (51). The finale of the play belongs to him; "facing the audience, with fists upraised," he shouts:

All you troglodytes, you cave dwellers! Stop killing one another! Stop preying on one another! Stop stealing one another's goods! Stop wrecking one another's happiness! . . . No more war! No more war! Get the nations together! . . . Tell all the people: There shall be no more killing! There shall be love, and kindness, and understanding! There shall be a world government, with the power to keep order! Let the government have the weapons, and let no other government have them! Let no government get ready for war! Let no government invade, or threaten to invade. There shall be peace and disarmament, so that men can work at constructive things. Down with war, and the war makers! Down with them for all time! (52)

The abrupt violation of the naturalistic fourth-wall convention here, so much more off-kilter than that in, say, Odets' *Waiting for Lefty*, wrenches the play's dramaturgy out of its previously consistent mode. The fatuousness of the highminded but totally unrealistic sentiments expressed (Shaw would have called Bub an Impossibilist) lifts the play off its previously down-to-earth conceptual moorings. The effect of this disruption in both form and content is disconcerting, to say the least.

Two other dimensions of the play that undercut its realism are veins of overdone soap opera and incongruous satire. Barry Harding's wife, Elaine, is a hedonistic, self-centered woman who considers it dull to live with a nuclear physicist and condemns what he has accomplished, but still resents his prolonged absences bitterly. Before he returns from "secret war work," she spends much time with a divorced man and seriously considers his offer to marry her. After he returns and the war starts, Barry assumes he cannot leave with the family because the Army will summon him, and Elaine threatens, "If you don't come with your wife, you won't have any wife" (29). He does flee with them (for sheer survival), but after months in the cave the Army summons him through the revived postal system and he prepares to go. Elaine dismisses him forever in a blast of withering invective (40–41). After flirting with the other husband, she finally works out her destiny by offering herself to an "underworld romantic," Bugs Gigotti, a few minutes after he arrives with two armed henchmen to loot the place (45). A radio serial about Lucy Dare's "sexual entanglements" is heard from time to time in the play, pointing up the comparison (42). This soap opera, along with obnoxious commercials and patriotic appeals, is part of the play's satirical attack on the banality and manipulativeness of radio. A jingoistic radio announcer periodically comments that this is a war for democracy and free enterprise—and that God is on the side of both (37, 51). Ridiculous advertisements alternate with sober sum-ups of the world situation. Bub, once a radio addict, has matured by Act III to the point that he denounces those who allow their minds to be manipulated by "the big business crowd" and the slogans of "political stuffed shirts" (51). The author's earnest motive is to show how "the minds of the masses become as clay" in the hands of the corporations and politicians who control radio (Preface). This strategy works well enough before the war begins, but after that it backfires. Not that Sinclair is blind enough to suggest that commercial radio has survived a virtual holocaust, or that "free enterprise" is still actively manipulating the few people who own working radios to purchase products that are not available; the play itself informs us that "the financial system is kaput" and American industry will have to "start from scratch" (33, 51). Radio is now government-controlled, and the President himself not only prompted the jingoist cheerleading but urged that advertisements for inaccessible products be broadcast to "keep up morale" by giving the illusion of "Business as usual" (35). But the effect they have in the present state of affairs points up the flaw in Sinclair's (as well as the President's) strategy: virtually everyone is immune to their appeal. The grim survival situation itself makes morale strictly dependent on local, not national, circumstances. Moreover, although one character comments that the ads for products make her "feel at home," the person who was once a slave to them, Elaine, says that now they simply make her think of all the things she left behind (35). Sinclair's anti-capitalist satire, like his alluring soap-opera plot, is misplaced and inappropriate. It is understandable that a demanding reviewer such as Eric Bentley might call *A Giant's Strength* one of the London season's worst.[30] Nevertheless, the play remains the pioneering attempt to deal with all-too-conceivable nuclear disaster in the familiar medium of naturalistic drama, and Sinclair is to be commended for the breadth of vital and interesting information and ideas that permeate the play in adequate, if not scintillating, dramatic form.[31]

In 1955 Sinclair completed a three-act drama about "the father of the atomic bomb," J. Robert Oppenheimer, which he never published (possibly to avoid lawsuits for libel).[32] This mixed-genre play, "Doctor Fist," merges the legend of Dr. Faustus with facts and fantasies about Oppenheimer and his associates. The propagandistic premise of the action is that the key advances on the road to the fission and fusion bombs were diabolical gifts of a figure from hell (Mephisto) to gratify the scientific cravings of stand-ins for Oppenheimer (Walter Fist) and Edward Teller (Joe Haggis). Sinclair wrote the play shortly after the Atomic Energy Commission had investigated Oppenheimer for possible Communist sympathies and declared him a security risk. The determinant factors in this process were almost surely revelations about the scientist's proximity to former members of the Communist Party (among them his wife) and his strong opposition to developing the hydrogen bomb. Sinclair concocts a hypothetical scenario which makes Dr. Fist's wife, Lila, partly responsible for atomic secrets falling into Soviet hands during World War II. A former close friend in the Party, Marila Rubin, visits her home and tries to reawaken her Communist sympathies to the point of enlisting her as a spy. Lila resists, but when Fist unexpectedly returns from work she conceals Marila and lures her husband into the kitchen. Her ruthless friend betrays her by seizing the opportunity to abscond with Fist's briefcase, which is improbably laden with top-secret documents. A scene set in 1947 depicts Fist arguing with Haggis about the moral and strategic import of an as-yet theoretical fusion bomb. Mephisto first tempts a scornful Fist with the missing link in the superbomb's formula, then sneaks it into Haggis's pocket, enabling him to become "the father of the hydrogen bomb." After Fist's reputation is ruined by the AEC hearings, the play concludes with a despairing, guilt-ridden Lila committing suicide in her husband's presence (prodded by Mephisto) and the great scientist resigning himself to the devil-figure's summons of death. Throughout, the Soviet system is portrayed as a simplistic dictatorship that gulls its adherents and aims at world domination. In a scene that veers disconcertingly from the play's dominant mode of domestic drama (in which the chief element of fantasy, Mephisto, functions as an internal tempter), Stalin appears as a caricatured tyrant surrounded by robotlike yes-men. Mephisto materializes, flatters him, and urges him to match the Americans' intentions by inventing a hydrogen bomb. The scene ends with a ballet of red-clad child-sized "hellions." The play is stageable but fascinating only as a curio, and may well remain unpublished as well as unperformed.

WOUK'S DISCURSIVE SPY MELODRAMA, *THE TRAITOR*

Herman Wouk was not yet the best-selling author of *The Caine Mutiny* and its long-running stage offshoot, *The Caine Mutiny Court Martial*, when in 1949 he ventured to hit Broadway with a play on the politics of the current nuclear situation, *The Traitor*.[33] The Soviet Union had generated a Cold War mentality with its absorption of several Eastern European countries and its threats toward Turkey and Greece. It had not yet revealed that it had developed an atomic bomb (the first test came later in 1949, followed by the revelation that an atomic scientist, Klaus Fuchs, had been passing on secrets for years), but it had resisted attempts to have nuclear materials put in control of an international agency. *The Traitor* focuses on an idealistic atomic scientist who is about to give the secret of the latest nuclear technology to the U.S.S.R. so that both superpowers will realize they must cooperate to prevent war. Wouk's play was accepted, performed at the Forty-Eighth Street Theatre, reviewed prominently (by Brooks Atkinson, John Mason Brown, and Harold Clurman, among others), and kept on stage for over two months. It thus became the only American nuclear drama of the decade after Hiroshima to have a significant theatrical impact. As we might expect, however, *The Traitor* achieved its modicum of commercial success less as a result of its subject matter than in spite of it. Reviewers attributed the play's appeal to its adeptness as spy melodrama, conceding only that its thrills were enhanced by the higher stakes of possible atomic war. The most critical of them traced the play's shortcomings to its treatment of serious topical issues. Atkinson wrote that Wouk is "out of his depth. He has written a shallow melodrama about the most sensational aspect of the most important subject in the world today."[34] Clurman goes as far as to accuse Wouk of crass exploitation: "[*The Traitor*] is an effort to cash in on a topicality that is related to the audience's mental confusion—compounded of prejudice, indecision and *Reader's Digest* information or ignorance. The play touches on Communism, academic loyalty tests, atomic spies and the Soviet menace with an irritating cleverness which serves to make it an evasive, catch-all thriller."[35] More representative is Wolcott Gibbs' temperate view: he found the play entertaining enough to recommend "in spite of the obscurity or evasiveness or possibly just the naiveté of its political thought."[36]

The Traitor does indeed rely heavily upon the features of classic spy melodrama. Professor Allen Carr is the brilliant young co-discoverer of a process by which thorium 233 can be produced as a nuclear fuel "at one-fifth the expense of plutonium, rendering all our atomic installations obsolete" (77).[37] He is maneuvering to transfer a sample of the material and information on its use to the chief Soviet agent in America, code-named "Baker." His attempts to deflect go-betweens whom he cannot trust and to confront the elusive Baker are countered by the efforts of Naval Intelligence to incriminate him and capture both spies. Carr is unmasked, to the horror of his mentor and oldest friend, Professor Emanuel, and his fiancée, Jane Bailey, who just happens to be Emanuel's secretary. Carr agrees to help snare the Soviet agent but dies in the culminating shoot-out. The professor speaks his epitaph: "He made a terrible mistake. He gave his life to correct it. He was a good boy" (108). His fiancée weeps—in the arms of a young intelligence officer who is more than ready to console her. This plot involves several clichéd gimmicks of detection, from a dictaphone concealed in a radio to a "just-visiting" friend who is really an American counterspy. The play also exploits a choice ingredient of the new Atomic Age for added titillations: "the new scientific divining rod," a Geiger counter (56). This device clicks sporadically as agents search for signs of radioactivity near the end of Act I and builds to "maximum intensity" at the curtain. John Mason Brown, heralding the revitalization of melodrama on Broadway, considered it the highlight of the play.[38]

Despite its melodramatic qualities, *The Traitor* is far from a stock example of the genre. The play reflects no simplistic categories of right and wrong, and thus has no clear-cut villains and heroes; on the contrary, characters' motives are treated in a disarmingly open-minded and realistic fashion. Key figures who would be especially susceptible to stereotyping in the Cold War milieu of the day are characterized so that they defy reductive presuppositions. These include the two main antagonists in the superpower spying game, the engaging Soviet secret agent who turns out to have no Party allegiance but is all the more efficient for being purely mercenary, and the anxiety-ridden chief American investigator who can only see the bumbling in his successes. The focal center of this stereotype-debunking strategy is of course the "traitor" himself. Allen Carr has every intention of committing treason, but he is a firm anti-Marxist whose motives are at once highminded and politically astute. He expresses them most concisely to the arch-spy Baker: "I have a motive. You think you're using me. But I'm using you. I want to prevent another war. I believe if your side has the bomb, there won't be one, because each side will be afraid to start" (102). Underlying this line of reasoning is an analysis of the current political situation which might have made the general public bristle but which reflects sound, independent thinking of the day such as that in Walter Lippmann's *The Cold War*.[39] Carr tells Professor Emanuel that the colleague who finally invited him to become a spy didn't convert him to Marxism—far from it—but

rang the changes on ideas I already had. That the cold war is due to fear and suspicion. That the U.S.S.R. thinks we delayed the second front two years in order to bleed them to death. That they're grabbing off small countries and acting mulish and truculent because they're scared sick of the bomb and trying to cover up. That sooner or later they'll work out the bomb, but meantime a *ghastly war* can explode from this stalemate of bullying. (76)

Carr also deduced that the economic devastation of a prolonged arms race could be avoided only if the U.S.S.R. first achieved equity by getting the bomb and then agreed to put atomic power under international control (29). This thinking led him into a crisis of conscience which he resolved by choosing what he clearly perceives as the higher good: "In the end, I found myself between conflicting loyalties—loyalty to the United States and my oath of secrecy—loyalty to all mankind and my *own reason*. I decided that one was provincial and limited, and the other eternal and right" (76).

Carr's principled motives have a surprisingly tenacious quality, so much so that they are difficult for other characters to undermine. Yet the conventional spy-melodrama framework of the play demands that they be undermined. The latest secrets of nuclear power must *not* reach the Soviet Union, and the agents countering the attempt must *not* seem like suppressors of the way, the truth, and the light. Oddly for a melodrama, *The Traitor* contains a significant component of argument about ideas. Carr's motives are of course the center of attention: spectators who might incline to his views must be reassured that good intentions such as his might pave the road to hell. The chosen instrument of this ideological exorcism, his name (and grey hair) rippling with implied credentials, is Professor Tobias Emanuel. He is not only "President of the Faculty Association, eminent author, man of principle, and so forth," as the admiring Carr advertises him (24), but an apparently flexible thinker capable of respect for Communism and contempt for loyalty oaths. That is, he is portrayed as the kind of person who could topple Carr's arguments if anyone can. Unfortunately for the intellectual integrity of the play, he is not up to the job, though the job must be done. Whereas Wouk managed to find well-founded and striking arguments for his principled transgressor, for his instrument of correction and admonishment he resorted to conventional sentiments that surely echo the preconceptions of the average person in the audience of 1949. When Emanuel challenges Carr about what he has done, the professor shows that he does not consider the morality of those actions an open question:

EMANUEL. Why, Allen—why?

CARR. Because I believe it was the right thing to do.

EMANUEL. Right to be a traitor to your own country? (74)

Later Emanuel challenges Carr to help capture Baker or "Stand your ground as a traitor . . . because you believe in what you did" (82). His attitude reflects a basic assumption of the play, announced in its title and earlier manifested when Jane Bailey grants Carr her best defense: "In some perverted way he means well, whatever he's done" (50). Emanuel's arguments to counter Carr's turn out to be mere emotional assertions:

> Supposing you're wrong? Supposing what you've done lets loose the horrors of hell on the world?
> . . . .
> You arrogant boy—Are the United States and Russia guided by logic? . . . They're nations, led by men, haunted by illogical impulses of anger, suspicion, envy and fear.
> . . . .
> The bomb in Russia's hands simply doubles the chance of an outbreak of atomic war. (75)

Carr responds like Antigone to Creon: "What guide has a man for his actions, but the lights of his own reasoning and good conscience?" He might have added that the United States, "led by men, haunted by illogical impulses," might be much less tempted to let loose "the horrors of hell" upon Russia if Russia also had the bomb. Emanuel's final argument is an even more mushy recitation of presumed audience sentiment:

> EMANUEL. Your mistake was contempt for the people, and that's the Communists' mistake. They think the common man's too dumb to vote himself a just society. It has to be imposed on him by the clever few.
> CARR. I saw a chance to bring world peace and I acted. Every day that passes is a day nearer to the end of the world, Toby. What was I supposed to do, wait for a Congressional Committee to hold hearings?
> EMANUEL. Yes, that is the way we live.
> CARR. Congress—Parnell Thomas, Rankin, Marcantonio, Taft—is world peace to hang on the honking of these geese?[40]
> EMANUEL. You see the flaw—and you miss the diamond. Our democratic process, which you call the honking of geese, has changed a wilderness into the happiest, strongest, most powerful nation of all history. (81–82)

Emanuel's admonitions have been anticipated by the chief investigator, who has voiced one of the cruder elements of audience sentiment by jeering at Carr, "So you were going to bring about world peace single-handed, eh?

Sort of a combination Jesus Christ and Benedict Arnold" (79). The Russian spy simply dubs Carr a "crank" (102).

An important sub-plot further exposes the a priori nature of Emanuel's thought processes, along with Wouk's underlying adherence to the conventional mind-set of the era. The trustees and president of the university at which the professor is the leading light (Columbia is implied) have sent him a questionnaire about the desirability of a loyalty oath for faculty. If he signs it, as Carr makes clear, every faculty member will follow him except those with Communist sympathies. By 1949, although McCarthyism per se had not yet emerged, Truman had established a federal loyalty-review program and the House Un-American Activities Committee was in full swing. Required loyalty oaths for teachers were common; highly distinguished educators—including James B. Conant of Harvard and Charles Seymour of Yale—"had promised legislators and alumni they would not appoint a Communist."[41] Before Professor Emanuel learns that his virtual son has gone astray, he is portrayed as a firm opponent of the oath. Carr "clasps his hand in an attitude of filial pride and confidence," and says "You'll let them shoot you before you'll sign"; in response, Emanuel "pats him on the shoulder affectionately" (25). The trustee who instigated the questionnaire, a titan of industry with a Cold War fix on the world, asks him to "sacrifice some self-respect in the cause of victory" (26) and reminds him that he could endanger his pension. Emanuel lives up to his billing: "If it's right to sign, I'll sign. If it's wrong, shall I do it to gain a pension?" (30). The *scène à faire* of the play involves not only the discovery of Carr's full complicity but also the side-effect of Emanuel's change of mind on the loyalty-oath issue. The professor had reluctantly agreed to draw Carr out while agents listened surreptitiously. The moment he is sure Carr is guilty he views the questionnaire in a new light and signs it. Wouk's stage direction is revelatory: Emanuel "seems to realize for the first time what he holds in his hand" (71). Responding to Carr's fury, he says he signed it because "I believe it's the right thing to do" (72). Later he explains to Jane: "I'm not happy about it. These questionnaires at best are like fever therapy—infecting ourselves with one illness to cure another. But it now seems a serious public danger to me to allow Communists in the guise of educators to recruit among the immature for their secret work" (92). The play has not in any respect implied that Carr was one of the "immature" successfully recruited as a spy by "Communists in the guise of educators," much less one of the "reducators" themselves; his anti-Communist stance and independent thought are stressed throughout. But if his complicity is to be claimed as the catalyst for Emanuel's change of mind, he must fit into this category. A reviewer who found the "inner logic" of the piece "shaky" put his finger on the deep flaw in Wouk's dramaturgy.[42] An underlying allegiance to prevailing Cold War sentiments, plus the desire to come up with a smash-hit melodrama, made the sound part of the intellectual fabric of the play an inconvenience that had to be negated somehow. Geiger counters, navy uniforms, and a shoot-out did not wholly disguise the feeble means employed to this end.

LENGYEL'S ALLEGORICAL FANTASY, *THE ATOM CLOCK*

The last American play that can be accurately termed a dramatic reaction to the birth of the Atomic Age is, appropriately, an abstract dramatization of attitudes toward developing atomic power. *The Atom Clock* was written in 1950 by Cornel Lengyel, a jack-of-all-genres creative writer in his mid-thirties.[43] The play won Stanford University's Maxwell Anderson Award for poetic drama.[44] Lengyel's half-poetic allegory focuses on emotional rather than scientific or political issues involved in the intensifying Cold War arms race. By early 1950, the news that Russia had exploded an atomic device had dissolved whatever complacency Americans may have derived from their nuclear monopoly, and the United States had made public its determination to create intercontinental ballistic missiles and a "Superbomb." Paul Boyer outlines the change in attitude since 1945 succinctly: "For a fleeting moment after Hiroshima, American culture had been profoundly affected by atomic fear, by a dizzying plethora of atomic panaceas and proposals, and by endless speculation on the social and ethical implications of the new reality. By the end of the 1940s, the cultural discourse had largely stopped. Americans now seemed not only ready to accept the bomb, but to support any measures necessary to maintain atomic supremacy" (334). In Lengyel's play the operation of a stylized atomic weapons plant, with its Establishment slogans and military control, represents the prevailing attitude of the time toward the arms race. The plant becomes a catalyst for the expression of attitudes that differ sharply from the norm or lie concealed beneath it. The central character is an employee, the Young Miner (delver?), who is spurred to grope for "an answer" and is bounced from one extreme point of view, and one extreme emotion, to another.[45] His progress is that of an Everyman figure confronting abstract alternatives that can be discerned as Despair and Hope, Evasion and Rebellion, with Compliance always beckoning. The play largely abandons surface reality in its search for a deeper human truth: an attitude toward the present nuclear situation that is both valid and viable. Realistically, no easy or gratifying answer emerges.

The closest *The Atom Clock* comes to depicting the actual state of the Atomic Age is in its first few moments of exposition, when the dramaturgy is flagrantly non-naturalistic. Choral voices from offstage poetically capsulize the essence of the era:

> Pursuing destruction he found the great treasure,
> Double-edged weapon for good or damnation,

Key to an Eden no prophet foretold,
Door to infernos none dare to describe.
How shall he master it? (436)

The voices also lay the basis for the play's allegorical device of a questing
Everyman: the "he" who must ponder how to "master" atomic power,
clearly mankind, is epitomized as a "lad" who is "not yet ripe for it."
Abruptly a loudspeaker over the gate of the weapons plant announces the
latest news: "the enemy" (never specified) has developed "a new simplified
weapon to supersede our latest rocket missile," and as a result the Atomic
Weapons Department, which "already controls more than half the national
budget," will receive further appropriations to "regain our margin of
safety." This exemplum of the arms race in action draws two sharply contrasting reactions. The newscaster himself (as in Sinclair's play) speaks for
the hawkish Establishment, inadvertently reducing its position to absurdity
by carrying it to logical extremes: "If bigger and better weapons alone will
preserve our freedom, let's get behind the program. . . . Whatever the risk,
we'll retaliate. If the cost is mutual annihilation, we're ready for mutual
annihilation. Let's build the best and biggest hell-bomb of them all!" (436–
37).[46]

This expressionistic trumpeting is countered by the humane admonitions
of a "scholarly old gentleman" who rises from the audience and climbs on
stage. He turns out to be another physics professor who regrets having
helped to develop nuclear weapons—this time, however, not a member of
a domestic circle but an abstract voice of reason. Addressing the spectators
directly (in the first and last "theatricalist" episode of the play), he points
up their complicity: "All of you are part of the show, more important than
any on the stage. . . . We each play a part in building the infernal machine
that's bound to blow up in our faces." He tries the persuasion of eloquence:
"Each of you who hears me now may also hear the irreversible blast of a
man-made judgment day. The final fatal moment of thunders, the mutual
surprise attack, to wrap our cities in the radiant vapors of ruin." He applies
the rhetoric of authority: "Each of you must understand four facts. There's
no real defense against the new weapons. We hold no secret the enemy
cannot duplicate. We must stop the suicidal race to develop more dreadful
weapons. We must free atomic energy for the benefit of all men on the
planet" (437). But the Establishment prevails; he is not permitted to read
a petition he has prepared and is dragged off by guards.

Finally hearing the professor's petition will mark the end of the quest
for the play's Everyman, the Young Miner. Being thwarted from hearing
it now prompts his quest. When he shows his determination to a man who
checks employees into the plant but is also a secret plotter, the Timekeeper,
that figurative pointer to "the atom clock"[47] hints at one clear alternative,
Rebellion. Insisting that he knows what goes on "inside" and what should

be done, the Timekeeper tells the youth: "When we take over, we'll run the works for all of us. It's man who'll ride the atom and rise to the stars, not bankrupt himself on a doomsday binge riding his fellow men to hell!" (440). The Young Miner derides his words as party-line "slogans for suckers" (which the end-justifies-the-means context strongly implies), but he absorbs the repeated message that "the time is ripening." Another alternative emerges unexpectedly in the figure of his mother, who serves mankind as a nurse but turns out to be the voice of Despair. In somnolent blank verse cadences, she puts the worst construction on the "facts" the professor had enumerated: since our weapons and defense systems are in effect obsolete,

> There's no more need for heroes,
> No more need for mothers.
> We're obsolete, too, now. (443)

The Mother claims to be uttering "the truth which everyone knows / Yet none dare believe" (444). Lengyel seems to be using her to expose and discredit an increasingly prevalent tendency of the time, escaping nuclear fear by abandoning hope and receding into an attitude that I. I. Rabi called "the complacency of despair" (Boyer, 351). As greater weapons and delivery systems were developed by the superpowers, an evolution the play takes for granted, this reaction of refusing to think about, much less do anything about, the nuclear situation became more widespread and crippling. The Mother's tone of bitter depression as she says such things as "The carrion smell from the fields of tomorrow / Already pollutes the air we breathe" (441) seems calculated to undercut Despair as an alternative for spectators with any degree of resiliency.

Its immediate effect on her son is to prod him to resist further complicity. He decides to take no further part in the plant's business and to seek out the professor's more positive alternative. What he encounters instead is a figure willingly involved in the production of more and more destructive weapons, but paradoxically an embodiment of Hope. An attractive woman clad in white, she appears carrying a Geiger counter and shepherding an atomic warhead to its stockpile. The warhead is a highly stylized super-bomb: two portable hemispheres that need only to be joined to attain "the critical mass" and "kill a million" (445).[48] The Mother likens the "Young Technician" to a priestess in a satanic ritual—

> The virgin of errors who swings the Geiger counter
> Blessing the bright chalice for unholy communion.

She is one of those "chained to the altars they built" who

> . . . finger the future in leaden bottles,
> Transmuting the wine and the wafer, . . .
> But never transmuting the heart of man. (446–47)

The Mother's fiercely ironic analogy does not apply well to the Young Technician's attitude, however. In line with popular opinion about the arms race at the time, she believes that the more dreadful the weapons, the less likely they are to be used: "That's why we must build the weapons, / Match terror for terror, in hope of peace" (448). This of course is the rationale that evolved into the full-fledged policy of Mutual Assured Destruction, which proved so economically and ethically debilitating for nearly four decades. But the "lovely and wise" young woman (446) has a vision that extends far beyond an image of stalemate. She envisions the arms race as indeed "transmuting the heart of man," hastening the day when "reason shall prevail." Her voice is that of sheer, abstract Hope as she addresses the skeptical Everyman:

> In reason's our hope. The men of reason
> Shall overcome the men of violence.
> Believe me, it's coming, the day, the hour,
> The long-awaited unpostponable minute
> When all the forbidden gates will spring open,
> When men will join hands,
> Step forward a thousand years
> And convert the secret stockpiles of death
> Into storehouses of rich new life for all! (448)

The allure of the young woman's wishful thinking—and good looks—sways the Young Miner for a moment, and he decides to stay on the job. But, in an ironic peripeteia, he does so just as word arrives that he has been fired for suspected disloyalty. This provokes him (with the Time-keeper's nudge) to recall the blighting features of the "infernal machine" that he had almost rejoined, chief among them the demand for unthinking Compliance. Thoroughly frustrated, he tries the alternative of Evasion, asking the Young Technician to leave with him and share a "private road to freedom." Her response is convincingly sound: "There is no private path. None may escape the shadow [of 'looming mushroom clouds'], not in our time. But each must do what he can do to remove the cloud from those who are yet to come" (452). In lurching reaction (again spurred by the Timekeeper), he tries Rebellion, seizing the atomic warhead and threatening to create "A 'No' to be heard around the globe!" (453). As he holds the two sections of the bomb aloft, his mother exults in this gesture of utter Despair: "Clap your cymbals, my son. It's time to celebrate." The Young Technician has little trouble showing him that such a gesture would be useless in practical terms ("Who'll know what really happened here, if none survive?"), and he realizes there are no simple or sure-fire alternatives. He laments: "Then what's to be done? Whatever I do is wrong. Chance has given me choice, yet choice itself is loaded, loaded with death" (454).

The final crescendo of *The Atom Clock*, punctuated in fact by the clock's distant resounding, suggests that a viable attitude does exist after all; the professor's petition still hovers in our minds, waiting to be heard. The Young Miner recalls it and, still brandishing his "sheaf of thunderbolts" (453), forces the authorities to relinquish it. While it is read, however, he becomes engrossed and gradually allows the two halves of the bomb to move apart. Having emblematically eschewed violence, he is shot. This second ironic peripeteia is a counterpart of the first, when the woman's wishful thinking turned him toward loyalty just as he was fired for disloyalty. This time, or so the dramaturgy implies, his search is terminated just as he has found his answer. The attitude reflected in the petition written by a man he—and the audience—must respect and sympathize with, a developer of the bomb who deplores his involvement and who was forcibly prevented from delivering his full message, is surely the attitude that the play recommends to Everyman. The reading of the petition brings out the best in the Young Miner and the worst in the Establishment. Moreover, the attractive young woman reads it, while the assembled plant employees inject the refrain, "Do not deny our petition!" Even though the young man is killed, the woman is seized as a rebellious accomplice, and the play ends by echoing the beginning—"Our lad's not yet ripe for it," the impression of the professor's words remains imprinted on the audience's consciousness.

The play would be almost fully satisfactory if this impression were strong and positive. The "message" embodied is sound enough: halt the arms race and turn nuclear efforts toward benefitting rather than destroying mankind. Lengyel expresses this with some of his best poetry:

> Make chain-reactions not of bright destruction
> To blind the last small witness-eye of heaven.
> Make chain-reactions of new
> Enlightenment to spread from man to man.
> Help integrate our alphabets of hope,
> Unite our atomized vision
> In one great universal stream of light—
> . . . .
> Let all who would live become
> As one man with two billion hearts in his breast.
> In union, not in fission, our faith.
> Do not betray the future and beggar the unborn,
> Designing the end-world weapon,
> The bomb with two billion deaths in its belly.

Transmute the old terrors and let
Our green planet become an island of hope
In the interstellar seas of the night. (455–56)

This would be an unequivocally stirring peroration if a flaw in dramaturgy
did not blur and confuse it to a significant degree. The speech is a structural
counterpart of the Young Technician's plea for the arms race to continue:
"Match terror for terror, in hope for peace." Yet the woman must read
the professor's words as if they were her own—that is, as if she had been
converted to his view before being exposed to it. Furthermore, in effect
both speeches are "alphabets of hope." That is, the general tone of wishful
thinking pervades this speech as it pervaded hers, so that it may be "undercut by association," as it were, in spectators' minds. These factors are
at least mildly disconcerting. Nevertheless, Lengyel's experiment in treating
the nuclear situation through non-realistic, poetic allegory contains more
depth and richness than the other varied experiments we have examined.
The Atom Clock perhaps deserves to be recognized as a kind of capstone
to early American dramatic reactions to the Atomic Age.[49]

CHAPTER 4

British Playwrights and the Birth of the Atomic Age

Of the British playwrights who recorded their reactions to Hiroshima, perhaps Noël Coward showed the least apprehension: two days after the event he wrote in his diary, "The papers are full of the atomic bomb which is going to revolutionize everything and blow us all to buggery. Not a bad idea."[1] His characteristic flippancy contrasts notably with Somerset Maugham's haughty detachment, but Maugham's view is equally insulated from nuclear angst. He does not share Americans' jitters about the atomic bomb, he stated in a reassuring letter to his nephew Robin: "One destructive weapon after another has been invented during the world's history, and filled people with terror . . . , and yet the world has gone on and things, bad as they were, were never quite as bad as was feared."[2] These were by no means typical British responses. Charles Morgan spoke for many when he observed that the Bomb filled people with "wonder, even proud wonder, at the prodigy, and horror at its destructive power."[3] Bernard Kops, only eighteen when he heard the news, registered a similar degree of awe but could not get beyond a strictly negative point of view: "I walked into the countryside alone and climbed a small hill and just sat there, feeling completely drained of all emotion. We were on our own now. Mankind. Terribly alone, growing beyond evolution."[4] A contrast in age but not in perception, eighty-nine-year-old Bernard Shaw ruminated over the possibility of "an end of our civilization and its massed populations."[5]

The sentiments of these five British playwrights might have come from civilized people in any country. But the birth of the Atomic Age also affected the British people in ways peculiar to their own situation. Unlike their closest ally, the United States, England was preoccupied with rebuilding its cities and coping with serious shortages of everyday necessities. The newly installed Labour Party government was intent on establishing a welfare state despite scanty resources. "The main public debate on atomic weapons, such as it was," one commentator said, focused on "the problem of international control" and on "the recriminations of the physicists over the manner in which the decision to drop the bomb was taken."[6] Although British scientists and political leaders had been involved in the development of the atomic bomb, they had been excluded from the crucial last phase of deciding to drop it on Japanese cities.[7] Thus the British did not share the same elation at having ended the war victoriously—or the same conscience-rattling for being countrymen of those responsible for the means. Moreover, as an English journalist noted bitterly, during the development stage of the bomb "the Americans were very happy to obtain from the British all the help they could and the British were only too glad to give it," but by August of 1946 the U.S. government had enacted a law which prohibited the sharing of atomic secrets, creating "a fantastic situation in which the United States completely slammed the door on her British friends."[8] This occurred at the same time that America was issuing noble proposals for international control of atomic energy (notably the Baruch plan)—and advertising its exclusive nuclear muscle with A-bomb tests in the Bikini atoll.

These mixed messages from America left many Britons feeling left high and dry on their "offshore island" (the metaphor invoked in the first full-fledged British drama of the nuclear age). In October 1946 Bertrand Russell explained this common perspective: "Great Britain is peculiarly vulnerable to atomic attack, owing to the smallness of its area and the density of its population. It is to be expected that during the first day or two London, Glasgow, and all the major centers of population will be wiped out; industrial production will be paralyzed, and about half the inhabitants will perish. To carry on the war after such a blow would be totally impossible."[9] If an atomic war came, the editor of the New Statesman wrote, "Our only hope is that by atomic neutrality we should avoid provoking either side to destroy us either as an arsenal or as a base."[10] Thus far, writers were only prophesying that the Soviet Union would soon join the United States as a nuclear power; two sides were necessary for a cataclysmic war. The air of speculation dissolved much sooner than expected when Russia exploded an atomic device in September 1949.

Not surprisingly, most of the earliest British literary treatments of the Atomic Age assume post-disaster scenarios. Three by prominent English novelists are illustrative. Aldous Huxley's widely read *Ape and Essence* (1948) pictures a small community of deformed people who have survived an atomic holocaust of a century ago which left most of the world intensely radioactive. Huxley presents this scene not as his own hypothetical vision of things to come, but rather as the product of a filmwriter's attempt to hit Hollywood: his rejected script is recovered from a garbage truck. Still, the novel clearly links atomic war to the recent assassination of Gandhi as equally logical outgrowths of "the subhuman mass-madness" of nationalism and power politics.[11] Two other well-known English novels of the era share the premise that a nuclear war has taken place, though in each case the fact receives little explicit attention. In George Orwell's *1984* (1949), Goldstein's book reveals that an atomic war had partly devastated Oceania in the 1950s. The book turns out to be a fabrication of the thought-controlling state, but this part of it is verifiable: Winston Smith recalls atomic bombs falling thirty years ago. Nothing is made of this fact overtly. Nevertheless, the novel's framework of a tripartite world in a state of constant belligerence, with only conventional weapons being used in skirmishes over disputed borders (plus sporadic rocket attacks on major cities), surely emerged from the hopeful commonplace that full-fledged wars are inconceivable in the Atomic Age.[12] Similarly, William Golding's *Lord of the Flies* (1954) merely mentions that the boys' plane was evacuating them from an atomic attack on England that almost surely left all the parents dead.[13] But the novel features a theme that applies just as well to adults living in a civilization with fatal buttons to push as it does to boys cast onto a primitive island: "[The boys] don't understand what beasts there are in the human psyche which have to be curbed."[14]

Bernard Shaw's reflections on the Atomic Age began to emerge only a week after Hiroshima and were partly embodied in two tiny dramatic exemplars, the second of which leads up to a worldwide, though non-nuclear, holocaust. The next two relevant English plays feature post-nuclear devastation scenarios, one as an almost peripheral event, the other as the central experience in the characters' lives. The first is *Summer Day's Dream* (1949) by J. B. Priestley, later a leading spokesman for the antinuclear movement and author of a propagandistic television fantasy on the subject. Priestley posits a disastrous atomic war in the recent past but concentrates wholly on the near-idyllic mode of life that eventually emerged from the ashes. The other play is Marghanita Laski's *The Offshore Island* (written in 1954). This is an impressive, sorely neglected "survivalist" drama set in a still-radioactive England victimized by superpowers who wisely refrained from decimating each other with atomic bombs.[15]

SHAW'S REACTIONS TO THE BIRTH OF THE ATOMIC AGE

From August 12, 1945, three days after the Nagasaki bomb, to August 6, 1950, the fifth anniversary of Hiroshima (and just three months before his death), Bernard Shaw offered numerous reactions to the new era, some of them in dramatic form. Richard Nickson and Michael Holroyd have

exposed us to most of Shaw's published journalism on the subject, and
Alfred Turco has recently edited an unpublished item.[16] But no one has yet
discussed his dramatic reactions, small segments of *Buoyant Billions* and
Farfetched Fables, in the context of the Atomic Age. These bits of plays
are unspectacular in themselves but prove quite fascinating when set side
by side and viewed in the light of his nondramatic comments, especially
the late 1945 preface to *Geneva*.

After a false start on *Buoyant Billions* in 1936–37, Shaw restarted it on
August 2, 1945. We can only imagine how his conception of it must have
changed after he heard the news of Hiroshima four days later. In any event,
he completed the play in 1947, and Act I now contains a brief argument
conveying the positive implications of atomic discoveries.[17] This became
the first British dramatic treatment of the new era to be staged in the United
Kingdom, beating Priestley's *Summer Day's Dream* by a month. Shaw's
second play-segment also contains a brief discussion, this one weighted
toward negative implications of atomic power. It appears in the first fable
of the six in *Farfetched Fables*, which he wrote in 1948.[18] (The second
fable is indirectly relevant, since it presents the plot dénouement of the
first.) Since Shaw was in his nineties when he wrote these scenes, it is not
surprising to find that the conceptions they embody are largely new appli-
cations of ideas he had already formulated in essays and letters. But his
mode of presenting them through the cut-and-thrust of debate emerging
from real-life situations, with each point of view expressed in the character's own idiom but with heightened articulateness, is still distinctively
Shavian.

Act I of *Buoyant Billions* touches off from an all-too-familiar excuse for
debate: a problematic son on the threshold of maturity confronts his prosperous, conventional father about his future. But Shavian twists keep the
situation from being hackneyed: the young man, acknowledged by his father to be brilliant, declares his intention to pursue a career as "world
betterer," which he considers all the more feasible with the advent of the
Atomic Age. The father, who has long profited from the status quo, can
see nothing but the dark side of the new era: soon not only America and
England but many other nations will wield "irresistible" power simply because they "can afford to make atomic bombs, and wipe out a city and all
its inhabitants in a thousandth of a second" (320). The son naively replies:
"What does that matter if they can build it again in ten minutes? . . . Hiroshima and Nagasaki are already rebuilt; and Japan is all the better for
the change." His retorts that focus on the potentialities of atomic power
to benefit mankind display little rashness of youth, however: "All the scientists in the world are at work finding out how to dilute and control and
cheapen atomic power until it can be used to boil an egg or sharpen a lead
pencil as easily as to destroy a city" (320). The son's Shavian propensity
to exaggerate extends to following such ideas "as far as thought can reach."

His rhetoric attains a glowing crescendo as a result: "When atom splitting makes it easy for us to support ourselves as well by two hours' work as now by two years, we shall move mountains and straighten rivers in a hand's turn. Then the problem of what to do in our spare time will make life enormously more interesting. No more doubt as to whether life is worth living. Then the world betterers will come to their own" (320–21).[19] A sharp exchange of radically opposed views puts the cap on their argument:

FATHER.   Damn the atomic bomb!

SON.   Bless it say I. It will make world bettering possible. (322)

A reconciliation of sorts ensues when the son (rather absurdly) proposes that his father finance an around-the-world trip to investigate the chances of atomic science "ridding the world of the anopheles mosquito, the tsetse fly, the white ant, and the locust" (322), and the father agrees—more to get rid of him than anything else.[20]

The son's optimistic notions about what Shaw later labeled "atomic welfare"[21] had been in the air at least since the discovery of radioactivity. Shaw himself attributed his early knowledge of atomic power to the writings of his friend H. G. Wells.[22] Wells's novel *The World Set Free* (1913) depicts a disastrous atomic world war but gives equal time, and final victory, to the conceivable Utopian benefits of atomic energy. Both possibilities were also heralded in *Wings Over Europe* (1928), which Shaw might well have known (especially since the hero is partly modeled on Eugene Marchbanks). The vein of extravagance in the son's rhetoric is present in both of these works. After Hiroshima the promising side of atomic power was flaunted conspicuously in government press releases and mass-circulation outlets as counters to the widespread shock and horror the event produced.[23]

The tiny first scene of *Farfetched Fables* uses the pretext of a boy-meets-girl situation to convey largely negative ideas about the Atomic Age. Here the conflict that creates the few dramatic sparks does not arise from disagreement on the issues but from the impact of the new situation on the male-female relationship. In a public park on a promising day an attractive young man and woman meet for the first time. In the late Shavian style, both fly in the face of convention by stating nakedly what they feel:

YOUNG MAN.   . . . I've got into this conversation with a view to our possible marriage.

YOUNG WOMAN.   Nothing doing. I'll not marry. (430)

We learn quickly that she equates marriage with bearing children, and that she will not "bring them into this wicked world to kill and be killed." Later the young man argues that wars will not be fought with atomic weapons because of their indiscriminate destructiveness (in his cockney idiom he refers knowledgeably to the effects of their blasts, firestorms, and radiation). He adds, pointedly, "Besides, bombs kill women. Killing men does not matter: the women can replace them; but kill the women and you kill the human race" (432).[24] This could be construed as a subtle appeal to the maternal instinct. It is preceded by a startling event that might also sway the woman: the United Nations countries have agreed to abolish war and make the manufacture of atomic weapons a capital crime. The newspaper extra announcing this development calls it "a new chapter in the history of the globe. The atomic bomb has reduced war to absurdity; for it threatens not only both victors and vanquished but the whole neutral world. . . . [No] nation will ever venture on atomic warfare again" (431). Unfortunately, the young woman is skeptical that wars will cease to exist. She visualizes a further step in the evolution of genocidal weapons: a new kind of poison gas that is lighter than air so that it will disperse. "It may kill the inhabitants of a city," she says; "but it will leave the city standing and in working order" (432). The second startling turn in this eight-minute sketch occurs when the young man shows intense interest in the woman's idea—and no more in her. He reveals that he is a chemist in a chlorine gas factory and begins contemplating how to create the weapon she imagined. This settles the less-than-promising romance once and for all:

YOUNG WOMAN [*rising wrathfully*]   So that is what you are! One of these scientific devils who are destroying us! Well, you shall not sit next me again. Go where you belong: to hell. Good day to you.

She goes away.

YOUNG MAN [*still thoughtful*]   Lighter than air, eh? [*Slower*] Ligh—ter—than—air?

The scene fades out. (433)

The next scene in *Farfetched Fables* refers in no way to atomic power, but it completes the young man's story by fulfilling the young woman's prophecy. He invents the usable poison gas and sells it to a dictator, who destroys the population of the Isle of Wight to demonstrate its potency. Other countries who also got the formula (no doubt from the inventor) start a cataclysmic world war. After peddling his profitable commodity, we learn, the young man had moved to the Isle of Wight as a safety measure.

The connections between the subject matter in this little play and Shaw's published comments on the new Atomic Age are remarkably close. His earliest articles in the press assert that the absurdity of the institution of world war was highlighted when the atomic bomb proved "too deadly to be used as a weapon, though it has had its momentary success by finishing the war with Japan."[25] A fortnight after Hiroshima he was prescient enough to raise the double specter of the proliferation of nuclear weapons and the invention of much more devastating ones: "What we have just succeeded in doing at enormous expense is making an ounce of uranium explode like [a supernova]. The process, no longer experimental, will certainly be cheapened; and at any moment heavier elements than uranium, as much more explosive than uranium as uranium than gunpowder, may be discovered."[26] By late 1945, when he composed his preface to *Geneva*, Shaw had refined these ideas markedly. He states flatly that "if another world war be waged with this new weapon there may be an end of our civilization and its massed populations" (23). He now speaks of countries *consoling* themselves "with the hope that the atomic bomb has made war impossible" (24), and shows little confidence in governments being competent enough to forge international agreements banning the bomb and enforcing the ban. He echoes his fear that more devastating nuclear weapons may be devised (22), but goes far beyond this in his peroration:

> Meanwhile here we are, with our incompetence armed with atomic bombs. Now power civilizes and develops mankind, though not without having first been abused to the point of wiping out entire civilizations. If the atomic bomb wipes out ours we shall just have to begin again. We may agree on paper not to use it as it is too dangerous and destructive; but tomorrow may see the discovery of that poisonous gas lighter than air and capable . . . of killing all the inhabitants of a city without damaging its buildings or sewers or water supplies or railways or electric plants.[27] Victory might then win cities if it could repopulate them soon enough, whereas atomic bombing leaves nothing for anyone, victor or vanquished. It is conceivable even that the next great invention may create an overwhelming interest in pacific civilization and wipe out war. You never can tell. (42–43)

The amusing tale of the young chemist is clearly a dramatically compressed equivalent, a "farfetched fable" or theatrical exemplar, of these grimly serious statements.

Neither *Buoyant Billions* nor *Farfetched Fables* is a full-fledged "drama of the Atomic Age." The Son's main objective in his argument with his father in the former play is not to convince him (or us) that world-betterment is more feasible than ever now that atomic power can be employed to that end, but to talk him into financing the first stage of his quest. The rest of the play, including the early part of the Act I argument, focuses on the Son's pursuit of *financing*, not world-betterment. The new possibilities of the Atomic Age are never again mentioned. Similarly, the first two fables in the latter play show hypothetically that curbing the atomic bomb will not necessarily prevent world destruction, but their main function is to establish the start-from-scratch situation for the ensuing futuristic episodes. These carry the chief thrust of the play, successively dramatizing the possible workings of Creative Evolution from restoring the human race (in amended form) to attaining the "vortex of pure thought" envisioned much earlier in *Back to Methuselah*. The significance and fascination of Shaw's varied reactions to the advent of a radically new stage in world history lies partly in their marked "Shavianity," but also as phenomena of a still-fertile mind in its nineties. That they exist at all is a farfetched fable in itself.

PRIESTLEY'S *SUMMER DAY'S DREAM*: "ROUSSEAU FOR THE ATOM-AGE"

A brief look at J. B. Priestley's play will suffice, since his focus in *Summer Day's Dream*[28] is so remote from the realities of atomic war as generally perceived in 1949 that the basic premise of his plot is highly improbable. We learn that in 1960 a "Third War" occurred in which "a thousand cities vanished in flame and dust and a hundred million bodies were consumed in agony" (473). The play sets up a sharp contrast between upper-middle-class life in England before this holocaust and fifteen years hence. The war deindustrialized the country and forced survivors into an existence more dependent on natural resources than technology, more inclined to cooperate than to compete. (Significantly, the largest city in England is now upcountry, nonindustrial Shrewsbury.) The gentleman-farmer life of the Dawlish family, on which the play centers, has supplanted a hectic, profit-oriented existence. As Stephen, the family's patriarch, deftly puts it: "I spent more than half my life . . . arguing and planning and running round like a maniac, all to sell a lot of things to people I didn't know so that I could buy a lot of things I never had time to use. Sheer lunacy. And it took nothing less than an atom bomb to blow me out of it" (410). The *Times* heralded the play as Priestley's "vision of an England which has come through atomic disaster to a quiet wisdom," but another reviewer panned its basic premise as "Rousseau for the atom-age."[29]

The plot of *Summer Day's Dream* hinges on the attempts by a triad of foreigners to restore a semblance of the prewar way of life to the area. An American capitalist, a Russian bureaucrat, and an Indian scientist arrive to lay the groundwork for exploiting the land in the old manner: having discovered that the chalk in the area (the South Downs) would enable them to make a new synthetic product, they want "to dig out the chalk, to erect a manufacturing plant, to build a whole industrial town—" (443). (Secretly they also plan cafés, TV palaces, gambling joints, and perhaps brothels [427].) Stephen sums up the conflict eloquently: the inhabitants of the area are "survivors from a wreck, from the war of split atoms and split minds—who crawled out of the darkness into the daylight. A dark clutter of rubbish was cleared away for us. Now you come to dump the rubbish back on us again" (463). The antagonists turn out to have some heart after all; the "idyllic picture of countrymen living in a haze of benevolence, barter and blank verse," as Peter Fleming dubbed it,[30] prevails upon them and they abandon their project.

After informing their compatriots back home through an efficient communications system, the intruders leave—in an "atomicar." Priestley is extremely vague on the recovery process that allowed such state-of-the-art technology to be available, not to speak of the miraculous ecological and psychic recoveries of the land and people. Part of the regeneration is credited to a benevolent "World Settlement Plan," and this must also account for the regeneration of American business, Russian bureaucracy, and Indian (or world) science. At any rate, the play exhibits a blitheful unawareness of the disparity between its nuclear catalyst for radical change and the varied transformations that it depicts.

LASKI'S NEGLECTED POST-HOLOCAUST DRAMA, *THE OFFSHORE ISLAND*

Like Priestley's *Summer's Day Dream*, Marghanita Laski's *The Offshore Island*[31] takes place several years after a nuclear holocaust and focuses on a small group of survivors who reject the kind of "civilization" that intruders offer them. But the resemblances end there. Laski takes the consequences of a devastating atomic war much more seriously, keeping an appropriate focus on the grim negatives while still allowing for regenerative side effects. The result is a vivid, moving piece of tragic naturalism with a mildly upbeat finale that saves the play from utter pathos. If Priestley's play unmistakably evokes the atmosphere of *A Midsummer Night's Dream*, *The Offshore Island* anticipates the mingled horror and hope that characterizes Edward Bond's post-holocaust drama, *War Plays*. Laski's ingenious, daring, and markedly feminist vision of a crisis that faces some very human survivors of the bomb, conveyed through the medium of a traditional but surehanded dramaturgy, makes her play by far the most interesting and impressive English-language drama of the first phase of the Nuclear Age.

The play belongs securely to this era. Although written in 1954, when the United States and the Soviet Union had already exploded fusion (hydrogen) bombs, *The Offshore Island* posits a war that involved saturation bombing with fission bombs. The play is set on an offshore island—a term often applied to Great Britain as a whole.[32] There, Rachel Verney scrapes out a primitive agrarian existence with a teenage daughter and son and receives occasional visits from another survivor, Martin, who lives with four people in the only other habitable enclave she knows about. Because of geographical peculiarities, these two small areas escaped the direct effects of bombs and the ensuing heavy radiation. The rest of the island (but not the water) is presumed to be dangerously contaminated. Laski states in a prefatory note written in 1959 that the world situation she based her play upon "has changed only in that bombs have got so much bigger that pockets of survival in England seem even dramatically improbable." Her play is in one sense an exercise in flirting with dramatic improbabilities, and when a squad of American soldiers turns up, and later a Russian one, it takes a convincing background scenario to induce us to accept these extraordinary turns of plot.

The scenario we learn about from the intruders not only seems like a reasonable hypothesis for the time, but contains some strikingly imaginative elements. Ten years ago the two superpowers, by then equipped with ample stockpiles of atomic weapons, reached a political crisis that erupted into war between NATO and the Communist bloc, a war that is still going on. Showing unusual prudence, the United States and Russia used only non-nuclear weapons on each other's countries. Asked why, the American captain shrugs: "Obvious reasons. No one wants them back, so no one cares to begin" (51). But the superpowers' prudence extended to ruthlessness: they used atomic bombs to destroy each other's less potent allies. The American explains this to Rachel as a military necessity:

CHARLES: Sooner or later all the satellites got treated alike by one side or the other.

RACHEL: But we weren't a satellite.

CHARLES *(With raised eyebrows)*:   Weren't you? (51)

Among other things, this exchange reflects England's apprehension that America was treating their country as a mere base for bomb storage and delivery—a handy but dispensable ally.[33] Rachel shows an almost irrational distrust when she asks the captain which country *did* bomb England. His reply justifies her intuition:

CHARLES: Why don't you assume it was the enemy?

RACHEL: I don't know.

CHARLES: You're too intelligent for your own good. I'll tell you the truth. I don't know either. If *they* bombed you, it was because you were allied to us. If *we* bombed you, it was to forestall some move or other on their part. Little countries got bombed for all sorts of reasons, and which it was in your case, I honestly don't remember. After all, it was ten years ago.

RACHEL: But we were your friends.

CHARLES: Military considerations are more important than friends. (51–52)

Moving this viewpoint to the outer edge of probability as the basis for her plot, Laski depicts the residue of this policy in action: the Americans are searching out and destroying minimally contaminated pockets of land (after removing the few people who agree to leave) so that the enemy cannot use them to their advantage. As Charles tells Rachel, "my orders are that this land has got to die" (81). Startlingly but not unreasonably, given the assumed dominance of wartime policy-making, America has been cooperating with Russia in this process, each pursuing "Operation Neutralizer" on one side of the fifty-first parallel. When a truce is called between the countries, Russian soldiers join the Americans at the Verney homestead. Captain Baltinsky has agreed to cooperate by dropping the "very small tactical bomb" needed to destroy the house and land.[34] Why the truce? Reminiscent of Orwell's *1984*, with its abruptly changing alliances between Oceania, Eurasia, and Eastasia, the United States and Russia are forming a new alliance because "the Eastern menace" is now a greater threat to the two warring sides than they are to each other (71).[35] In sum, former enemies have collaborated in the past and are cooperating even more efficiently in the present to complete the destruction of an offshore island, a microcosm of the larger entity, Great Britain.

Within this plausible framework, a three-part tale of the preservation of humanity and humanistic values unfolds. Act I reveals not only the dismal conditions of survival the Verney family and Martin have dealt with more or less successfully for ten years, but the psychological and moral states of mind which have naturally evolved. After Rachel's children, Mary and James, idly speculate about someone coming to rescue them, Martin arrives on his biannual visit—hardly a savior, but a welcome replenisher. He and Rachel soon go upstairs. Mary expresses intense envy toward her mother and desire for Martin—or any male, including her brother. Before he leaves, Martin reveals that he has talked to other survivors (Frenchmen in a boat) and that they saw an airplane. He gets the Verneys to promise that if anyone comes they will pretend he does not exist. At the curtain, grotesquely clad American soldiers burst in, brandishing tommy guns, as their leader announces "We come as friends." Act II gradually exposes the background of war and militarism that originally caused the survivors' plight and now pervades life in "uncontaminated" America. Rachel and James grow increasingly leery of their potential saviors, who seem to be hiding something ominous, while Captain Charles senses that Rachel is holding back information about other survivors. After the soldiers go outside for the night, Martin sneaks in (the water was too high for him to make his way home) and vainly urges the family to leave with him. The captain reenters just as Martin departs. An enemy plane is detected; Charles tells his men about the truce; and at the curtain, grotesquely clad Russian soldiers enter cautiously as their leader announces "We come as comrades."

In the brief final act, Rachel and her children learn what their alternatives truly are: extinction along with their land, removal to another type of severely limited existence, or (if possible) flight to Martin's enclave. Their land will be "killed." They are all classed as "C.P.s"—Contaminated Persons—and as such will be sterilized. They will live in glorified concentration camps and work for the war effort. As the Neutralizer plane approaches, James insults Charles enough to get shot, and Rachel decides to stay with her dead son. Mary also wants to stay, but Rachel convinces her to flee to Martin and try to have children.

The thematic conflict involved in this melodramatic but engrossing plot can be stated oversimply as a clash between thoroughgoing militarism and gutsy humanism. Captain Charles not only stands firmly on the side of military necessity as an agent of a superpower at war, but often displays the psychic makeup of the "military mind" at an aberrant extreme. With the children present, he tells Rachel that he will take them back to civilization "Depending on which side you're on." When the precocious sixteen-year-old son asks why he must choose a side and thus an enemy, Charles responds:

> You've got to have an enemy because that's the condition of mankind. A lot of fools wonder . . . whether it isn't possible to live in peace. . . . It isn't. Peace corrupts you, makes you soft, makes a fool of you. If you want to protect the values you stand for, you've got to fight for them. It's the fighting, I tell you, that proves the civilization, that tells a man where he stands in his own private battle. . . . What we don't need are neutrals, peace-mongers. They're the real enemy, the enemy of both sides, the enemy of all that's fine and decent in mankind. (57–58)

Captain Charles is portrayed here as a professional military bureaucrat who has gone off the deep end. He has internalized the qualities distinctive to his profession so that he can now justify its necessary functions, beneficial or ghastly, in terms of a self-serving ethic that elevates fighting to "all that's fine and decent in mankind."[36] Symptomatically, he views a battle between enemies as "his own private battle." The play translates this into the cat-and-mouse game that he plays with the Verneys to smoke out other pockets of survival. It is vital that they own up so that he can complete his military assignment and also determine if the family is "on his side" and thus worth saving. In the end his efforts are frustrated, largely because his extreme militarism manifests itself so nakedly.

The chief spokesman for humanism in the play is Martin. He is characterized as an unrefined west-country fisherman, "very brawny, very tough, very gentle and likeable" (10). Although the more cultured Verneys share his general outlook, only Martin goes to the extent of valuing the simple, ultra-humane life which he loves so much that he does not want to give "civilization" a chance. He has a wife who has been blinded and severely brain-damaged in the war, but for "selfish" reasons he and his daughter have refrained from putting her out of her misery:

> You see, we keep her for our sakes, not for hers. It gives us a chance to be kind, sort of—. . . . It's as if we were forever saying to ourselves that there's those that hold human life cheap but not us. You might say that keeping the poor thing alive is our way of saying that we're human beings in a different way to them people, real human beings the way we was meant to be. (11–12)

This touching declaration reflects both the basic gentleness of Martin and the rough edges. His humanism is idealistic but tinged with narrowmindedness: he views survivors like himself in direct opposition to "them people," which he defines as those who "hold human life cheap." This turns out to embrace everyone who might come to rescue him, and by extension (though he does not grasp it) all the still-civilized world. When James utters hopefully, "if they do come, real people, O God, we can begin to live—," Martin retorts: "Then live for yourself, young James, and don't drag me in. I've had enough of the kind of life those kind of people can give me" (26). After James has seen enough of the kind of rescuers who do come, he announces that he will not leave with them, and consciously echoes Martin:

> JAMES (Stammering as he tries to remember): Captain Charles, people like us—we've got to show what we stand for. There's those that hold life cheap, but they're not our kind. We've got to show we're different from people like that. (80)

In this brave assertion of manhood, James manifests Martin's aggressive humanism. Laski hints at a resemblance between the militarist Charles and the humanist Martin. In the opposed points of view of both, the world consists of like-minded friends and "those kind of people"—enemies. Both men embody the basically masculine mind-set that leads to war.

Rachel Verney, who at forty is about as old as Laski was when she wrote *The Offshore Island*, has complex and at times ambivalent views, but their core is a typically feminine one: the desirability of living in peace. She is indeed a "neutral." To a degree the American and Russian captains sum her up when they generalize derogatively about the survivors they have met:

CHARLES . . .   Leave us out, they say, let us live in peace. Let us rear our families and raise our crops and you keep your ideals to yourself.

BALTINSKY: They think mankind is— . . . families. (74)

This applies to Martin almost as well as to Rachel, of course. But what distinguishes her from him is that although she too is skeptical, she does not rule out the possibility of finding a better life for her family. Martin abruptly makes his decision to stay and, in effect, imposes it upon his wife, daughter, and two neighbors (who will never hear about the potential rescuers). Rachel keeps an open mind and prompts her children to do the same. After Martin's declaration, James is strongly influenced toward staying and continuing to cultivate the small farm he has lovingly nurtured. But when he manifests his mother's flexible attitude, she subtly encourages it:

MARTIN . . . :   You don't think they've come for anything that's good?

JAMES: *I* don't. But there's just a chance—

RACHEL: That's it, Martin. There's just a chance. I daren't let it slip without finding out. (64)

A moment later James says, "I think I've got to wait here and see" (65). Rachel's daughter Mary, at eighteen, is physically mature, but her mind has been shaped more by some leftover popular magazines than by her mother's balanced realism. She has become an escapist with a romantically warped idea of the world she might escape to. Rachel gently puts the damper on her enthusiasm:

MARY: . . . Martin's mad not to want to be rescued, isn't he, Mummy?

RACHEL: I suppose he is. *(Doubtfully)* I wish I was sure. (28–29)

When Mary proposes a toast to "The rediscovery of civilization," Rachel replies: "No, I won't drink to that. I'll drink to the rediscovery of people, if you like" (29).

The crucial factor that makes Rachel more positive than Martin about choosing to leave is that he has always lived a life not very different from his present one, whereas she has experienced a genuinely civilized life as an architect's wife in London.[37] When Captain Charles notes that the survivors he has met, "people living like animals," nevertheless exude "some kind of peace" and "rightness," Rachel rejects the idea that this aura may derive from living away from "all the corruptions of civilization." Without civilization, she insists, "life's nothing more than just keeping alive. These past years, you don't know how often I've wished to God I *could* be a peasant, not think, just rear children and grow food and stay alive without even knowing I was alive. But I'm civilized. I've got to have music and books and people—*(Angrily)*—and I don't think that's corrupt" (54–55). Near the end of the play Rachel finally realizes the source of her "rightness" and relative peace. She expresses it to Charles as absence of guilt:

> I've enjoyed civilization too much to be happy in a new stone age. But for ten years I've been free from guilt. I've lived at no one's expense. The things that have been valuable have been truly valuable, not a matter of making money and spending it, showing that you've made it and spent it. I've had no part in hurting and killing for words. I've lived in peace with my family. (84)

She sums up this state simply as "freedom." It is partly freedom from the "ideals" that Charles told Baltinsky the survivors reject: Rachel has lived where capitalist ideals cannot apply and has had no part in "killing for words." Charles has a hard time grasping that firm ideals do not seem to underlie the survivors' pacific tenacity. Yet they do not even believe in God any more,[38] much less nationalist or militarist bywords. And Rachel is not even a rigid humanist, like Martin. She has "family values," but they are flexible, tolerant, and natural.

Natural, Laski would have us recognize, for a strong, self-enlightened woman. Act I reveals Rachel's ways of coping with the conditions which have been her lot for ten years. Deprived of her husband, her habitual milieu of cultured society, and all but minimal resources for subsistence, she has adapted courageously rather than succumbing to despair. Inflicted with severe loneliness and no appreciable hope of rescue, she has raised "living in peace with her family" to the stature of the highest good attainable. Her children have been imbued with this ethic, as an interesting exchange (with feminist import) demonstrates early in Act I:

JAMES *(Casually):* O, women are different.

MARY *(Strongly):* That's just a phrase out of a book. . . . You don't know any women but me and Mother. Of course we're different from you, and we're different from each other too. How do you know we're different in a special way because we're women?

JAMES *(Seriously):* I don't of course. You're quite right. (5)

Elsewhere the children show that they have learned to place great value on the activities they must perform, as a group forced into self-sufficiency: care for the pigs and chickens, nurture and harvest the plants, organize meals. Mary remarks how much it satisfies her to prepare food for the family: "I mean, it's preparing food, no not just preparing food, but doing it for people, people you love" (17). James feels a special pang when he learns that "his" land will be killed.

Perhaps the most notable adjustment Rachel has made in her present circumstances relates to her liberation from "ideals," in this case social and moral conventions concerning the family, marriage, and reproduction. Rachel is at her most independent—and Laski at her most daring—when she and Martin discuss ways to produce "someone to carry on." They have been trying, but the only result has been miscarriages. Martin proposes bringing his twelve-year-old daughter to James in three years. Rachel readily answers, "I think that's a very good idea." Then Martin raises the ante:

MARTIN: And Mary—(He stops, embarrassed.)

RACHEL (Looking at him steadily):   Yes, Martin? And Mary?

MARTIN (Looking away from her):   The way I see it—(He breaks off, confused, and tries again) You know how it is with my wife. I'm not really married. And I'm not so old yet. I can still have children, you said so yourself.

RACHEL (Clearly):   You are suggesting that I should give you Mary for yourself.

MARTIN: Yes.

RACHEL: I've thought of it, of course. (21)

In a moment Rachel says she will talk to Mary about his idea, and adds, "I think she will be pleased." But before this Rachel digresses into another possibility she has considered seriously: incest. Here Laski courts instant rejection at the hands of the Lord Chamberlain's Examiner of Plays. In discussing this utterly forbidden topic with Martin, again it is Rachel who is the more open, he the more reticent:

RACHEL . . .   They used to do it in ancient Egypt, you know, and so long as it's pure line-breeding, they say it's all right.

MARTIN (Shamefaced):   I've thought of it with me and Jenny, but I wouldn't never be able to bring myself to it, somehow.

RACHEL (Deliberately light):   I didn't fancy it either. It's silly, isn't it? I mean, our ideas on those things, they're just conventions society has made up, and now there isn't society any more, there's only us. (22)

Laski has already laid the realistic basis for this tense consideration of alternatives, which is of course tempered by both parents' rejection of incest. Earlier in the act she shows how badly Mary wants a man and points up her lack of conventionally acceptable choices. When Rachel and Martin go upstairs, Mary reacts just as a physically mature young woman in this situation might: she becomes preoccupied with sexual desire, and expresses a fierce desire for Martin, whom her mother is monopolizing. Her frustration leads her into the most forbidden territory of all:

MARY *(Intensely)*: I want to, overwhelmingly, and nobody thinks of it. She's old, she could do without.

JAMES *(Shocked)*: Do you mean you want *him*? . . .

MARY *(Looking down at her hand)*: Or anyone.

JAMES: There isn't anyone else.

MARY: No, there isn't, is there? *(She raises her head and looks at him.)*

JAMES *embarrassedly fumbles in the sack.* . . .

MARY: Have you ever thought what you'll do when you come to want it overwhelmingly like they do?

JAMES *(Frightened)*: No, I haven't.

MARY *(Frightened, too, but resolute)*: The pigs, yes, and the chickens too, they don't bother who's who. . . . Which of us are you going to choose—or both?

JAMES *(Standing up, tortured)*: Mary, I don't know. I've thought about it. I've lain awake thinking about it, but I couldn't. It seems horrible and unnatural, I don't know why, but it does. There used to be those people, monks, who never had anybody. I think I'll have to be one of them. I don't want to be, but I'll have to be. . . .

MARY *(Despairing)*: Then what about me? (15–16)

This episode is a highly ingenious and striking means of placing before the audience some of the blunt realities the Verneys must deal with. In turn, it reflects the relative openmindedness Mary and James have absorbed from their mother when "family values" are involved. At the end of the play, when James is dead and Rachel awaits the bomb with Mary, a pathetic but tender final affirmation occurs. Rachel, herself mildly disabled, urges Mary to flee to a not-too-distant cave, then go to Martin when she can.

RACHEL . . . He's a good man, he wants you. Quickly, go quickly.

MARY: But Mummy—I can't leave you—I'll help you—I'll drag you—

RACHEL: I can't—you know I can't. We'd both die. Mary, it's right. You must keep alive. Whatever kind of children you have, they'll be good. (87)

Mary hesitates, then caresses her brother, kisses her mother, and leaves. Rachel has given her blessing to a union between her daughter and her fifty-year-old lover, whose wife will still be present, a union which might well produce deformed or mutant children. But a new family may emerge as a result.

Rachel's general strength of character emerges most clearly from her interaction with Captain Charles. Here, feminine humanist values compete with masculine militarist ones in a complex, deftly handled conflict that also involves mutual attraction. Charles is more than an extreme representative of his profession; like Rachel, he is intelligent, cultured, and self-conscious. Underneath his bravado he questions his chosen role and hopes to discover a more valid way of life. Rachel is the first person he has met whom he thinks may have "something really important" to say. Telling her this prompts a revealing exchange:

RACHEL: Is that what you want, a message? When you've got everything else in the world?

CHARLES (Deeply moved): If I could be sure—I know what we've got, what we're fighting for. I shouldn't doubt, I don't doubt really. But I volunteered for this job, because I thought, I hoped—I don't know what I hoped, only that if you were alive, people, I mean, they'd have found something worth knowing.

RACHEL: What about the other people you found?

CHARLES: They were peasants, I tell you. It didn't matter what they said. But you—you must have had something to keep you going all these years, something worth living for. (53)

Rachel's explicit answers do not satisfy him: he cannnot live in peace with his family because he has none, and his life has passed the point where he might feel free of guilt. But in a moment he tells her tormentedly, "you've got more than I have," and kisses her "greedily" (55). Charles has come to believe that Rachel holds a magnetic power over him, so firm is her sense of "rightness" compared to his own. If he can induce her to go to America, his dubious mission—emblematic of his whole way of life—will receive some sanction. If he cannot, the temptation to call off the mission and stay with her will be genuine. Rachel acts as an inadvertent Siren to Charles's Odysseus. Baltinsky asks him if this family will go with him, and he answers "*(Savagely)* By God, they'll come if I have to drag them." The Russian perceptively adds, "Why do you care?" Charles evades the question and launches into a flailing reassertion of his militaristic ethic: "They're the real enemy, I tell you. Without them, you'd have a clean decent fight"— a "personal battle," that is, with no doubts that it might be dirty or indecent. Again perceptive, Baltinsky divines what underlies this outburst:

BALTINSKY: Fortunately few of my men know any language but their own.

CHARLES: But you do.

BALTINSKY: Yes, you and I both understand what they say.

CHARLES: "What song the Sirens sung"—Christ, I know now what song the Sirens sung—(74–75)[39]

Just as Odysseus had to lash himself to the mast in order to resist the sirens' lure (while manfully exposing himself to it), Charles has been tying himself to the staunch mast of his own convictions while exposing himself to Rachel. In his next encounter with her she is preparing to leave with him, not yet knowing what is in store for her. He remarks that he never really had the option of staying with her but confesses that he was strongly tempted:

CHARLES . . . There's never but the one thing to do.

RACHEL . . . : What was the other thing you thought of doing?

CHARLES *(Explosively)*: Thought?—No, that's not right. Dreamed? Imagined? I don't know. Only wanted like hell to stay here, live here with you the way you do, say "Include me out" to everything I'm committed to.

RACHEL: We'd have welcomed you. I'd still welcome you. *(Pause)* It's not going to happen—is it?

CHARLES: No, it couldn't happen. Why did I have to meet you here? (79)

After Rachel learns the grim truth of what would face her family in America, Charles still tries to convince her to go. The finale of their intricate conflict is the emotional crescendo of the play:

CHARLES: . . . *(Pleading)* You said you wanted people to talk to.

RACHEL: I wanted more than that.

CHARLES *(Angrily and brutal)*: Well, you can have that too. I wasn't good enough for you, was I, but no doubt some husky C.P. will be delighted to oblige. (85)

James intrudes with a counteracting jibe that proves fatal: "My Mother doesn't need you or any C.P. either. She's got a better man." This humiliation provokes Charles to strike the boy, then shoot him when he remains defiant. Tender pathos ensues:

> JAMES *(In childish surprise)*:   Mummy, he's hurting me.
>
> *He dies.* RACHEL *kneels beside him, not touching him.*
>
> RACHEL *(In quiet agony)*:   My son, my son.
>
> CHARLES *(Starts to speak, breaks it off, then speaks curtly and officially)*:   We're leaving now. You ready?
>
> RACHEL *stands up clumsily, facing him.*
>
> RACHEL: I'm staying here with James.
>
> CHARLES: There's no need, you know. We've met this situation before. *(Laughs)* I ought to be more used to it. But I thought that you—*(His voice breaks.)* (86)

Once again, Charles's excessive assertion of manhood only results in intensifying his frustration and self-doubt. Rachel has given him her last word already by choosing "freedom," such as it is.

> CHARLES: You don't call this freedom?
>
> RACHEL: Yes. Freedom is what it is. (85)

Laski's *The Offshore Island* was given a short run at a small leftist venue in London, the Unity Theatre, in early May 1960. Television versions were aired in England and Canada, but the stage version has apparently never been revived.[40] Yet the one substantial review of the Unity production said it was "written with rare intelligence and restraint," and praised it for accomplishing what it set out to do: "Few subjects for a play or a novel can be more daunting than that of the world after an H-bomb war [*sic*]. Marghanita Laski in *The Offshore Island* has succeeded extraordinarily well without ducking any of the problems—sexual, physical, intellectual and moral—which would in fact face an isolated family which survived in contaminated Britain."[41] The play has also been ignored by serious critics. The only extended discussion I have found is several pages of introductory material in a high school text.[42] It is clear that the play was virtually stillborn. The major reasons, I would contend, derive from qualities which are now irrelevant or grant it a distinctive interest. Surely the script, as published, could not have passed the stage censor without having some of its most absorbing and functional passages lopped out. Its antiestablishment theme that Britain had become a mere strategic pawn for the United States in the Cold War against the Soviet Union actually resulted in the author being "reviled as a communist," according to Doris Lessing.[43] Then its thoughtful treatment of a hypothetical situation that was considered quite probable when the play was written, in the pre-thermonuclear Atomic Age, would not have struck contemporary sensibilities nearly as much a half-decade later when the play was published and performed; the focus of terror in the H-bomb era was total annihilation. Still, like Bond's *War Plays*, *The Offshore Island* is a sophisticated and highly effective re-creation of a past chapter in the annals of all-too-possible events. As such, it has far more literary appeal than mere sci-fi or fantasy fiction, not to speak of its historical and cultural import. Finally, it is at the very least a minor landmark in the total body of feminist drama, if a fine play written by a female with a strong, liberated woman at its center admits it to that category. Especially if this quality was one reason for its neglect, it is certainly a good reason why it deserves resuscitation.

O'CASEY'S EVOLVING REACTIONS TO THE ATOMIC AGE

Crisp pronouncements on the nuclear situation from a gadfly to the English, Sean O'Casey, provide a striking and convenient bridge from the sudden birth of the Atomic Age to its replacement by the Thermonuclear Era. Although a resident of England well before the atomic bomb was dropped, O'Casey retained his inimitable Irish flavor, well conveyed by his projection of himself as "the green crow," as well as his dogged allegiance to Soviet Communism, which made most British socialists seem like timid gradualists in contrast. (Once he trumpeted publicly, "May God damn the one who raises a voice for war against the Soviet Union."[44]) His immediate reaction to the shocking emergence of atomic weapons, recorded in letters written not long after the event, was that he was "not a bit frightened."[45] Assuming with many thoughtful people that Russia would soon match the United States in destructive capacity, O'Casey found an audaciously positive point of view for favoring the new bomb:

> Everyone seems to be worrying about the atomic bomb. I think it's the best thing yet. It's too dangerous for anyone to use. "I dar you! You blow me up, an' I'll blow you up!" . . . When they didn't dare do it with gas, they wouldn't dare with the atomic bomb. It puts Capitalism in the worst position ever: here they are with the power to blow Communism out of life, & they daren't use it! Why? Because in blowing out Communism, they'd be blown out too; & the one & only thing a Capitalist values more than his money is his life.[46]

When O'Casey learned that the United States was going to produce a hydrogen bomb, he changed his tune. Again assuming that the Russians would quickly catch up, he found no consolation in the idea, but rather shared the world's fear that the new weapons may destroy us all.[47] "The whole world is frightened and suspicious, and no wonder. If the atom bomb—not to mention the H. brother—is loosed on us, then it will be a toss up as to what may happen to all or any of us."[48] He put his sentiments in bold, bald terms for his Communist compatriots in a letter to *The Daily Worker* entitled "Let It Rot Where It Lies"—"It" being the Bomb: "We need a lot of things, we do that; but the first thing of all these things is our need for peace. . . . Nothing is any good if we let ourselves be plunged headlong into war. . . . To do things, we must be sure of life. To be sure of life, we must first ban the atom bomb. Let it rust away, let it rot away where it lies on its stockpile. . . . To hell with the atom bomb!"[49]

Reflecting a more knowledgeable pessimism, O'Casey's last words on the subject at this time were to jeer at the idea that public and private shelters might alleviate the problem. "[D]esperate efforts" were going on in England to scrape together a Civil Defence program, "though all in their hearts know there can be no defence in the next war. . . . [It] is clear that neither brown paper nor steel can shield a soul from atomic concussion and flash."[50] In turn, O'Casey took whatever positive measures that he could, joining the Atomic Scientists' Association, giving speeches at peace conferences when his health permitted and sending messages when it did not.[51] In a time when peace "was a hated outcast," he became one of twelve writers (among them the playwrights Laurence Housman and Christopher Fry) to risk public castigation by signing a call for "international settlement through peaceful negotiation"—an open letter printed in the *Daily Worker* and *Pravda*.[52] These contrasting reactions to the advent of the atomic bomb and then its "H. brother" are thoroughly typical of Sean O'Casey. They are also clearly symptomatic of the way heightened nuclear terror could impose itself upon a strong-minded person determined from the first to resist it, and finally able to overcome it by constructive action.

CHAPTER 5

American Playwrights in the Early Thermonuclear Era

Shortly after President Truman announced the program to develop a superbomb, Maxwell Anderson exemplified the basic mind-set that would evolve among humanitarian thinkers in the new Thermonuclear Era. In the late 1940s he had viewed the Cold War in naive, conventional terms as a competition between totalitarian Communism and a wholly democratic "capitalist group" of nations (even telling Elmer Rice that he considered American Communist Party members "agents of a foreign power who wish to defeat us").[1] But in a speech accepting the Brotherhood Award from the National Conference of Christians and Jews on February 2, 1950, Anderson declared that although we are competitive animals, "we can no longer afford to be that way."

> We can't afford it because men are beginning to get their hands on the powers that used to be possessed by the gods of Olympus. . . . So long as weapons of war were comparatively inefficient men could afford to hate each other and whole nations could try to blow out each other's brains. There were always survivors. But when we begin to use hydrogen bombs it's possible that the survivors will be few or none.[2]

Anderson's views would continue to evolve, but in a circular path. By 1959 his mood was again symptomatically competitive: he asserted publicly that

America is "so spoiled, so luxury-minded, so carefree, so devoted to the pursuit of happiness, that we have let Russia get ahead of us . . . in the armament race. If Russia gets far ahead of us with ICBMs she will probably bury us,[3] and then proceed to take over the earth." Thus, Anderson concluded, America must excel in the arms race for as long as Russia competes.[4]

A more consistent humanist, Thornton Wilder, reflected an unusual degree of freedom from doctrinaire views, right or left, at the height of the McCarthy era. His statements in a 1953 interview make him seem like a throwback to the enlightened but ineffectual advocates of world government in pre-Cold War days: "If the planet Earth begins to understand its basic unity, . . . it will be full of promises and wonders. East and West have so many very important things to give each other. . . . This double track, this parallel noncooperative existence of the two hemispheres, is pernicious." Commenting on the arms race, Wilder conveyed his view by speculating about a hypothetical addition to *The Skin of Our Teeth*:

> As far as the question of scientific developments and discoveries (such as nuclear physics, A-bombs, etc.) which have outstripped the moral strength of man is concerned, I would like to express the problem figuratively as follows: The as yet unwritten fourth act of my tragicomedy *The Skin of Our Teeth* would deal with the painful lessons man still has to learn in the process of adapting scientific and technological advances to the demands of freedom, dignity and the ultimate destiny of mankind.[5]

Even in mid-1962, after the Soviet Union had erected the Berlin Wall, broken the moratorium on nuclear testing, and exploded a fifty-eight-megaton H-bomb in the atmosphere, Wilder still warned against "those who are overwrought with fear and are atavistically distrustful," whether Russians or Americans. Remarkably, he called for trying to understand why the Kremlin must distrust the United States: "I am fairly certain that the Soviets believe that the Western World is planning to surprise, seize and divide that great country." The problem for both sides is "how to allay the fears of the fearful."[6]

Unconciliatory by nature and leftist by experience, Lillian Hellman at first approached the Cold War with more sympathy for Russia than for America. When Henry Wallace ran for president on the Progressive Party line in 1948, she chaired the Women for Wallace committee "and took part in drafting the party platform, which asked for greater cooperation with the USSR, arms reductions, [etc.]."[7] In 1952 she became irate at the U.S. government because of her ordeal with HUAC and subsequent blacklisting. Later in the decade, however, she became sorely disillusioned about the Communist leadership after their brutal suppression of Hungary and the revelations of Stalin's atrocities. Hellman finally arrived at a comfort-able position of evenly divided scorn: "They [the Russians] condemn Vi-etnam, we condemn Hungary. But the moral tone of giants with swollen heads, fat fingers pressed over the atom bomb, staring at each other across the forests of the world, is monstrously comic."[8] This is the most striking caricature of the Cold War by an American dramatist of the time. In con-trast, one of the least striking revelations of nuclear consciousness is a state-ment Tennessee Williams made in a 1960 interview when the famous Japanese writer Yukio Mishima mentioned the atomic bomb. Apparently groping for an element of kinship, Williams commented: "We show both the light and the shadow, and the shadow is the violence which we live threatened by. I mean we're threatened with world extinction through vi-olence."[9]

At least three prominent American dramatists in this period planned dra-mas of the nuclear age but failed to complete them: Arthur Miller, Thorn-ton Wilder, and Clifford Odets. Miller wrote "page after page" of a play focusing on a tormented Oppenheimer figure but found it turning out to be "interesting when it should have been horrifying" (see Chapter 3). Thornton Wilder's journals record that while he was working on *The Al-cestiad* he was asked to write a play for the 1955 Edinburgh Festival.[10] He sketched out evolving scenarios for an Aristophanic comedy about a man taking absurd measures—and dragging his family into them—in order to escape living under the shadow of thermonuclear weapons. According to the two tentative scenarios (222 and 225–26), he refuses to let his daugh-ter(s) marry because "the world is about to come to a cataclysmic end," or because "it was dishonest to bring a child into the world in our time."[11] Then he moves his family to a cave "to await the end," or simply "because of the H-bomb." Finally, he takes his chances on a voyage to Mars; a flying saucer lands in front of the cave, or he has arranged a trip somehow and prepares to embark. Meanwhile (at least in the second version), photog-raphers and sacks of mail arrive, showing that his extraordinary actions concern the world—deeply or shallowly, as the case may be. Wilder wanted to adapt this unsettled sequence of actions to the "basic moral" that "many of the problems which seem insurmountable to us in our present world would find their solution if we could bring ourselves to face them supra-nationally" (222). On the face of it, this does not seem like a promising fusion of plot and point, and Wilder seems to have grown more and more skeptical of his idea. At one juncture he noted enigmatically: "Have written openings of Parts One and Two. It's all right, I guess. Only not funny enough—and by *funny*, I mean, *appalling*. But it's fairly appalling" (224). A later journal entry registers genuine discouragement. The necessary in-gredient of keeping women from having children in an H-bomb world would not "permit development as comedy"; it would violate "the spirit of Aristophanes" (226). Wilder soon gave up on the play, and seems to have destroyed the notes and drafts. He ultimately contributed an early version of *The Alcestiad* to the Edinburgh Festival.[12]

Clifford Odets had already written a fantasy-drama with analogies to impending nuclear destruction, *The Flowering Peach*,[13] when in 1961 he mapped out a play which might have dealt with the entire nuclear age to date. Described vaguely in two interviews,[14] the play was one of a group which Odets projected to search out and express "what has been happening here in the last fifteen years. And this isn't going to be anything to dance and shout about, because what happened here in fifteen years is really frightening." One play in particular, *An Old-Fashioned Man*, will itself "almost cover the American scene from the time of FDR's death to today. I think the play is of considerable import, but really the kind of import that makes you sit there and think, rather than the kind that makes you get up and burn with zeal" (83). In the second interview nearly two years later, Odets again speaks of a group of plays in process and says that he wants to write "the most serious play first," *An Old-Fashioned Man*. He adds, with tantalizing vagueness: "But then I think, if I write that play . . . it will lay me open to all sorts of charges of immodesty, of lopsidedness. It's the kind of play you simply cannot get on one viewing" (65). Unfortunately Odets died two months after this interview was printed, leaving his project in limbo.

Apart from Upton Sinclair's unpublished 1955 play about Oppenheimer (see Chapter 3), the varied group of completed American plays that reflect the first stages of Thermonuclear Era consciousness begins with Arch Oboler's *Night of the Auk* (1956), a full-length sci-fi parable. A successful American expedition to the moon led by a vainglorious capitalist/patriot touches off a global nuclear holocaust when enemies visualize the United States making the satellite an impregnable nuclear base and launch preemptive strikes on the country. The next play is a compelling little theatricalist fantasy about nuclear terror, Ruth Angell Purkey's *Hangs Over Thy Head* (1956). A nebulous playwright asks a group of actors to suggest an ending for a brink-of-disaster script, but the only "plausible" finale comes from reality when air-raid sirens scream. Dore Schary's *The Highest Tree* (1959) is realistic from start to finish. Basically a domestic drama revolving around an atomic physicist coming to terms with his life, the play incorporates a one-sided argument on a burning issue of the day, nuclear testing. Jules Feiffer's *Crawling Arnold* (1961) is a witty one-act farce that uses a family fallout shelter and a civil defense drill as springboards for satirizing generational and racial conflicts. Lorraine Hansberry finished a preliminary draft of a post-holocaust fantasy, *What Use Are Flowers? A Fable in One Act*, in 1962. A charming, unpretentious object lesson for those caught up in nuclear angst, it presents a band of wild children being dragged toward civilized behavior and values by an old hermit-educator they happen upon. Ray Bradbury turned a piece of science fiction he wrote in 1963 into an effective one-act, *To the Chicago Abyss* (1964), and inadvertently provided a complement to Hansberry's play. Here, years after a nuclear war an aged "rememberer" confronts people clinging to existence not with the highlights of civilization but with images of ordinary, everyday objects which might fuel their aspirations for recovery. Stage versions of three popular novels with nuclear-age themes were also produced during the period.[15]

OBOLER'S FUTURISTIC FANTASY, *NIGHT OF THE AUK*

[Note: The following section has been recomposed under exceptional circumstances: the refusal of Arch Oboler's literary executor to permit this author to reproduce any part of the playtext for scholarly analysis.]

Night of the Auk: A Free Prose Play[16] is one of the few significant stage works of Arch Oboler, familiar to radio listeners of the early 1940s for his series of scary radio dramas, "Lights Out Everybody," and to motion picture fans for his 3-D experiments and the 1951 post-holocaust film "Five." Drawing on such science-fiction staples as the voyage to the moon (including the imperiled journey home) and the probable end of the earth (subgenre: man-made cataclysm), Oboler composed a futuristic fantasy based much more on imaginative hypotheses than on actual developments in science and technology.[17] Enough relevance to the nuclear situation in 1956 exists for the play to work as a parable with an antinuclear point. However, it is far from "realistic" in the sense of giving the illusion that real things are happening to real people in a contemporary environment. Oboler intended it as an impressionistic, abstract, lyrical drama and attributed its failure on stage to the jarring incongruity of elaborate hi-tech sets and naturalistic acting.[18] Its failure as a theatrical as well as literary work, however, might more accurately be traced to its conflicting modes of parable and melodrama, the first compatible with Oboler's nonrealistic treatment, the second not. Most critics attacked its "pretentious" verbal style[19]; in large part, they may have been reacting to the incongruity of that style with the melodramatic vein in the play.

The plot of *Night of the Auk* is designed as a warning not to allow capitalistic self-interest and nationalistic fervor to upset the delicate balance between nuclear powers. The world's first rocket trip to the moon (presumably in the early 1960s) has led to a startling discovery: the surface is permeated with radioactivity (32). A Nobel Prize-winning atomic scientist aboard, Dr. Bruner, deduces from the widespread craters and radiation that an atomic war may have produced this deadly wasteland (60). He points the moral: the moon most likely went through a stage of evolution that is now possible on earth. The play unfolds one conceivable scenario of that dreaded event occurring. Capitalist greed is one of the villains, jingoistic pride another. The mission was financed by an offshoot of an industrial fortune, the Albert Rohnen Foundation; Rohnen's son Lewis conceived the expedition and became its leader. A co-sponsor, The Associated Newspapers, has offered a prize of $500,000 to be split among the astronauts if someone sets foot on the moon. Despite knowing about the perilous conditions, a great admirer of Rohnen, Major Lormer, left the spaceship and claimed the moon for America by planting a flag. Unfortunately, he failed to get back to the ship before a timer signaled an automatic takeoff. The play begins as the ship sets off on its journey home and the crew members brood over the cost of their good fortune. Rohnen tries to keep them focused on their great success, adding that the price they paid was surely worth it (24–25). Contacting the President later, he conceals the truth of the moon's irreparable state and announces that the moonwalk gave America a priceless new colony (91). When Rohnen eventually comes within view of earth, he sees enormous fireworks rising from it (131). At first he thinks they are an improvised greeting, but a fragmentary message from earth makes it clear that his false claims triggered a worldwide atomic conflagration. The military expert aboard, Colonel Russell, berates Rohnen (in some of Oboler's most stirring free verse): his arrogant rhetoric struck such fear in America's enemies that they risked a collaborative atomic attack (142). The astronauts' triumph turns out to be hollow and their source of rewards decimated, all because of their leader's desire for self-aggrandizement. If he had reported the truth, he would have insured that he and his crew would reap no harvest of money or glory; instead, he reported a lie that provoked a nuclear holocaust.

Oboler portrays Rohnen as a pride-driven capitalist with only the narrowest sense of the political impact he might exert. Using deft phallic metaphors, Colonel Russell sums him up as an over-rich nonentity who financed this daring mission to demonstrate his masculinity (165). Rohnen thus becomes an object lesson in the wrong way to serve one's nation in the Cold War climate. This would seem sufficient to make him a representative villain in a parable for the Thermonuclear Era. However, Oboler muddies the terms of this pattern by mixing in a conventional melodrama with Rohnen as a conspiratorial murderer who must be exposed. Late in the play we learn that he engineered the heroic sacrifice of Major Lormer, urging him to drink too much of the celebratory champagne, then to don a spacesuit and leave the ship to plant the flag at a time when he would not get back before the takeoff mechanism started. One man aboard observed this, however: Lieutenant Jan Kephart, who turns out to be a bit of a conspirator himself. His German father was a jet expert whom the Americans "liberated" after World War II to exploit his technical expertise (on the model of Wernher von Braun). Kephart conceals his knowledge of Rohnen's crime for possible use as blackmail to insure that his father is publicly credited for his contribution to the mission. The plot keeps twisting with further improbabilities: Rohnen learns that Kephart knows his secret and manages to get him killed by accident, but the others find a notebook in which Kephart had recorded what he observed, and the villain is unmasked. The source of this dimension of Rohnen's villainy is still a self-centered, sexist drive for glory, but the means to the end which Oboler has him adopt not only distract from his exemplary function in the parable, but necessitate a complicated underplot that is hardly amenable to the nonrealistic treatment or stylized dialogue which Oboler has imposed upon the play. The villain's black heart needed to be cut out. Even the final disposition of Rohnen seems incongruous: he poisons himself in despair.

The fateful main events imply that mankind, along with the crew, has little chance of surviving, though a degree of hope is pumped into the play at the finale. For the military-minded Colonel Russell, any number of mishaps might have triggered the war; their own misadventure just happened to be the inadvertent cause of a disaster that was, and in real life is, waiting to happen. The wise and philosophical Dr. Bruner puts the entire tragedy in broader, but no less grim, perspective when he reflects on the inception of the nuclear age and its significance in an eloquent variation of Einstein's famous telegram, "The unleashed power of the atom has changed everything save our modes of thinking and we thus drift toward unparalleled catastrophe." It is symptomatic of the confused nature of *Night of the Auk* that the great scientist has just looked down upon the fires exploding on earth and identified their source as fission bombs (138): after 1956, and surely by the early 1960s, they would be fusion (hydrogen) bombs. But the finale of the play is the clinching symptom. Dr. Bruner transcends his grim prophecies to envision long-term hope for mankind, predicting that remnants of humanity will develop physical resistance to intense radiation, absorb the lessons of the present holocaust, and generate a more durable world (174–75). Even his fact-defying vision (has he forgotten the condition of the moon?) doesn't leave room for himself and other crew members to survive, yet the ending evades despair by implying that they will at least reach the earth. The auk's night may be followed by a dawn, or the bird may prove not to be extinct after all. The play remains fuzzy on its crucial issue.

PURKEY'S THEATRICALIST FANTASY, *HANGS OVER THY HEAD*

In Ruth Angell Purkey's interesting one-act, *Hangs Over Thy Head*,[20] an unfinished drama encapsulates the sword-of-Damocles situation that ordinary people in America, England, and Russia were experiencing intensely for the first time in the mid-1950s. Five actors have been invited to a theatre to read "an exciting new play" by an unidentified playwright (157). Sirens warning of H-bombs wail, but it turns out to be a civil defense drill—"a rehearsal," an actor in this theatricalist exercise calls it (159). An elderly man with a gentle face and searching eyes enters, obviously the mysterious playwright. (Asked later if he has an "angel," he replies: "Yes. Yes, I believe I do" [173].) He informs the group that his play is not yet finished, and requests their help with the climax. Assuring them that the characters are "much like yourselves," he describes the situation: "the world is facing possible destruction, and these people are trying to save themselves. *How* shall they save themselves?" (169). Weird, unearthly music sounds offstage and the lights dim, evoking "the haunted present." Late in his play, the author continues, "the characters are standing [at an airport] in an attitude of terror. In their eyes we see panic at the thought of death. Destruction threatens the world." The playwright explains that he envisions "a kind of parable" about a "modern Noah" facing a "deluge of man's own creation" (174)[21]; his tentative climax begins with an airport dispatcher offering everyone a place on a space-ark headed for Venus. But that idea poses a dilemma: would people prefer the risk of an unlikely interplanetary voyage to that of a nuclear holocaust? As one person puts it, "Wouldn't death be grinning over your shoulder either way?" (171). Finally, a modest young actress proposes the only resolution that meets general approval: "Perhaps it's only a symbol—that rocket ship. . . . Maybe the characters realize there *is* no escape. The sirens are wailing! . . . They begin to see there is only one choice: they must face their problems and learn to live together in peace or— . . . or die together in conflict" (172–73). The playwright thanks her for that ending and prepares to leave, but then he turns abruptly and says: "There's one thing that still bothers me. . . . I'm afraid I won't be able to make it sound plausible." On that enigmatic note he departs.

The actress's resolution is, in effect, as remotely possible as moving mankind to Venus, though it is certainly meant to strike the audience as potentially the most effective remedy in the long, long run. But the curtain scene warns that the short run is all humanity may have: "Well, what are we all waiting here for? [*An air-raid siren starts faintly in the background.*] After all, it's only a play, isn't it? [*A great host of sirens begin to shriek wildly;—a horrible, unearthly wailing. The players all start in terror. . . .*] ISN'T IT?" (174). Well, yes, of course it is, but then the opening of Purkey's play has likened an empty theatre to an empty world and the curtain coming down on a last performance to "a world coming to an end" (157–58). And, as a comic-relief half-drunk actor says about the game Forfeits, "Somebody'd come up behind you and say: 'Heavy, heavy, hangs over thy head.' . . . That was a nice game then. Lots of fun and nothin' to be afraid of. 'Heavy, heavy, hangs over thy head'—but it was only Mary's gold locket or Pete's aggie. [*Sadly.*] Now it's a bomb" (161). The sentiment that remains as an alternative is the one that we and the young actress would "like to believe—possible" (172).[22]

SCHARY'S ANTINUCLEAR DOMESTIC DRAMA,
THE HIGHEST TREE

As a realistic play, Dore Schary's *The Highest Tree*[23] stands in sharp contrast to *The Night of the Auk* and *Hangs Over Thy Head*. It directly reflects a specific public preoccupation of its time in regard to the nuclear situation: dangers to health produced by atmospheric nuclear tests. The play was first presented on November 4, 1959. Schary might not have been aware of the fact, but this date was the first anniversary of a respite from a long siege of nuclear tests. A year before, the three nuclear powers had finally put into effect voluntary moratoriums on testing and were meeting in Geneva to work out a firm test ban treaty. President Eisenhower had called for the moratorium largely because of much-publicized new information on probable carcinogenic and mutagenic effects of fallout from tests.[24] Ironically, anticipating the halt led all three countries to "a last-minute flurry of testing" that caused "a sharp increase in radioactive fallout during the early months of 1959" (Divine, 262). Schary responded to the alarm these events created by writing a domestic drama that incorporates a strong argument against resuming nuclear tests.[25] For several reasons, the play managed only twenty-one performances. The main factor was certainly negative reviews based on real weaknesses in the play,[26] but a contributing element was the *decline* in radioactive fallout which inevitably occurred after April 1959 and which the government eagerly advertised (Divine, 277–78). The half-year "fallout scare" left many Americans convinced that above-ground nuclear testing should cease once and for all (280), but their sense of urgency had declined along with the fallout, and may have left few to think of the play as an occasion for shared protest.[27]

The Highest Tree is much more than a didactic play. It contains a web of domestic involvements that critics considered largely superfluous to the main business at hand and which are not germane to this study. Insofar as it contains a two-sided debate on a topical issue, however, it clearly stacks the cards against the resumption of testing. The protagonist, Aaron Cornish, has become famous as one of the physicists who originally developed the atomic bomb, and by the end of the play is about to become infamous as a big-name speaker on the protest circuit. His son Caleb is a geneticist who has studied the effects of fallout and can therefore cite concrete scientific evidence that accentuates the danger of testing. A former colleague of Aaron's, Bronislaus Partos, is a kind of comic-relief figure who fortifies Caleb's points with irony and paradox. The only significant defender of testing is the head of Aaron's present project at the missile testing center on Cape Canaveral, John Devereaux. He gives a formidable personal impression at first, but his standard Establishment rationales are no match for those of the team arrayed against him.

The debate is strategically organized to give Schary's view the advantage. Aaron Cornish appears to be a reticent fence-straddler who needs convincing that tests should not resume. This device allows Schary to start the debate in the audience's mind by bringing in Caleb first with his strong geneticist's arguments:

CALEB . . . :   In the lab we see changes from radiation that won't be lost for hundreds of generations.[28] And if the strontium load gets heavier—

AARON: Caleb, we really don't know how heavy it is or how much we can take.

CALEB: Father, we do know that the rate of leukemia has increased three hundred percent since the first atom bomb fell.

AARON: Yes, I know that.[29]

CALEB: And the rate will keep increasing—more people will die— and the cold political logic is paralyzing all of us. (45)

Partos, a fellow insider, next visits Aaron and presents the basic framework of the anti-test position in appeallingly graphic terms: "You and I know that there will be no atomic war and the Russians know it. But it isn't war we should be afraid of. It's peace. A peace where they keep blowing up bombs to frighten each other and keep each other from making war. . . . Ahhh! A beautiful peace—with fallout and sickness and death" (65). He concludes pointedly: "I talk too much . . . —and you, Aaron, not enough." Schary saves the antagonist Devereaux for the forensic *scène à faire* late in Act II of this conventionally structured three-act play. As Aaron attacks and Devereaux defends the atomic assaults on Japan and the spiralling arms race, we gradually realize that Aaron has concealed his real opinions because he has been enmeshed in a conspiracy of silence which his job has necessitated for years. Alone with Devereaux, he is not restrained and rational but passionately indignant: "I'm indignant with all the lies—the hundreds of lies we all tell. . . . It's all piled up inside me here—like sick vomit! Why not tell the truth about how the air and the sea and the earth is being poisoned—of the places where man can no longer live? Why not! Then the fears would come bubbling up—and out of it would come a wave—a tide of indignation . . ." (99). Aaron and Devereaux meet once more, and even then the spokesman for the government does not attempt to counter this specific accusation, stating only general principles that he thinks keep the issue in perspective. When he does, Caleb rubs salt in his wounds:

DEVEREAUX . . .   For me, the scientist, in political terms, must remain an arm of defense—not a philosopher.

CALEB . . .   The fight against strontium ninety *is* in the domain of the scientist. As he builds atomic power, he fights against it and—since he finds himself wearing two hats—can he *help* becoming a philosopher? Is it moral to plan destruction and immoral to think of tranquillity? (115)

Aaron announces that he will quit his job, throw off the "muzzle" he has worn on his conscience for years, and work with Caleb (and other prominent scientists, we presume) on an activist committee to insure that nuclear tests are not resumed.

Several elements more connected to personalities than issues follow a similar strategic development and thus play strong supporting roles. Aaron has just learned from specialists that he will die in six months or so from leukemia.[30] His doctor wonders if the illness may derive from his exposure to radiation at Los Alamos; Aaron replies that his reason tells him it is "merely a risk of the times in which we live" (32). But when he and Devereaux meet, we realize that he was dissembling. He tells his superior: "It's acute leukemia. We both know what that means. We both saw it happen to Margoti" (90). Revealed as another victim of insufficiently controlled radiation, Aaron adds sympathy and pathos to the emotional weight of anti-test appeals. Schary exploits this further by injecting a poignant love affair into the play: an attractive young woman proposes to the aging scientist before she learns of his malady, and when the truth leaks out she not only promises to give him "six wonderful months" but vows to campaign by his side against testing (129). A subplot involving the pasts of the three nuclear scientists also supports this strategy. Bronislaus Partos was investigated during the "security hysteria" of the early 1950s and was "branded and stamped and dismissed" (63). He visits Aaron to repay him two thousand dollars he had borrowed when he became desperate. We learn, first, that Aaron was "the only colleague who was generous and brave enough" to help Partos, and second, that Devereaux "made no effort to defend him" (62, 93). Partos characterizes Devereaux as an "old iceberg" and Aaron calls him "glacial" to his face (64, 96), an *ad hominem* argument that the staunch upholder of government policy inadvertently verifies whenever he voices what Aaron (redundantly) calls "the cold implacable logic that takes us so logically, step by step, to disaster" (99). Devereaux's "calm, rational view" that we must learn to live with the arms race, even if it results in "some mutative changes" (45), is trumped by Aaron's "But if we can effect any change, then it's a sin to 'live with it' " (114). Aaron's heat of indignation and warmth of purpose (and personality) easily win out over the "paralyzing" cold of Devereaux's political logic, as Caleb has termed it (45).

Reviewers of *The Highest Tree* pose a fascinating case study in their comments on its topical argument. For once, a morning-after review proves

the least indefensible. Brooks Atkinson complains that the play unfortunately reminds us how difficult it is to write "a persuasive drama on a
political theme. . . . High principles need passionate and original statement." Schary is indeed no master rhetorician. But the famous drama critic
is wrong, I think, when he concludes that Aaron's decision to campaign
against the resumption of nuclear testing seems "feeble" after the argument
that precedes it. Atkinson at least is not downright puzzling, as Henry
Hewes in his review repeatedly is: Schary "has bent over backwards to be
fair to both sides of the argument" (quite the contrary); "To make matters
worse, Mr. Schary draws Aaron as nauseatingly good-hearted, omniscient,
and reasonable" (when he counters reason with burning indignation?).
Worst of all: "Mr. Schary could easily have gained our admiration for a
brave attempt to dramatize a subject to which only a great playwright could
do justice ('Sing Me No Lullaby' and 'Time Limit' are two examples of this
sort of thing). But a dramatized essay which at its end reveals that its author
has no charges to make or no new insights to offer is downright madden-
ing." The "great playwrights" that Hewes refers to are Robert Ardrey and
the collaborators Henry Denker and Ralph Berkey.[31] Kenneth Tynan's review is stranger still. He sneers that Schary's play "recommends merely
that nuclear tests should be stopped—which at present they have been—
and that the air should never again be impregnated with the man-made
poison of strontium 90. This is about as uncontroversial as liberalism can
get" (114).[32] He seems unaware that the public controversy on the issue
was at the time heavily weighted against "liberalism."[33] Perhaps it was
Tynan who told Gore Vidal about the play, leading to one of the most
spectacularly perverse judgmental essays in the annals of journalism:

> I did not see Mr. Dore Schary's *The Highest Tree* but I can imagine
> what it must have been like. In a burst of right feeling, Mr. Schary
> took an urgent theme—ban atomic tests—and fashioned a play to
> illustrate that theme. Now I am all for this kind of play, in theory at
> least. But there are dangers peculiarly inherent in the topical play. . . .
> Between the conception and the production of Mr. Schary's play fell
> an unexpected shadow: atomic tests were suspended. Yet Mr. Schary
> persisted, no doubt changing lines here and there to accommodate
> history: we must not allow these tests to start up again . . . something
> on that order, inevitably less urgent.[34]

Tynan and Vidal are so wrongheadedly flip that they make the *Time* reviewer look gracious in dubbing the play "a disaster of good intentions."
The only defense that Schary himself offered (in the early 1970s) was that
The Highest Tree "said many things that became more popular to say later
on."[35]

Schary's comment is accurate enough: in late 1961 the Soviet Union and the United States resumed testing in the wake of the Berlin crisis, the Americans staying underground (and thus only leaking radiation) but the Russians using the convenient atmosphere above Siberia. "Fallout alerts" around the world aroused a clamor of protest. Nevertheless, what a play says and when it says it are components that have little relevance to literary or theatrical quality (as Atkinson should also have recognized). Walter Meserve's retrospective judgment is well-founded and balanced: "Although the theatre can be a remarkably effective medium for presenting opinions, Schary has not shown either the theatrical talent or the intellectual subtlety to recreate his humanitarian questions or statements upon the stage."[36] This is almost surely why the play had little chance for a significant run in New York and virtually no chance to be remembered *except* for its content and timeliness.

FEIFFER'S FALLOUT SHELTER FARCE, *CRAWLING ARNOLD*

Revolving around a family fallout shelter as it does, Jules Feiffer's *Crawling Arnold*[37] was potentially as timely as a nuclear drama could be when it was first performed in mid-1961. Improved relations between the United States and the Soviet Union since Stalin's death in 1953, and more directly the moratorium on bomb testing, now two and a half years old, had lulled many Americans into a state of complacency (and denial) about the possibility of nuclear war. Then, the U-2 incident in May 1960 and the Bay of Pigs invasion in April 1961 restoked the dormant embers of the Cold War. One result was an increasing call for municipal and private fallout shelters. Attention of this sort did not lead to many shelters being built, but it did stir a debate that intensified for the next year or two. An episode of Rod Serling's "Twilight Zone" television series entitled "The Shelter" (discussed in Chapter 7) was one of two American dramatic works that capitalized on the attention in 1961; the other was Feiffer's one-act, *Crawling Arnold*.

The degree of seriousness with which Feiffer approached this issue can be easily conveyed. The Enterprise family boasts "the only shelter in the country to be written up in *Good Housekeeping*." The area they live in has regular nuclear attack drills; during them they "simulate the normal conditions of living," for example by projecting films they like through the frame of a television set and by rereading "articles of *lasting* interest" from carefully stored issues of the *Reader's Digest* (75). In preparation for the drill that occurs during the play, Millie the maid dispenses four air-raid helmets from a serving tray, then hands out cocktails. The patriarch of the family, Barry Enterprise (in his seventies), expresses his "old man's dream" for his two-year-old son: "A nationwide alert! All the American people mobilized as one, sitting it out in shelters all over the country. That's what I'd like Little Will to grow up to see" (76). The play touches on a problem of genuine interest involving family shelters, the treatment of racial outsiders, but treats it in the same spirit of sardonic triviality. The live-in maid is a Negro (the accepted term in 1961) who has been in the vanguard of black activism. Barry proposed building "separate but equal fallout shelters": "One for us and one for Millie and any friends she'd want to invite. Same dimensions, same material, exactly like ours in every way" (78). However, Millie resented the idea, demanding to share their shelter, so Barry built only one and invited her in. "Suddenly she wants her *own* shelter," he remarks; joining a riot at the United Nations made her a separatist. When the alert sounds for an air raid drill, Millie quickly enters the shelter, locks the door, and shouts, "Let the white imperialists wipe each other out" (80). The parents feel compelled by law to lie on their stomachs in the cellar until they hear the all-clear signal. Feiffer handles the troublesome dimensions of this issue in such a farcically extreme manner that anyone who reacted by worrying about them would be guilty of lacking a sense of humor.[38]

The main line of action in the play interconnects amusingly with the shelter plot but again cannot be taken seriously, even as satire. It concerns the older son, Arnold, a handsome and successful thirty-five-year-old businessman with a more independent mind and volatile psyche than his father's. Ever since his baby brother was born, he has chosen to crawl rather than walk (after he comes home from work). His parents have called in a psychiatric social worker, Miss Sympathy, to help. She learns that he can be quite rational about his behavior: "I find that in crawling like a child I begin to act like a child again. . . . As an adult my values encompassed a rigid good, a rigid evil, and a mushy everything-in-between. As a child I've rediscovered one value I had completely forgotten existed. . . . Being naughty" (81). When the test alert sounds, Arnold refuses to go down to the cellar and tempts the "young and pretty" social worker (75) to continue her interview. Soon she yields to his attractiveness and crawls over to him, they kiss, and she admits she was going to give herself to him in order to make him "feel like a man." Now her motives are less therapeutic, but she is concerned that the all-clear signal will interrupt them. Arnold tells her at the curtain: "It won't. It's broken. That's what I did that was naughty today" (83). One has to interrupt celebrative chortles to reflect that he has caused everybody in the *area* to remain in their shelters or on their stomachs indefinitely, the obscure serious note in this sheer-fun finale.

HANSBERRY'S POST-HOLOCAUST FABLE, *WHAT USE ARE FLOWERS?*

Lorraine Hansberry presents a sharp contrast in seriousness. Among the many causes she espoused during her short, active life was the cause of peace in a world threatened as never before by the potential consequences of war. Hansberry had keenly shared her generation's consciousness of Hiroshima and what she termed "the worst conflict of nerves in human history—the Cold War."[39] Her greatest play, *A Raisin in the Sun* (1959), addresses most of her other causes, but it also touches lightly upon bomb testing. Walter Lee glances at the morning paper and tells Ruth, "Set off another bomb yesterday," but draws only "maximum indifference"; later, Ruth elicits no reply at all from George Murchison when she comments, "Warm, ain't it? I mean for September. . . . Everybody say it's got to do with them bombs and things they keep setting off."[40] Drafted in 1962 but published posthumously, *What Use Are Flowers?*[41] deals with no such specifics of the nuclear situation; it is a modest, sentimentally generalized plea to avoid letting a nuclear confrontation occur. The play simply postulates a holocaust and presents a semi-realistic, emblematic "fable" (its subtitle) with a clear, uncomplicated point.

"Somewhere in the world," on a vast plain by a deep forest, an elderly man clad in tattered clothes and animal skin appears, crawls into a crevice in the rock, and goes to sleep (230). Identified as "Hermit," he turns out to be an English teacher who has just emerged after twenty-odd years of self-imposed exile in the forest. The light rises, and he is awakened by a band of long-haired children, all about nine or ten, who look like "naked beasts" (230). Unaware of the man, they stalk and kill a small animal, then fight each other violently until a few claim segments of it. They grunt but say no words. The Hermit startles them by emerging and talking. What he says reveals the false conclusions he has jumped to: "how significant, indeed, that the very first thing I should see upon my return is the sight of little hooligans abusing a creature of nature!" (231). He then asks for directions because he wants to reach what he sarcastically terms "civilization" (231). No one replies, so he explains that he abandoned civilization at age fifty-eight and, now that it is time for him to die, he is returning to observe what progress has been made (233). He has returned in "contempt"—"Not love!" When the children attack him to get his food, he exclaims, "I can see that nothing at all has changed. Damn you! And damn your fathers!" (235).

It gradually dawns upon the man that the children are not playing cruel games with him, but are predatory, wild creatures, unfamiliar even with the rudiments of civilization. Taking a clue from their reactions to his lighting a fire with a flint—their leader says "VAROOM!" and they "hit the dirt, face down, and try to bury their heads under their arms" (236)—the hermit deduces what has happened to the world:

What have they done ...?
(*Slowly turning about; his voice rising in its own eccentric hysteria, crossing down center to the audience*)

What have you finally done!...WHAT HAVE YOU DONE!
(237)

Later the group's leader, whom the Hermit has taught to speak and named
Charlie, confirms his supposition by indicating that "The sun fell down"
(258).

The old man's direct challenge to the audience can easily be translated
from a horrified accusation of something that has not, after all, yet happened in real life, into a half-despairing, half-contemptuous "What might
you finally do!" Hansberry is addressing the world of the very early 1960s,
with its truculent atmosphere of nuclear brinkmanship. Premier Krushchev
and President Kennedy had rattled their nuclear sabers in the Berlin crisis,
then both superpowers broke the bomb-test moratorium. Hansberry said
in a 1962 letter that *What Use Are Flowers?* is set in a wasteland "after
we have all gone and blown up the world."[42] We learn near the end of the
play that about five years before time present, a heroic woman "tried to
guarantee the human race" by bringing the children out of the danger zone
just before the bombs fell and then going back for more, never to return
(258). This is the improbable but engaging nuclear-age premise of Hansberry's fable.

In the same letter the author indicates the underlying strategy of the play
after the point that the Hermit learns of the holocaust: to leave us "at the
end, hopefully, with some appreciation . . . of the cumulative processes
which created modern man and his greatness" so that we will value life
enough not to "go around blowing it up." This aim is pursued by having
the man impart to the children "his knowledge of the remnants of civilization which once . . . he had renounced." To use the play's own terms,
this means that he must convince them of the *use* not only of technical
skills and higher forms of communication but also of poetry, music, invention, affection—in a word, the use of "flowers." In successive scenes, he
tries with varying success to teach them basic ceramics and basket-weaving,
choral singing, "socializing" as it used to be, and the means of perpetuating
the race. The children sometimes show amazing precocity—leaping from
"Greensleeves" to Beethoven's "Hymn to Joy" overnight[43]—and sometimes
revert to savagery, twice breaking into vicious fights (though ironically no
longer out of hunger, but rather out of envy at another's civilized accom-
plishments [260]). The Hermit, in turn, relishes the moments of successful
teaching to the extent that he forgets his disdain for the "old package of
passions and prejudices" that he knew as civilization (257); but he finally
curses the self-destructive "animals" and tells them, "FORGET EVERY-
THING I HAVE TAUGHT YOU—!" (252). As he nears death, he hopes
only that some of the children will experience grief born of affection, or
even love (255).

The resolution of the play involves a final shift on his part from affirming
that mankind should rekindle its dream of survival, to renouncing that

dream in a spate of Beckett-like pessimism.[44] He tells Charlie, as if the boy now represented all humanity:

> the vast majority of humankind over the centuries became committed to the notion that—that this particular unpremeditated experiment of the cosmos which was the human race—well—that it *ought* to go on ... It was a defiant notion, and only something as fine, as arrogant as man could have dreamed it up: only man could have dreamed of triumph over this reckless universe. . . . Ah, the things he perceived! You will be like them: heroes all of you, merely to *get on* as long as you do. (259)[45]

What transforms the old man's mood is a complicated incident which first elates him and then fills him with despair. A boy who has played second fiddle to Charlie, Thomas, interrupts the private lesson and demonstrates a miniature water wheel he has fashioned. With awe and gratitude the Hermit responds, "I should have christened thee 'Leonardo,' Thomas!" Unfortunately, the event goads Charlie into a jealous rage (259). He seizes the invention, hurls it away, and intimidates Thomas into staying away from it. His mentor pleads with him to *use* his jealousy and help Thomas build a bigger water wheel for the benefit of the group. "Of all things you must learn," he adds, "this is the most difficult and that from which you most will profit." But when Charlie remains resentful, it is the last straw for the frustrated, dying teacher, and he goes overboard: "The truth is, children, that I don't think you will survive at all. I have been indulging myself, no more. Engaging in a timeless vanity of man. . . . Pretending that I could hand to you the residue, badly learned and hardly retained, of— five thousand years of glory!" (260). He even berates the "silly sentimental female" who saved the children and left them "to torment me in my last absurd hours!" As the life seeps out of him, he relents a bit when Charlie holds a lily out to him, and he echoes a positive statement he made earlier: "*Use* ...What *use*? Charlie, the uses of flowers were infinite ..." But this time he says "were" instead of "are," relinquishing hopes for the future, and dies in pathetic despair. What the audience is led to focus upon, however, is the counteracting element in this final picture. Thomas has slipped over to his broken invention and the children have clustered around him as he patiently reconstructs it, too preoccupied to notice the old man's death. At the curtain Charlie quietly joins them.

When Lorraine Hansberry was asked in 1959 why she was so sure the human race should go on, she replied that

> man is unique in the universe, the only creature who has in fact the power to transform the universe. Therefore, it did not seem unthinkable to me that man might just do what the apes never will—*impose*

the reason for life on life. . . . I wish to live because life has within it that which is good, that which is beautiful and that which is love. Therefore, since I have known all of these things, I have found them to be reason enough and—I wish to live. Moreover, because this is so, I wish others to live for generations and generations and generations.[46]

This articulates the sentiment conveyed subjectively by the finale of *What Use Are Flowers?* The underlying postulate is of course avoid nuclear war. Hansberry expressed it with utter simplicity in 1964: "we don't fight. Nobody fights. We get rid of all the little bombs—and the big bombs."[47] A corollary is that we reject despair and the indifference that often masks it. In her play of 1964, *The Sign in Sidney Brustein's Window*, Sidney certainly speaks for the author to the world when he declares: "Is that all you can ever say? Who cares, who cares? Let the damn bomb fall, if somebody wants to drop it, 'tis the last days of Rome, so rejoice ye Romans and swill ye these last sick hours away! Well, I admit it: I *care*!"[48]

BRADBURY'S POST-HOLOCAUST PARABLE, *TO THE CHICAGO ABYSS*

By sheer coincidence, Ray Bradbury's short poetic drama *To the Chicago Abyss*[49] resembles *What Use Are Flowers?* in several respects, and its major contrasts make it a complementary play. As in Hansberry's scenario, well after a nuclear holocaust an old wanderer intrudes on a remnant of humanity, bringing with him an elixir of memory that might spur survivors to improve their level of existence. But whereas Hansberry's teacher brings knowledge of high culture and refined behavior to a group of ragamuffins who had no chance to be exposed to it, Bradbury's protagonist, a compulsive rememberer, brings recollected images of the lost world of ordinary things to a variety of suppressed people whose nostalgia (and thus aspirations) might be stimulated. If flowers have uses, so do weeds. The Hermit in *What Use Are Flowers?* wants to impart "some appreciation . . . of the cumulative processes which created modern man and his greatness"; the Old Man in *To the Chicago Abyss* hopes to re-expose humanity to "a trash-heap of the mediocre" in order to "ulcerate the people's half-dead desires with vinegar-gnat memory" (153–54).

Bradbury's play is a close dramatic adaptation of a story with the same title that he finished in 1963.[50] Most of the words in the dialogue and stage directions are taken straight from the story, although he refined the dialogue slightly to attain rhythm and sound effects appropriate to free verse.[51] The settings also become suggestive rather than naturalistic. The story is inherently dramatic, and gains power from being depicted as a series of stage images that put more emphasis on emotions than on ideas. *Seeing* a woman "stare in dreadful fascination" and later "reel . . . as if gun-shot" at the old man when he word-paints the sights, sounds, and smells of opening a can of coffee (130) is obviously more effective than reading that she does so; yet the idea that she has tasted succulent fruit which she knows is forbidden remains intact. The central scene of the play and the finale go farther than this, altering the staging implicit in the story to attain a distinctive theatrical impact without losing "point."

An old man in filthy rags, his expression reflecting the "desolation of the city," shuffles into a park searching for remnants of the past that attract his eye (129). Like a low-key evangelist, he places himself near people and induces them to absorb his poignant images of coffee, cigarettes, Milky Ways, oranges, and so forth. Such reminiscing is forbidden by law; we learn later that the old man is already a notorious "criminal fugitive" sought by the "special police" (143). The lady who hears his eulogy of coffee merely flees the pain of memory. However, a man too young to have much recollection of the pre-holocaust world reacts wildly, first beating the old man brutally, then sobbing loudly. The buffeted relic (eighty in the story) apologizes for having inflicted depressingly happy images upon the man's consciousness, then explains: "I just wanted people / to think where are we going, what / are we doing, what've we done?" (136)—a statement surely aimed at the audience. But the young man parrots his indoctrinated belief that it was "never nice" back then and runs off to find a policeman.

It turns out that a kind of underground railroad for rememberers exists within the city and elsewhere. A man of about forty who has been searching for the old man offers him refuge in his seedy apartment. He considers him "a very precious commodity" (138), and warns him to stop behaving like a "saint panting after martyrdom" (140). The special police suddenly arrive; remarkably, the protector and his wife show that they are fully prepared for such intrusions, quickly hiding their charge behind a sliding panel. The police offer tempting cans of soup and beans in return for "the old talking man" (145), but the husband does not betray his guest. As soon as the police are out of earshot, he summons everyone in the apartment house to experience the old man's presence. The climactic scene of the play ensues.

Strongly reminiscent of Ionesco's *The Chairs*, a crowd of people anticipating an enlightened speaker is presumed to be entering the apartment, but all that the audience can perceive is murmurs, shuffling feet, and shadows. This is surely meant to convey the nebulous idea of them that grows in the old man's mind, a touch of expressionism which the norm of nonrealistic setting helps to make viable. The husband has assembled the residents so that the speaker can touch many people at once and do it in relative safety—an occasion that seems to have occurred before. Prompted to explain why he risks his neck and provokes others to risk theirs in order to hear him, the rememberer proceeds to explain and justify his chosen vocation. Years ago, he "looked at the ruined world, the / dictatorships, the dead states, the empty / nations, and said, 'What can I do? Me, a / tired old man . . . ?' " Then he recalled an old song, "Remembering," and suddenly it "wasn't a song, it was a *way of life!*"

> What did I have to offer a world
> that was forgetting? My memory!
> How could my memory help? By
> offering comparisons! By tell-
> ing the young what *once* was. By
> *considering our losses!* (150–52)

"Like a sorcerer" he then mimes sample images: imitation flowers, a kazoo, a thimble, bicycle clips, antimacassars. Admitting he "never had / a head for plays or poems," he calls himself

> . . . a trash-heap of the
> mediocre, the third-rate-hand-me-
> down, useless and chromed-over
> slush and junk of a racetrack
> civilization that ran "last" over
> a precipice and still hasn't struck
> bottom. (153)

But he insists that the things people remember are things they will try to recover, "silly or not." Whereas he once would have raved, "Only the *best* is / best, only *quality* is true!," he now realizes that "Mediocre / must be, so most-excellent fine can / bloom" (154). The play is more of a parable than a thesis play, but this is certainly Bradbury's hypothesis presented by a fairly convincing spokesman.

The undefined assortment of survivors reacts blankly to the hypothesis and ambivalently to "the sad upheaval of old memory," just as the lady and young man had done (155). Sensing a threat from some, the husband hastens to steer the old man to safety. Each week a friend gives him a free train ticket "for some idiot I want to help"—some rememberer, we assume. Urging the old man to keep his "fine mouth shut" for a year, this kindly engineer on the underground railroad gives his guest a one-way ticket to the "Chicago Abyss," assuring him there's "life of sorts" around the "crater where the city once was" (156–57). The scene changes to the semblance of a train car crammed with "crumpled masses of clothing which must be people," a variation on the expressionistic staging in the apartment. What the old man now perceives is "hundreds, thousands" of people "fighting / to sleep, hoping not to dream" (158)—but perhaps susceptible to dreams.

A boy of ten or eleven claims his attention by gazing intently at him. The other figures recede while light shines brightly on the boy, who inadvertently becomes a compelling tempter. The old man tries to fight the boy's unblinking "look of great lost loneliness," but finally gives in and utters "once upon a time..." as everything "freezes in tableau" and the curtain falls (159–61). The boy has told the rememberer his name is Joseph, therefore becoming the only named character in the play. Of the several legendary Josephs that Bradbury may be evoking here, the most likely ones—the dream-interpreter of *Genesis* who rose from slave to valued patriarch; the husband of the mother of Jesus; and Joseph of Arimathea, who allegedly brought the Holy Grail to England—are all figures of authority and promise. Thus, perhaps, the boy's effect on the old man; thus, also, whatever perceptible hope the play may yield. Lorraine Hansberry's dying mentor finally loses faith in his restorative enterprise, whereas Bradbury's dauntless quester has no evidence at all, only faith, that his hypothesis will prove valid in the long run. But the last stage image in the first play shows the Hermit's program working better than ever, and the finale of the second shows the once-discouraged rememberer starting from scratch on a receptive harbinger of the future.

CHAPTER 6

British Playwrights in the Early Thermonuclear Era

In the early 1950s, the American/Soviet arms race took on a dimension that had terrifying implications for Great Britain. The hydrogen bombs that both superpowers created and tested were a thousand times more powerful than the atomic bomb that British scientists had just finished building, and were accompanied by treacherous radioactive fallout that drifted unpredictably. Within very few years a single nuclear exchange between NATO and Communist countries might leave only the largest nations partly intact, and would almost certainly turn the overcrowded "offshore island" into an uninhabitable mass grave. Prime Minister Winston Churchill told Parliament in February 1955, "The hydrogen bomb has made an astounding incursion into the structure of our lives and thoughts. Its impact is prodigious and profound."[1]

Playwrights registered a fascinating variety of reactions. Comparing the situation of his homeland with that of the Soviet Union, J. B. Priestley declared: "at the last dreadful pinch . . . the other side possesses all the advantages. If there is one country that should never have gambled in this game, it is Britain."[2] Robert Bolt, a historian as well as a playwright, confided to Arnold Wesker that he didn't think his children would live beyond thirty: "All history taught . . . that given a conflict of interests which could be resolved either by war or negotiated compromise, war had been chosen. Old-fashioned human stupidity in a nuclear age promised nothing but Armageddon."[3] Early in the 1950s a young Harold Pinter projected an imaginative vision of London streets after an attack: "Carthorses lugging Etruscan crockery to the fire. Saucers and daffodils broken in the moon. Some vomit of A-bombs and H-bombs."[4] In a preliminary draft of *Happy Days* Samuel Beckett pictured nuclear devastation in unlikely corners of the British Isles: an island off the north coast of Scotland, the Isle of Man, and (accidentally) Ireland. Willy tells Winny that his remnant of old newspaper reports that "rockets" struck the largest of the Orkney Islands, Pomona, leaving "seven hundred thousand missing" (of the 7,700 inhabitants), and the Isle of Man (which he calls simply "Man"), sparing only "one female lavatory attendant." He also reads: "Aberrant rocket strikes Erin, eighty-three priests survive." The wry doomsday wit in this sequence was apparently not alluring enough to Beckett for him to permit the diverting explicitness of a concrete reference to nuclear weapons: he noted in the margin of the draft, "Eliminate Rockets."[5]

Christopher Isherwood, the Anglo-American who collaborated with W. H. Auden on three prewar plays, had experienced the possibility that the Korean conflict might escalate into an atomic war which could involve the bombing of his home city, Los Angeles. Noting that he was finding it "very hard to realize the horror of all this," he lectured himself that "The danger of taking the war unseriously is a truly hideous spiritual danger."[6] But his horror grew spontaneously after Russia developed a hydrogen bomb. In a 1954 diary entry, he noted having heard that "atom scientists are pressing for a preventive war at once" since Russia is growing too strong, and reflected: "I can't altogether believe this, but I'm nevertheless depressed and alarmed. And my pylorus is busy manufacturing anxiety in case it's needed suddenly in gigantic quantities. I wake, most nights, around 3 a.m., fairly shaking with terror" (468). His rumination about his own future could stand as an epigraph for the era: "The problem: what to do with the next twenty years—H-bomb permitting—remains unsolved" (467).

The literary equivalent of this sentiment emerges in the most memorable speech of John Osborne's *Look Back in Anger* (1956). Jimmy Porter takes an ultracynical look at current prospects for zealous youths like himself:

> I suppose people of our generation aren't able to die for good causes any longer. We had all that done for us, in the thirties and the forties, when we were still kids. (*In his familiar, semi-serious mood.*) There aren't any good, brave causes left. If the big bang does come, and we all get killed off, it won't be in aid of the old-fashioned, grand design. It'll just be for the Brave New nothing-very-much-thank-you. About as pointless and inglorious as stepping in front of a bus.[7]

Jimmy's casual equation of the "big bang" with total annihilation is a hasty generalization that was apparently a widespread view at the time. Doris

Lessing muses in her autobiography about an inexplicable "pattern common to everyone marching, demonstrating, writing," one which "dominated our minds, our songs, the speeches, the manifestos," that the Bomb meant the end of civilization. It was perceived "as a final conclusive dead-end explosion which would at a stroke kill everyone in the world and lay it waste probably for centuries. . . . The idiot thumb presses down, the Bomb falls, and that is the end of everything."[8]

The Suez crisis of mid-1956 brought Great Britain (and France) to a crescendo of anxiety over the Soviet nuclear threat. Egypt, Russia, and to a lesser extent the United States all played troubling roles. Abdul Nasser managed to gain control of the Suez Canal and refused passage to British and French ships. The two nations sent troops to reopen it against the wishes of the American government, and they promptly received "a virtual Soviet ultimatum threatening, by clear implication, air-atomic destruction of both countries if they did not call off the Suez expeditions." When the American government failed to issue a timely counterthreat, it became the first time in history that major powers "were stopped dead in their tracks at the outset of a victorious operation which they considered absolutely vital for their survival."[9] America eventually asserted itself and the United Nations took control of the canal, but Britons from all walks of life had felt the keen edge of the nuclear sword of Damocles hanging over them. The tense affair convinced the government not to rely upon the United States but rather on its own thermonuclear deterrent, then in production.

The year 1957 might be characterized as a logical aftermath. The first British H-bomb test took place on Christmas Island in May. The Americans and Soviets began stepping up their own testing because they secretly anticipated a moratorium in the near future. On the literary front, the English novelist Nevil Shute made a tremendous impact on the popular consciousness with *On the Beach*, a mordant picture of the last stages of total genocide after a cobalt-bomb war. It is doubtless coincidental (since Shute began the book in 1955) that one of the main characters is a wry cynic named John Osborne, who quips that the coming end of humanity makes sense because the world will be "made clean again for wiser occupants."[10] A similar scenario is treated as pathetic farce in David Campton's 1957 one-act, *Then...*, in which a holocaust of "hetrodynamic deterrents" has turned to dust all but two people in the world, an intellectual Adam and a voluptuous Eve. The female, Miss Europe, laments: "I'd have been Miss World next year—only now there doesn't seem to be a world to be Miss of." Campton definitely intended a comic analogy to a serious world situation: he wrote the play, he said, "in the days before any international curb on the testing or proliferation of nuclear weapons was considered practical. There seemed a real danger that at any time the world might be destroyed by mistake."[11] Campton went on to write three more antinuclear one-acts in 1960, two of which were performed during a protest march that year. Perhaps equally symptomatic is the fact that a budding major dramatist, Peter Shaffer, made "sheer fun stuff" out of world tensions in a television spy thriller which he entitled *Balance of Terror*, though its plot simply deals with tracking down an intercontinental ballistic missile.[12] In contrast, the novelist John Braine found it impossible to deal with England's precarious nuclear situation: "In order to write novels it is absolutely necessary for me to forget the existence of the H-Bomb. At least, I do as far as is possible push it to the back of my mind. Most of us in what I'll call the target countries have to do this simply to preserve our sanity."[13]

PLAYWRIGHTS AND ANTINUCLEAR PROTEST

As the Cold War invaded everyday lives more and more, antinuclear activities that had little popular support in the early 1950s began to burgeon. A demonstration held at Trafalgar Square in the spring of 1958 featuring Bertrand Russell gave the movement visibility and notoriety. Protest organizations such as the National Campaign Against Nuclear Weapons Tests (NCANWT—a women's initiative), the durable Campaign for Nuclear Disarmament (CND), and its militant offshoot, Russell's Committee of 100, enjoyed a brief and tempestuous heyday. Among the sponsors and members of these groups were dramatists Priestley, Osborne, Bolt, Wesker, Campton, Benn Levy, Marghanita Laski, Doris Lessing, John Arden, Lindsay Anderson, Shelagh Delaney, Bernard Kops, David Mercer, and Spike Milligan. Most of these playwright-activists also wrote plays related to the nuclear situation, leading a social historian to conclude that "it was through the medium of the stage above all else that literary protest against the H-bomb was most commonly expressed."[14]

Four of these plays, two written for the stage and two for television, address the protest issue directly. Lessing's *Each His Own Wilderness* (1958) revolves around a habitual social reformer who is now giving full time to "hydrogen bomb work." Bolt's *The Tiger and the Horse* (1960) hinges on a family crisis which is first exacerbated and then resolved by the decision to sign a petition for nuclear disarmament. Priestley's unpublished television play, *Doomsday for Dyson* (1958), implicates an apolitical average citizen through a dream sequence in which he first dies in a nuclear explosion and then is accused by a mysterious tribunal of having caused the calamity.[15] Mercer's television drama *A Climate of Fear* (1962) depicts an acquiescent wife of a nuclear scientist being converted by concern for her children into sharing their anti-nuke civil disobedience. In a related vein, Bernard Kops overcame an extreme case of nuclear angst partly by participating in constructive protest; he was finally able to "Sing over the abyss" and portray both the abyss and the energizing defiance in his expressionistic fantasy-drama *The Dream of Peter Mann* (1960).

Attitudes among playwrights involved in protest differed markedly. Doris Lessing expressed general and fierce indignation:

> We are living at a time which is so dangerous, violent, explosive, and precarious that it is in question whether soon there will be people left alive to write books and to read them. It is a question of life and death for all of us; and we are haunted, all of us, by the threat that even if some madman does not destroy us all, our children may be born deformed or mad.
> . . . .
> Now, in March 1957, the British Government decides to continue the hydrogen bomb tests which threaten unborn children. Yet of the men who took the decision I am sure there is not one who says: Because of me thousands of children will be born crippled, blind, deaf, mad. They are members of a committee. They have no responsibility as individuals. They represent me. But I repudiate their act.[16]

An elder statesman of the movement, J. B. Priestley, called on the country to abandon "the idea of deterrence-by-threat-of-retaliation. There is no real security in it, no decency in it, no faith, hope, nor charity in it." If Britain would "go into reverse, decisively rejecting nuclear warfare," this would give the world "something quite different from the polarised powers: there is now a country that can make H-bombs but decides against them."[17] The atypical Sean O'Casey continued to rail against what he perceived as the chief motivation behind the nuclear buildup instigated by the United States: irrational fear and mistrust of the Soviet Union.[18] On the positive side, he welcomed the increasing calls for disarmament among trade unions, fellow socialist writers, and "the huge Co-Operative Movement in England," sensing that the " 'Wind of Change' is blowing in the direction of Peace."[19] In 1956 his incentive for protest was spurred by a family catastrophe that he attributed to radiation from H-bomb tests: his son Niall died of leukemia at the age of twenty-one.[20] A year before his death in 1964, the snappy old Irishman was still tormented by "the presence of the damned hydrogen bomb"; "This terrible and evil gadget held over us all by the finger and thumb of belligerent man can utterly ruin us all, root up life everywhere, down into the very bowels of our earth."[21]

Among the young-Turk dramatist-demonstrators, Arnold Wesker and John Osborne represent near-opposite poles in their attitudes, as their memoirs attest. Wesker participated enthusiastically in the first major CND demonstration, the gathering in Trafalgar Square and ensuing march to the nuclear weapons research station in Aldermaston on Easter weekend, 1958. He recalls proudly "this four-day mission to save the world from a nuclear holocaust," which started with only a few hundred people but grew to four thousand despite "the squelch, the damp discomfort, the hard floors of schools and churches upon which we slept."[22] At this time Wesker was still obscure as a writer, but by 1961 his trilogy of plays had been produced and well received. He now had visibility enough to be summoned for the Committee of 100 (which also included Priestley and Bolt). Wesker readily answered the call for "acts of civil disobedience unknown since the suffragettes," joined a mass sit-down in Trafalgar Square on September 17 and endured six months of "open prison" as a result (508). One passage of his 1959 drama *Roots* implicitly deplores indifference to the nuclear threat and advocates doing whatever one can.[23] The play follows the progress of a young country girl, Beatie Bryant, as she is drawn out of lethargy into self-improvement by a Wesker-like city friend, Ronnie Kahn. Beatie satirizes the complacent despair of the phlegmatic when she paraphrases one of her former cohorts: "She say she don't care if that ole atom bomb drop and she die—that's what she say. And you know why she say it? I'll tell you why, because if she had to care she'd have to do something about it and she find *that* too much effort" (146). Wesker's/Ronnie's/Beatie's rationale for activism is far from buoyant in the grim atmosphere of nuclear terror, but it is positive. Parroting Ronnie, Beatie pertly declares, "It's all going up in flames, . . . but I'm going to make bloody sure I save someone from the fire" (115). In sharp contrast, John Osborne was prominent enough in 1958 after *Look Back in Anger* and *The Entertainer* to be wooed for public protests, but was never comfortable in the role and became highly critical of such activities. He explains in distant (and perhaps jaded) retrospect that the reason why he attended his first CND demonstration in late 1958 was that his wife at the time, Mary Ure (Alison in the first *Look Back in Anger*), wanted them to "be seen together in the vanguard." Refusing her, he says, "would be interpreted as marital disloyalty, a politicized act of adultery. Convenience was more persuasive than conviction and I agreed. . . . I wished I was touting cheap umbrellas and briefcases rather than self-consciously hawking peace."[24] He accepted an invitation to the Committee of 100 in 1959, but realized he could not be a wholehearted participant: "I'd no intention of associating with lunatics intent on disrupting theatricals like the Trooping the Colour, still less of throwing myself beneath the well-trained boots of British squaddies" (150). Looking back, he resented being lured into activism: "Like many others at the time, and for many years to come, I had a sentimental, indulgent attitude toward the adherents of CND and even its militant wing. It was the popular view of a substantial minority of high-minded folk driven to unremitting extremity by their sense of helplessness in the face of the wickedness of those who had seized dominion of their lives" (213). Still, Osborne did sit down in Trafalgar Square with Wesker, Bolt, et al., and continued to serve the cause as at least a valued figurehead.[25]

Lessing's *Each His Own Wilderness*

The first of the three plays with protest themes, Doris Lessing's *Each His Own Wilderness*[26] greets the audience with the sound of an H-bomb explosion (we soon learn that it's on a tape to be used at a demonstration). The curtain rises on an untidy room featuring posters inscribed BAN THE BOMB, WE WANT LIFE NOT DEATH, etc. However, as the play's title implies, Lessing is much more concerned with portraying the inner lives of a galaxy of characters than with projecting her opinions of the nuclear situation in dramatic form. As T. C. Worsley put it, "Politics do, certainly, dominate the play because the characters are mostly political people but the play is about their humanity, not their politics."[27] Nevertheless, the broad subject of the hydrogen bomb and the specific one of protesting Britain's nuclear policies do gain prominence as stimuli for exposing the variety of personalities (and inner wildernesses) depicted. Enough representative attitudes on these issues are revealed, in fact, for a sort of cross section to emerge, and this in itself is an illuminating diagnostic of the temper of the times.

The plot revolves around the clash between a long-term pursuer of "good, brave causes," Myra Bolton, and her twenty-two-year-old son Tony, who, far from regretting that there are no causes left for him, would prefer an isolated life in a well-ordered home. This is a nice role-reversal twist of the trite "generation gap" conflict between rebellious youth and repressive parent, recently recycled as "angry young man" versus "pusillanimous" opponent of whatever age.[28] Myra also clashes with her former cohort in activism and love, Philip Durrant, who has given up politics and plans to marry a girl half his age who knows nothing about current affairs. Whereas Tony regards himself as a victim of the everyday chaos spun out of perennial activism, Philip has simply yielded to frustration and exhausted his reformer's zeal. Myra's needs for companionship in politics and passion are now served by one of her son's peers, Sandy Boles. He has aligned himself with her and with a veteran Labour Party politician, Mike Ferris, less out of sincere conviction than to advance his career. Mike is steadfast in his wistful belief that diplomacy can solve the nuclear dilemma—and in his devotion to Myra, to whom he proposes periodically. Lest this appear an over-simple diagram of contrasts and alignments, let it be noted that Myra's and Tony's sharply divergent attitudes are complex enough to be joined at the root—by despair.

Two polar points of view on the nuclear situation are elegantly dramatized in a low-key argument between the pessimist Tony and the optimist Mike, with the opportunist Sandy chiming in on his employer's side. Mike brings up the subject of "the big issue, the hydrogen bomb business," and raises Tony's eyebrows with his naiveté:

The more I think about it, the more I am convinced it is much more simple than we think. Simply a question of getting the Governments to agree, that's all.

TONY [drily]: That's all?

MIKE: Well, it really is hard to believe that people will be prepared to do things that will affect their own children, isn't it?

. . . .

I really can't believe—I can't believe that after all we've done, all the glorious achievements of humanity, we are going to consent to blowing it all up.

TONY [puzzled, more than derisive]: You can't?

SANDY [very smoothly, as it were testing a public voice]: Quite obviously, the first step is to stop tests everywhere, and then we can proceed to a general discussion on disarmament.

TONY [staring at him with disgust]: Oh, hear, hear!

MIKE: If the tests are stopped we still have the Lord knows how many hydrogen bombs stored here and there, waiting for some madman to set them off. But I can't believe humanity will be so stupid. (119)

Mike is a mellifluous proponent of confidence in one's fellow man, so much so that he does not digest what he has said: that a single member of the human race, "some madman," might violate the presumed collective wish of "humanity." Here as elsewhere, he undermines his own rose-colored view. Tony's challenges gain force as they become more articulate:

You seem to be constitutionally incapable of believing in the ultimate horrors. Why? You've lived through enough, haven't you? It gives me the creeps to listen to any of you when you're in one of your reminiscing moods—a record of murder and misery. Yet on you go, all jolly and optimistic that right will prevail.

MIKE [with great sincerity]: It's a question of getting agreement between men of good will everywhere.

TONY [laughing incredulously]: Good. Let's drink to that: the glorious achievements of humanity. (120)

Not surprisingly, Mike misses the irony and welcomes the toast. Tony has defined him accurately in telling Sandy why he can't help liking him: "he's so—bloody innocent. . . . Sometimes I think he's parodying the ordinary kind of political pomposity, and then, God help me, I see that he means every word. Every sweet silly word of it" (116). The play strikes few Shavian notes, but its incurable Polyanna is strongly reminiscent of Sir Ralph Bloomfield Bonington in *The Doctor's Dilemma*. His attitude is unparalleled in the play.

Tony clashes with Myra along somewhat the same lines, but Myra keeps an important dimension of her attitude hidden from him. The reason she does is exposed early when they argue about the efficacy of protest in general:

> MYRA: I'm going to demonstrate about the hydrogen bomb outside Parliament with a lot of other women. [*as TONY laughs*] Yes, laugh, do.
>
> TONY: Oh, I'm not laughing. I do really admire you, I suppose. But what use do you suppose it's going to be? What good is it?
>
> MYRA . . . :   Oh, Tony, but of course it's some good. Surely you think so?
>
> TONY: You've been demonstrating for good causes all your life. So many I've lost count. . . . And where are we now?
>
> MYRA: How do you know things mightn't have been worse?
>
> TONY: How could they possibly be worse? How could they? (108)

When Tony says this, he sounds "forlorn, almost tearful," and Myra impulsively renders motherly consolation. He laughs to keep from crying, and it would not help him to learn that she shares his deep despair about the state of the world, if not his sense of futility about protesting. She has given up her job to work for nuclear disarmament, and has even considered joining a group that intends to try to disrupt a bomb test in the Pacific. But when her friend Milly, an unreflective fellow demonstrator, hears her mope that she wouldn't mind getting killed, the kindly confidante must serve as the sounding board for Myra's suppressed nuclear angst:

> MILLY: Myra, love, we all of us get depressed.
>
> MYRA . . . :   Depressed. That word annoys me. Half the time we dope ourselves up with some stimulant—men, our children, work. Then it fails and we see things straight, and it's called being depressed. You know quite well that there's only one question that everyone's asking—what are we alive for? Why? Why shouldn't that damned bomb fall? Why not? Why shouldn't the human race blow itself up? Is it such a loss? A little dirty scum on the surface of the earth—that's what we are. (153)

Myra proceeds to relate a ghastly recurring dream in which the earth "is disintegrating in a cold white crackle of fire." She has come to terms with the horror by turning it into relief: "we stand there thinking, thank God. Thank God it's all over. Thank God it's all over" (154). Near the end of the play, Myra cries in frustration at her son's refusal to care and asserts that she has at least "been alive" in her years of social activism. But her parting shot faintly echoes her death wish:

> perhaps I'll go on that boat to the Pacific to the testing area—I wanted to do that and didn't, because of you.
>
> TONY: Mother, you might get killed.
>
> MYRA: Dear me, I might get killed. And what of it? I don't propose to keep my life clutched in my hand like small change ... (184–85)

The secret wilderness of the chief character, who labors to prevent what seems inevitable to her benumbed offspring, is a kind of excrutiating love/hate relationship with the Bomb. All Tony can say to the world at the curtain is a poignant "Leave us alone to live. Just leave us alone ..." (186).[29]

Bolt's *The Tiger and the Horse*

The next play that addresses the theme of nuclear protest resembles Lessing's in one major respect, its primary focus on the inner lives of complex, articulate characters. Robert Bolt's *The Tiger and the Horse*[30] is a three-act domestic drama in which the psychological complexities involved in the marital relationship of a College master and his wife are the central concern. The play devotes little explicit attention to the nuclear situation, but its plot turns on the responses of this highly intelligent pair to "a petition for unconditional nuclear disarmament" which is being circulated at English universities (226).[31] These responses evolve over the course of a year from conventional and expected to radically surprising, so that in and for themselves they yield a high degree of interest and suspense.

A bright, abrasive graduate student, Louis Flax, brings the petition to the professor, Jack Dean, and his wife Gwendoline[32] at an unspecified but venerable university (a Holbein hangs in the Master's office). Louis is backed by their daughter Stella, his girlfriend. He finds that he must confront not only the Deans but also the retiring Vice-Chancellor of the University, Sir Hugo Slate, who arrives with the news that Professor Dean will surely be elected for his position. With Jack absent for a while, Gwen vows to sign the petition. Her reasons seem predictable for a born mother who is also a biology scholar: making hydrogen bombs is "a devilish waste of human ingenuity" that would be better applied to the problem of starving people—"among them, small children"; radioactivity from atmospheric testing can stimulate mutation—"In other words it produces monsters. Babies that are monsters" (227–28). Slate takes Gwen aside and seemingly dissuades her from signing the petition until after Jack is elected. "If it would do Jack harm," she deferentially replies, "I won't sign it, of course" (231). When Jack enters, he reacts negatively to the petition. His daughter challenges him to declare whether or not bomb-testing should continue. The response he gives marks him as a virtual stereotype of the wise but conservative academic: "How could I possibly know? The diplomatic and military considerations must be grotesquely complicated. I haven't the facts, Stella" (237). In turn, he challenges Louis to say whether he believes that such petitions would induce the Prime Minister to change his policy, and Louis replies, "Probably not." This lures Stella into asking, "Then ... what's the good of it?" (238). We must wait until just before the final curtain, when a year has passed, for Stella to issue the standard counterargument:

DEAN: My dears, nothing will stop humanity from using that thing. Nothing *you* can do. What, a folly of those proportions within our very grasp, and you think you can turn us back with a petition? . . .

STELLA: Probably not. But this is something we can do. When we've done what we can do, then's the time to worry about what we can't do. But I don't know anyone who's done even what he can! (306)

By this time, however, a remarkable evolution of Jack's response to the petition has occurred as the result of an illuminating redefinition of Gwen's.

Through an astonishing deed and an equally astonishing explanation of it, Gwen has revealed the deep psychic grounds of her opposition to nuclear weapons. The "splendid Holbein of two adults and a row of children," valued at forty thousand pounds, has hung in full view throughout Act I (215). In Act III Jack learns to his horror that Gwen has slashed the painting beyond repair and displayed it in the College courtyard, with the newly signed petition pinned to the fabric. Stella assumes she must be mad, but Jack resists that conclusion, evidently believing the act was an extravagant political gesture. He challenges Gwen, and her response shakes him:

DEAN: . . . Gwendoline, I *insist* on a reasonable answer: Why did you do it?

MRS DEAN (*cries out*):   I had to!

DEAN (*furiously*):   You did not 'have to'. You wanted to perhaps—

MRS DEAN: Yes. I wanted to. I told myself it was for Mr Flax's petition of Peace. But in fact I wanted to! I ripped across their little faces, and it rejoiced me! (292)

Later she expands on this, even negating what everyone supposed was her reason for not signing the petition a year ago. She had kept it secretly, and she began to have delusions that she had signed it: "I could have taken my oath that I'd taken it out and *looked* at it, a score of times, and seen my signature on it. How's that for the Powers of the mind? (*Sadly*) How's that for the Powers of Evil?" (294). In a moment a startling exchange between herself and Louis occurs:

LOUIS: . . . You've signed it now, Mrs Dean.

MRS DEAN: Yes, I've done everything necessary now.

LOUIS (*gently*):   Aye, but you *wanted* to before.

MRS DEAN: Oh no, I didn't. These atomic explosions; have you noticed how beautiful they are? There's your clue. The venial sins can be very plain but the mark of outright evil is this ... extraordinary ... beauty—And I didn't get that out of a book. That picture was beautiful, and often moved me by its beauty; but when I ripped it across, it was I who was beautiful—as Lucifer, Louis, for a moment I was as beautiful as Lucifer ... (*Briskly*) I didn't sign the petition against the Bomb, because I want the Bomb to happen. That's very clear to me. (296)

Not incidentally, this expression of extreme demonic fascination with the limitless power of nuclear weapons, capsulized as a single Bomb, is the first occurrence I have detected in English-language drama. Other manifestations of the general frame of mind that Joseph Conrad memorably described as "the fascination of the abomination" or, closer to the case at hand, what General Patton called "the cataclysmic ecstasy of violence,"[33] are not uncommon in modern literature, but Robert Bolt deserves credit for the first all-too-appropriate dramatic application of the concept to nuclear weapons.[34] Presumably, Gwen's perception of this Satanic impulse in herself, an intelligent and humane woman, has made her realize how extraordinarily important it is to work toward eliminating apocalyptic weapons which might be unleashed by people with similar impulses but fewer restraining qualities. Since her first intuitive sense that she wanted the Bomb to "happen," she has experienced further signs of what she calls the "evil" in herself. Feeling "as beautiful as Lucifer" when she ripped the Holbein was just the final eruption of her impulse to destroy what she loved. She relates manic fantasies of killing Stella's baby and her own husband as well, and shows dread that she may actually try. After living through this series of "dreams, abominations . . . Impulses! Desires!" (295), she declares that she has "always been evil" and is "now mad" (301).

Several years of thermonuclear bomb tests and publicity about the genetic effects of fallout seem to have inflicted an obsessive paranoia about mutations upon Gwen. She tends to see them everywhere possible and to pin the label "evil" on the makers and sanctioners of their source, nuclear weapons. Before she tells Sir Hugo Slate in Act I that she will certainly sign Louis's petition because radioactivity can produce monsters, she says that the bomb "is merely the high peak, the show place, of the wickedness that's in us" (227). When she repeats her rationale to Jack, she states that mutations "constitute an extension of our own wickedness into the future" (248). Stella confides to Louis that when her mother talked (offstage) about atomic deformities, "She was in a kind of ecstasy!" (251). In Act II, two or three months later, Gwen learns that her daughter is pregnant. As Stella moves toward her she reacts strangely:

MRS DEAN (*sharp warning*):   No, don't come near me!

STELLA: Why not?

MRS DEAN: One can't be too careful.

STELLA . . . :   Careful of what?

MRS DEAN: With a baby, like that ... one can't be too careful.

Stella moves toward her again, and she "dodges away" (269). This behavior spurs Stella to risk telling her father that Gwen may be mentally unbalanced. In Act III the baby has been born, and we hear that Gwen loves little Nicky and often visits him in Stella's flat. But when she goes into the bedroom where Nicky is napping and he cries, she emerges quickly and says, "I haven't done anything! . . . I didn't touch him" (294). Gwen did succeed in "killing" the children in the Holbein portrait, one of whom was a hunchback. There is no suggestion that she might actually kill Nicky— only that she has fantasies of being on the brink.

Gwen's feelings toward her husband that provoke similar fantasies are complicated, and this is not the place to deal with all their intricacies. Suffice it to say that she believes he has never exercised enough empathy to acknowledge the "evil" dimension in her character.[35] Thus, as she oversimplifies the case, his consistent sanity and goodness showed her by contrast what she really is, and her involuntary revulsion at his habitual attitude made him leery of getting close to her (300). She repeatedly calls him a "saint." She also mocks the ivory-tower purity in his behavior toward her: "The Master has never brought any kind of pressure to bear on me. The Master has never attempted to influence me in any way. The Master has always left me perfectly alone!" (297). Relating her fantasy of approaching him in bed, pruning shears in hand, she reveals that she cared less about killing him than about having him see the kind of person she is: "sometimes I would knock things over! (*She is now crying noisily.*) But he never heard! He never woke! He sleeps like an angel! (*Almost shouting through her tears*) Like a pig!" (296).

Gwen's fascinated horror at her own capacity for violence parallels her fascinated horror at the effects of nuclear explosions; Jack's aloofness toward the one parallels his aloofness toward the other. To Gwen, he is at once an angel perched on a remote cloud and a pig wallowing in a self-contained bed of mud. The epigraph of *The Tiger and the Horse* is one of Blake's *Proverbs of Hell*: "The Tygers of wrath are wiser than the horses of instruction." Gwen clearly represents the wrathful, intuitively wise tiger, Jack the stolid, bridled horse. The play's dynamics impel Jack to shed his blinders and perceive the reality that his wife embodies in both the domestic and social spheres.[36] Jack resists with every fiber of his pedantic self-respect: "For pity's sake, Gwen, it isn't you! Keeping one's distance, dissociation—it isn't you—it's my philosophy, Gwen, it's my belief. (*He is terribly distressed....*) It's in my books!" (301). But his extreme distress makes him admit, "Oh, now I'm mastered." Seeing into the soul of the person he loves makes Jack realize that he must "associate" himself with her. Obliterating the painting and signing the petition were two sides of the same coin for Gwen—the first demonstrating the impulsive wrath that might produce catastrophe, the second protesting the availability of catastrophic weapons. Even though Jack will ruin his career by lying to the press that Gwen was not solely responsible for defacing the Holbein, he declares: "*I* am going to say that the purpose of the action was to publicise the petition, that my wife and I had allowed the subject of, er, nuclear warfare to prey upon our minds to a possibly obsessive extent, and that we did it together!" (303). And even though Jack still believes that the petition is a futile gesture, he adds his signature to it with a "blaze of arrogance," provoking the formerly critical Louis to exclaim, "Oh, Stella, what a bloody marvellous man!" (304). These heroic gestures reflect Robert Bolt's idea that Jack behaves as "a man who'd do anything rather than have his wife hurt. What I was trying to say . . . is that someone who is really engaged with another human being will find willy-nilly that he is interested in the bomb. Not that he ought to be, but *is*."[37] This is a vague statement (from an interview), but it conveys perhaps more clearly than the dialogue the central idea of the play's resolution. Jack has broken through his "philosophy" of dissociation—no doubt the natural outgrowth of his personality and conditioning—and has felt a genuine association with humanity through the feelings Gwen has aroused in him. This, in turn, made the nuclear situation personally crucial to him. His last words on the bomb—"nothing will stop humanity from using that thing" (306)—stress a side-effect, a more deeply felt pessimism.[38] But the last words for the audience are Stella's "When we've done what we can do, then's the time to worry about what we can't do." The play's thrust toward protesting nuclear weapons remains intact.[39]

Mercer's *A Climate of Fear*

David Mercer's *A Climate of Fear* was written for performance on television, but was published in a fully intelligible script as the second part of an imposing trilogy.[40] It is worth a close look not only because it reflects the nuclear-age concerns of a respected political dramatist (and member of the Committee of 100) but also because it contains some near-miss parallels to *The Tiger and the Horse*. The play focuses on the Waring family, headed by a stodgy atomic scientist, Leonard. His wife, Frieda, defers to her husband in deploring the antinuclear activities of their protest-veteran son, Colin, and their aspiring-novice daughter, Frances. Leonard parallels Jack Dean in his flat opposition to demonstrating, but lacks the capacity that Jack finally shows for self-contradictory, sacrificial action, given proper impetus. Accepting his role as an Establishment functionary (and exuding none of the aura usually granted nuclear physicists at this time), Leonard parrots the standard anti-red, pro-Bomb rationale even when responding to his mature, intelligent son:

COLIN: . . . It's precisely the things you stand for that I can't value. What have you done? Built a house and put a wife and children in it—put your gifts as a scientist into weapons of mass murder—isn't there something inconsistent there?

. . . .

LEONARD: . . . As for being against the bomb, aren't we all? Isn't everybody? Scared out of our wits. And that's why we're still alive and still free, because we've *got* it! (125–26).

Colin clearly parallels the Deans' prospective son-in-law, Louis Flax, as a severely left-wing socialist and ban-the-bomb advocate. But whereas Louis only peddles a petition and then seems unfazed by having lost it for a year, Colin begins the play by being sentenced to three months in jail for a sit-down in Kensington Palace Gardens and ends it by getting arrested for a sit-down in Trafalgar Square.[41] Frances, a simplified Stella, seconds Colin in his derision of their father and accompanies him at protests. Only seventeen, she is more of a knee-jerk rebel than an independent political thinker.

The central character in Mercer's play, as in Bolt's, is the wife and mother. Frieda is not a person of hidden depths and mixed motives, but she matches Gwendoline's development from ostensibly submissive wife to one willing to damage her husband's career through public protest. And she does so in response to the emerging dominance of her basic motherliness. Frances sums up her progress in Mercer's sequel to *A Climate of Fear*: "We have a charming woolly liberal for a mother, whom we shamed into sitting in protest against nuclear weapons because she respects what she calls the sanctity of human life."[42] Frieda's main stimuli for this change seem to have been growing empathy for the nuclear anxieties of the younger generation, plus feelings of disgust at her husband's boorish treatment of Colin and Frances. Speaking to Leonard at one point, she expresses the disparity that she senses between their own fears and those of the young: "We live, but we have no real connections with life. What are we afraid of? Fire? Burglars? Burst pipes? Accidents? Human beings should have more dignified fears! *(Pause)* Why do we find it so easy to live with the idea of extinction when our children find it so hard? We don't believe it. They do. *(Pause)* A lot of people believe it" (112). Leonard's reply is, in effect: "I'm going to sleep. I don't know why you're raking all this up" (113). A few days before joining her children in Trafalgar Square, Frieda defends her passivity to Frances and, in the process, discovers a malady in herself that can be remedied:

> I really do believe you're all wasting your time. *(Pause)* If people were determined to live, then they would insist on it ... demand it ... but they accept the possibility of annihilation already. And they're learning to live with the certainty. . . . There's only one conclusion. Death must be less of a strain on us than our humanity! *(Pause)* I see your beliefs as an emotional trap. I don't reject them—I've no energy left for them. No hope. I feel as if my life has—flickered out. (145)

It is not until the morning of the demonstration that Frieda completes her conversion. Her husband's contempt for what Frances is going to do ("I'm damn well past caring. I hope they give her six months" [149]) makes her realize that, although she has no energy to invest in her children's beliefs, she does care about them as human beings enough to stand—or rather sit—by them when they are putting their bodies on the line for a cause they consider worthy. After she is arrested, she explains her motivation with the utmost simplicity: "I don't know what it was. *(Pause)* But rather this than anything else. I'm sure of that. No one should leave it to someone else" (156). Ironically, it is Colin who ultimately abandons the movement (as we learn in the sequel).[43] Frieda divorces Leonard and demonstrates with the CND. When Frances asks Colin why he loves Frieda, he replies, "She has courage" (165).[44]

Kops's *The Dream of Peter Mann*

In the first stages of the Thermonuclear Era Bernard Kops was an unlikely candidate to write a nuclear drama with any kind of positive implication. But by 1960 in *The Dream of Peter Mann*[45] he at least managed a positive *carpe diem* thrust. After the devastating effect the news from Hiroshima had on him at eighteen, he developed an obsession with death which, by 1951, became one cause of a serious nervous breakdown. "For me the world was empty and destroyed already. The bomb had exploded in my brain."[46] An anarchic lifestyle dragged him deeper into the mire. Even at twenty-six he had "recurring dreams of destruction. I had no sheets on the bed and I always slept in my clothes and shoes. One had to be ready for the holocaust" (223). Then, in 1954, the new hydrogen bomb increased his anxiety: "I saw a picture of the H-bomb on television. It looked like a great monster crawling towards the world. I was obsessed with an ugly vision of the impending holocaust" (234). The ultra-ominous year of 1956 actually marked a significant upturn in Kops's life; he met and married Erica Gordon. "The clouds of war got thicker and blacker as did the news-paper headlines," Kops recalls; "Yet we were very happy. Never once did I question the value of bringing a child into the world" (256). His wife even got him to demonstrate against nuclear weapons, and he was to con-tinue his activism into the 1960s. The mode of defiant buoyancy and con-structive action in the face of nuclear terror became the signature of his early plays. He expresses it rhapsodically in his memoir: "Sing you silly sod! Sing over the abyss. . . . Sing because we are for no apparent reason suddenly illuminated in the darkness, reaching up for the sun. Even if we are going to be annihilated that was no reason to die before you died. Sing to wake the living and the dead. Just sing. Say yes to life. Yes! yes! yes! and yes again. Spit on the darkness" (258). Then, in a more personal vein: "I knew that if I had but a few days left on earth I wanted to embrace those days, not curse them. . . . To achieve dignity through affirmation. And for three days, at a white heat, I wrote the first draft of my first play" (259). That play was *The Hamlet of Stepney Green*, but the same singing spirit, toned down for public display, infuses *The Dream of Peter Mann*.

Kops designed this semiexpressionist parable primarily to convey how not to conduct oneself in a climate of impending nuclear destruction. The play is set in a stylized London marketplace, a microcosm of middle-class capitalistic existence. The protagonist, a Peer Gyntish representative of free enterprise, dreams that he is trying to exploit the nuclear situation for all it is worth. After a futile quest for uranium with two companions, he re-turns home, organizes a collective search which is successful, then shrewdly develops a lucrative business making shrouds, including varieties "designed specially for the Cobalt war—one for Russia, one for America, and one for England" (75). These shrouds sell extremely well because they can serve the double-edged purpose of protecting wearers against fallout and cover-ing their dead bodies. Peter has his comeuppance at the peak of his for-tunes, however: the fatal bomb falls, and he perceives his own complicity. His own death is a wakeup call. Wiser from his dream, Peter urges everyone to reject profit-motive activities and make the most of life while it's still there. This message, Kops's mildly positive *carpe diem* for the thermonuclear age, is lost on the over-conditioned people of the marketplace (who end up chanting "MONEY IS TIME AND TIME IS MONEY"), but remains to influence whatever spectators have become receptive to it.

As in Ibsen's *Peer Gynt*, the protagonist's relations with women parallel the stages of his mental misadventures. Before his dream, he spurns his ever-faithful true love, significantly named Penny, to pursue his infatuation for a more expensive item, Sylvia (read "silver"). She will only accept a stable rich man as a husband, so Peter adds this to his list of motives for joining the contemporary version of the gold rush. To finance his quest for uranium, he steals his mother's life savings—or so he imagines, since her safe falls on his head and prompts his hallucination of seventeen years in league with the military-industrial complex. Within his fantastic and tangled dream, Penny begs to accompany him. He grudgingly concurs, first to enjoy her sexual favors and later, when his money runs out, to parley them into the only source of capital available. Peter is also accompanied by Alex, an amoral vagrant who exploits *him* (and turns out to be his father). Alex has promoted the quest, but is clever enough to grasp what the "great uranium fever" really signifies: "We can't wait to blow ourselves to smithereens" (24). On his far-from-triumphant return to the marketplace twelve years later, Peter is treated as an intruder and nearly executed, but his sympathetic mother saves him. He uses his hawker's skills to make the people cooperate in digging a massive trench on the premises, promising them the "Superstore" of their dreams. After another five years pass we learn, somewhat bafflingly, that they did locate uranium but that Peter told them "so much uranium made the world a dangerous place to be" (66) and redirected their slavish energies toward the shroud factory. Since no Superstore materialized, Kops may want us to infer that Peter made a big killing from the dig and realized that an exploitative industry with less competition would reap more profit in the long/short run. In any event, the self-styled "supermann" (39) transformed the huge hole into a luxurious fallout shelter for himself, created the shroud business, married the now-bloated and gaudy Sylvia, and settled down to wait for the inevitable bomb. Before it falls and he awakes, he realizes that he wants Penny in the shelter with him rather than the capitalist trophy Sylvia. Penny refuses to join him, but his feeling survives upon his return to reality, and of course she accepts him then. Similarly, in his dream he sees his mother die just after her chemistry reconnects with Alex's, while in real life their reunion is not lachrymose but gratifying.

These developments move the play close to the mode of romantic comedy, with the obstacles to happiness removed and multiple unions to celebrate. The ghastly devastation of the hydrogen bomb, the failure of the shrouds to protect—"There's not a person left in the world, just shrouds . . . covering the dead world" (79)—have proven to be delusions, and in fact salutary ones since they woke Peter up in more ways than one. However, by no means does the play end happily for all. The oppressive forces that existed before, the money-making drive and the nuclear weapons poised to strike, still predominate. Lest we forget, Kops inserts reminders of this into the play's finale. Alex bellows to his newfound love, "COME, LET US WRITE OUR LOVE UPON THE SKIES—LET'S DREAM TILL DOOMSDAY" (83). After Peter and Penny agree that their love is all that matters, Peter proclaims: "I know what I do want—I want Penny—I know what I don't want—Superstores and Uranium." But he sees the market-people "working furiously" and hears them chant:

MONEY IS TIME AND TIME IS MONEY;
IF YOU'RE BROKE IT ISN'T FUNNY—
. . . .
MONEY IS TIME AND TIME IS MONEY,
MIGHT AS WELL DIE IF YOU HAVEN'T ANY—(85)

Peter *is* broke. His last exhortation to his neighbors puts just as much accent on the downside of the *carpe diem* theme as on the upside. Moreover, to sway the people the only way he knows how, he casts it as a hawker's spiel, with the rosebuds to be gathered "while ye may" turned into commodities up for auction: "What will YOU bid for LIFE? Here it is. A kiss in the dark. The one and only—all shapes and sizes—lovely, lousy, terrible, terrific. Magnificent! Ridiculous! But it's the only one we've got. A great opportunity never to be repeated—a unique bargain—going—going—so make the most of it before it's gone!" (85–86). His punch line is hardly more positive than the dismal children's song that starts the play:

Apricot, Peach, or Plum!
We may get blown to kingdom come.
Let us eat our fruit before
Our parents go again to war. (15)

The assembled parents respond enthusiastically to Peter's declamation, but as soon as he leaves they "stop cheering and laughing and go back to work as if their lives depended on it," chanting their habitual refrain as the curtain falls (87).[47]

ABSURDIST WITH A SOCIAL CONSCIENCE: DAVID CAMPTON

Although David Campton has kept his long, prolific career as a playwright in relative obscurity by writing mostly one-acts which are rarely seen in London or published prominently, he is a significant figure in the context of this book. Four of his short plays have a direct bearing on the nuclear situation of the late 1950s, and distinctively, all four have qualities in common with absurdist drama. In them, Campton displays the political, social, and psychological consciousness that we expect from dramatists of the early nuclear age, but unlike any of the others, he often employs the techniques and effects of Theatre of the Absurd. His 1957 post-holocaust play, *Then...*, is a mini-tragic farce à la Beckett, with a bleak landscape and even more bleak prospects for the caricature-like survivors. The other three plays, all of which date from 1960, touch corners of the nuclear situation that had not yet been dramatized in the English-speaking world. They also directly manifest Campton's discovery of Eugène Ionesco's early plays, which he attests that he greeted "with whoops of delight," saying "Yes, this is the sort of thing I've been waiting for."[48] *Out of the Flying Pan* is a pun-rich parody of arms/peace negotiations, in effect if not in intention a "comic bomb" dropped on the year-old Geneva test-ban conference. The tiny play skillfully adapts the structural patterns of Ionesco's *The Bald Prima Donna*. *Mutatis Mutandis* is a gently farcical treatment of parents' reactions to their newborn mutant child, whose green hair suspiciously matches the twilight's radioactive glow. A farce tinged with pathos, its dramatic movement progresses from realism to the surrealistic absurdism of Ionesco's *Amèdèe or How to Get Rid of It*. *Little Brother: Little Sister* takes place in a fallout shelter twenty years after the Bomb destroyed London. Amid echoes of Beckett's *Endgame* and various Ionesco plays, it depicts the efforts of a boy and girl in their mid-teens to overcome a tyrannical nanny-cook and begin their mature lives outside the constricted world of their youth. Commentators justifiably exclude these plays from the ranks of Theatre of the Absurd because of their purposeful thrusts[49] (and Campton concurs, adding that his preference for upbeat endings also violates the spirit of the Absurd[50]). Still, it takes only a slight qualification to dub him a small-a absurdist with an active social conscience.

Then...

The basic situation in the first of his relevant plays, *Then...*,[51] is ludicrously improbable: all the world's people except one man and one woman have been "granulated" by a nuclear force which, in the style of a ray gun, affected only living organisms (and a statue of Eros). The two survivors find each other in Piccadilly Circus and realize that they, and they alone, took the protective measure that authorities urged and put brown paper bags over their heads in time. Although outrageously mismatched as candidates for the roles of the new Adam and Eve, the two fall in love and, as a step toward union, consider taking the risk of baring their heads. The man makes a tentative gesture toward his bag and utters an ambiguous "Then...," but his ellipsis fades into darkness as the play ends. The all-important finale is left dangling much in the manner of Pinter's *The Dumb*

Waiter.[52] David Campton makes a highly illuminating observation about the impact of this moment: "The reaction of audiences to the ending . . . acted as a peculiar barometer to the political atmosphere when any particular performance took place. At times of international tension a majority of the audience would be convinced that removing the bags would prove fatal, but during a period of comparative stability the majority was sure of a happy ending."[53]

The underlying dynamic of *Then...* is a kind of whimsical send-up of certain elements in Britain's current nuclear situation, especially the development of their own hydrogen-bomb deterrent. The physics professor/protagonist, Phythick, identifies the product of nuclear research that all but undid the human race as "hetrodynamic deterrents" (31). Reducing an established government policy to its frighteningly absurd reality by applying typical Shavian logic, Phythick declares: "Whitehall blundered. They gave the fanatics in hetrodynamic deterrents *carte blanche.* Can you imagine that? They deputed absolute authority for the world to be destroyed" (34). The familiar irony that a nuclear weapon cannot fulfill its deterrent purpose unless it is powerful enough to cause what it is supposed to prevent, mutual annihilation, is pointed up by the weapon itself being called a deterrent. (The invented adjective "hetrodynamic," by the way, would sound almost exactly like "heterodynamic" in the theatre and thus suggest a fusion device roughly equivalent to a thermonuclear ray gun.[54]) The hilarious ploy of having a brown paper bag that covers only the head—and has holes for the eyes and mouth—serve as a flawless fallout shelter is another exposé via reduction to absurdity, this time directed at government attempts to delude people into thinking that minimal civil defense measures will save many of them from the worst after-effects of an atomic attack. (I have not found the source, but apparently some British survival manual specifically recommended covering oneself in brown paper.[55]) The reason why so few people put the bags on affords Campton a satirical attack on government-managed nuclear complacency:

PHYTHICK. Everyone had heard the propaganda so much that they were used to it. They weren't afraid of the hetrodynamic deterrents any more. . . . It appeared on every television screen in every home. It was a household pet.

GIRL. It was a clean bomb. . . . It sounded so hygienic. Everyone said that it was a good thing. And it was on our side. (42)

Finally, the couple's dilemma after they want to look at each other's faces derives from a logical hitch with analogies to civil defense policy: the television told them how, why, and when to don their paper bags, but it cannot now tell them if it is safe to remove them. The all-clear signal is no longer manned.

The farcical pathos of the couple's dilemma, accentuated by the indeterminate finale, is one of a few noteworthy affinities with Theatre of the Absurd in the play. The two have no way of knowing whether they will take a giant step toward normalcy if they remove their bags—or decompose on the spot. It is a little like Didi and Gogo wondering if Godot will turn out to be a savior if he ever does come. Even with a favorable outcome, another element keeps the situation problematic: the miracle of love has occurred, but will *it* survive close looks at each other? The male is "a wisp of a man in an old macintosh several sizes too large for him" (29), sufficiently advanced in years to have had a few of his students become "chiefs of nuclear research" (31). The female is "smartly dressed with a good figure" (29), so young and gorgeous that she has been chosen Miss Europe (32). Physically they are incompatible fugitives from a burlesque show, and this would strike them both. What happened to the statue of Eros in Piccadilly Circus may happen to their bond: "Eros disappeared," Phythick comments; "I don't know why" (31). Their love affair progresses from an imitation of Jack and Gwendolyn in *The Importance of Being Earnest*—

> PHYTHICK. Miss Europe ... I want you to understand that this is no hurried statement. Although it may appear to be composed on the spur of the moment, it has a lifetime's reasoning behind it.
>
> GIRL. I know perfectly well what you are going to say, and I might as well tell you here and now that I agree with every word of it.

—to farcically repetitive speech patterns—

> PHYTHICK. I warm towards you. Do you know that? I ...
>
> GIRL. I feel something about you too. I ...
>
> PHYTHICK. I feel your proximity glowing in me like old wine. I ...
>
> GIRL. I felt it the very second I heard you call me. I ...

—finally to a sequence that betrays an acquaintance with Ionesco's *Bald Prima Donna*:

> *He clasps her in his arms. Their heads come together, but do not touch. They freeze in this position for a few seconds. Then they straighten. . . . [T]here is a long pause between each of the next few speeches. He laughs. A short, dry, nervous laugh.*
>
> PHYTHICK. Ridiculous.

GIRL. Silly.

PHYTHICK. For one minute ...

GIRL. I thought so too.

PHYTHICK. That I was making love to a brown paper bag.

GIRL. It's a good bag.

PHYTHICK. I've never seen a better bag. . . . (37–38)[56]

The farcical pathos of their relationship escalates when they briefly decide, like Didi and Gogo, that it would be better if they parted, then realize "We are the only ones. We are the only ones in the world. We are the world." In a moment "They turn and run into each other's arms" (41), but the ludicrously problematic bags remain in place.

Out of the Flying Pan

Out of the Flying Pan[57] is an ingeniously composed parody of peace/ disarmament negotiations between Cold War nuclear powers. In the comic opening, a British diplomat awaits an aircraft. One approaches; he becomes attentive. It passes; he lapses into idleness. When another approaches, he pays no attention; of course it lands. He "collects himself hurriedly" as an identically dressed Russian diplomat disembarks (47). Both men, labeled simply "A" and "B," have been given authority to make agreements on arms reduction and disputed territories to the end of establishing "Peace and Friendship." They make a show of amiability for the media, then get down to serious business. After examining each other's proposals they prepare to sign a treaty, but both suddenly become indignant at the other's "double-talking" and alternately repeat "No" at "a fantastic rate" (52). The Briton's civil offering of tea mollifies the Russian and saves the negotiations, but wrangling over faulty maps of territories renews the conflict. The angry diplomats escalate their threats all the way to "devastation" and "annihilation" (56). But it dawns on the Russian that his threat would bring *mutual* destruction, so this time *he* saves the negotiations by offering wine. The two over-imbibe. The resulting congeniality results in a hasty agreement to exchange the problematic territories, and both actually sign the treaty. However, their mood soon turns to petulant distrust; realizing that the territories are still ill-defined by the maps, they denounce each other, tear up the charter and the documents, and again repeat "No" after each other "with fantastic rapidity." The logical consequence that they hypothesized then ensues, at least in their imaginations: "They toss the torn paper about until the air is filled with fluttering pieces. Amplified 'no's' give way to sounds of war—guns and sirens. . . . The sounds of war are amplified to a climax. As A and B cease to speak, there comes the roar of a cosmic sized explosion" (59–60). Both are now able to voice a genuine point of agreement: "Nothing left." The Russian leaves the stage and the Briton cleans up the litter, doing "a little semi-ballet" to the tune of gentle classic music (60). The finale surprisingly duplicates the comic beginning, with a Russian diplomat played by the same actor again arriving in a second airplane and greeting his British counterpart. The implication is clear: exactly the same thing will happen again.

The general pattern of this action strikingly resembles that of *The Bald Prima Donna*. Ionesco's play puts the hosts (the Smiths) and their guests (the Martins) on a rollercoaster of harmony and disruption, the latter caused each time by the sudden intrusion of "a wrench in the works."[58] Finally, just when the two pairs are getting along better than ever, a great crescendo of conflict occurs. Mr Smith suddenly interjects, "Down with polishing!" (which we can imagine a fed-up diplomat saying). This leads to the four characters "shouting at each other, raising their fists, ready to hurl themselves at each other's throats" (116–17). As darkness slowly falls before the curtain, they chant faster and faster in unison, "Its not that way, its this way, not that way, its this way, not thatter way, thisser way, thatter way, thisser way. . . ." The tumult ceases, the lights come on, and the play begins again with the Martins saying exactly the same things as the Smiths did in the first scene (119). This cyclical finale, which also occurs in Ionesco's *The Lesson* (and in Beckett's *Act Without Words II* and Fernando Arrabal's *The Architect and the Emperor of Assyria*), is a dramatically potent element of absurdist structure which Campton adapts effectively from Ionesco's example.

A trademark of the absurd comedy in *The Bald Prima Donna* is its frequently nonsensical dialogue. An exchange will often strike spectators as barely intelligible, while the characters behave as if they are communicating famously. The Smiths discuss a doctor who considerately had his own liver operated upon before operating on a patient's. Mr Smith wonders why the doctor survived and the patient didn't, and insists that a doctor "should perish at the same time as his patient, like the captain and his ship."

> MRS SMITH: Ah! I hadn't thought of that! ... Perhaps you're right ... What do you make of it all, then?
>
> MR SMITH: It's very simple. All doctors are charlatans. And all their patients too. The only respectable thing left in England is the Royal Navy.
>
> MRS SMITH: But not sailors.
>
> MR SMITH: No, of course not! (88)

This mode reaches its most extravagant point just before the explosion caused by the host's "Down with polishing!"

MRS MARTIN: I would give you the slippers of my mother-in-law if you gave me the coffin of your husband.

MR SMITH: I am looking for a monogynist priest to marry our maidservant.

MR MARTIN: The pine is a tree, whereas the pine is also a tree, and an oak breeds an oak every morning at dawn.

MRS SMITH: My uncle lives in the country, but that's none of the midwife's business. (116)

This pretense at communicative harmony represents a form of "social polishing," the butt of Ionesco's implicit satire in the play.[59]

The butt of Campton's satire in *Out of the Flying Pan* is diplomatic polishing, and his equivalent of Ionesco's linguistic technique is semi-intelligibility through punning. His puns are strategically warped words and phrases designed to transform meanings into near-opposites, such as "greedment" for "agreement" or "hate stations" for "great nations." Neither character lets on that he notices the transformation. B first states the phrase "Peace and Friendship" and then garbles it into "Piece of Fiendship," but A lets it pass (48); A changes "Freedom and Democracy" into "Three ton of Mockery" (49) without drawing a reaction from B. On the point of signing the treaty, A pontificates: "Never before in the mist re-exhume an affair [in the history of human affairs] has such a purple and a staining [perfect understanding] been achieved between beef steaks [big states?]. We underhand the other, and will truss the other illicitly" (51). They actually do underhandedly trust one another illicitly. Addressing the media, A speaks for his counterpart as well as himself when he declares, "Today we prove the tooth of the old saw 'The Gun is Mightier than the Word'" (49)—warping truth, pen, and sword, and thus half-consciously exposing a belief that the two have in common. When A notes that the treaty provides for "substantial disarmament," he accepts B's clarification: "Ban of the comic bomb" (54).

As in *The Bald Prima Donna*, some of the dialogue in *Out of the Flying Pan* is free of such devices so that the absurd effects they yield do not become diffused or stultifying. And like Ionesco, Campton often employs these intelligible stretches to satirize more or less meaningless social and diplomatic "polishing." A and B exchange friendly boasts about their countries:

A: Our rainfall is the envy of civilised society, and we have mountain ranges which could hardly be manufactured elsewhere in the world.

B: Our building programme includes ice houses, boiler houses, light houses, dark houses, power houses, and sand castles.

They proceed to shake hands (53). At one point Campton directly borrows the device of blatant self-contradiction from *The Bald Prima Donna* (as in Mr Smith's description of Bobby Watson's wife as both "too tall and too well-built" and "too short and too slight" [89]). In two successive speeches, A describes Britain's disputed territory as follows: "The Government Strip contains valuable mineral deposits, rich farm lands, thriving factories, and a contented population. . . . The Strip consists merely of uncultivated bush-land and arid stone crops. The natives are wild and unco-operative" (55). No wonder the maps of the territory are misleading. A last item worth mentioning in Campton's gallery of linguistic pleasures is a device he uses independently of Ionesco, but for the same satirical purpose. This is the substitution of intonation and body language for intelligible verbalization. The best example is the exchange that starts the play and is repeated ver-batim at the end, when the Russian diplomat(s) arrives:

A: How? [How was your trip?]

B: Nice. . . .

A: Jolly.

B: Time? [Did I arrive on time?]

A: Exactly.

B: Welcome? [ambiguous]

A: Ready. [eh?]

B: Press? [ah: he meant Is the formal welcome ready?]

A: Films. . . .

B: Ready? [ambiguous again]

A: Go. [clarified when the two "assume exaggerated postures of greeting" for the benefit of photographers]

Since Campton himself played both Bs in the first performance, his fellow actor would not have had to rely on himself to fill in these blanks—and diagnose the many puns—as I have tried to. Luckily it is not vital to trans-late the gestures or words instantly and accurately; the parodic *gist* of the dialogue, like that of the action, is unmistakable.

Mutatis Mutandis

In contrast to *Then...* and *Out of the Flying Pan, Mutatis Mutandis*[60] is downright realistic. But only in contrast; the little play is still skewed enough by grotesque and farcical elements to show Campton's affinity with Ionesco. The setting is a sitcom standard: the waiting room in a maternity clinic. The three characters in the play, the new parents and a nurse, have amusing foibles typical of characters in traditional comedy. The opening situation seems simply exceptional rather than fantastic or eerie: the nurse wants the father, who has already seen the baby, to prepare his wife carefully for her first view of it. "Break the news to her gently," she says (157). The tide of our comfortable responses begins to turn with his comically ominous reply: "Why me?" When the nurse explains, "you must make her want the child. *You* must [my italics]," alert spectators of the early 1960s would recall the play's title, connect it to the publicity recently given to the genetic dangers of fallout from bomb testing, and suspect that the baby is a mutant. The suspicion proves true. From this point on, the play discloses the comic but appalling details of this secret in a sequence of increasingly striking revelations, each one building anticipation for the next. Unfolding a semi-fantastic image of a possible byproduct of the Cold War by employing a much-used structural pattern of comedy, Campton achieves that amalgamation of realism and grotesquerie, pathos and farce which marks some of the best absurdist dramas.

The main business of *Mutatis Mutandis* is the confrontation between Douglas, the father, and his wife Celia, which concludes when Celia definitely wants to have Nurse Min bring the baby for her to see. But the play begins just after *Douglas* has viewed his child for the first time. We don't know this, so that when the nurse tries to console him and he responds "mechanically" and "dully," we have little to go on. With ambiguous foreshadowing, Min comments, "An amazing child for a first attempt, if I may say so" (155). Douglas learns to his surprise that Celia has not yet seen her baby (we learn later that it was born seven days ago); "The mother doesn't see the child until she's quite restored," Min explains darkly. When he realizes that it will be his job to prepare his wife, Douglas asks (in vain) for a double whisky to calm his nerves. The comic sequence that the rest of the one-act follows hinges on the fact that the parents need only ring for Nurse Min and the baby will appear.

After the two get together, Celia complains that she has not even been told if the child is a boy or a girl. Step one in the sequence occurs.

CELIA.   . . . It is a boy, isn't it?
DOUGLAS.   It's—a baby.
CELIA.   A boy?
DOUGLAS.   Sort of. (159)

This dubious note, along with the nervous twitching of her husband's nose, does not keep Celia from wanting to ring the nurse; an optimistic type, she is convinced that the baby must look like him. Douglas puts her off, then issues a more concrete warning signal (step two): "He's a healthy child. . . . You should see him laugh. Showing little white needle-sharp teeth" (161). This touches off what becomes the dominant verbal refrain of the play, the mixed consolation that "Our baby is unusual."

CELIA.   Because he has teeth?

DOUGLAS.   Because he—has teeth.

CELIA.   Then we have an unusual baby.

DOUGLAS.   Do you mind?

CELIA.   We have the most unusual baby in the world. And I love him.

Again she wants to ring for Nurse Min, but Douglas's nose again twitches. He tells her (step three) that the child has lots of hair: "Thick curly hair. Curly green hair" (162). The revelation of this markedly unusual detail leads to prolonged speculating about causes and consequences (a whole new line of humans with green hair?), and Douglas must finally come out with the crucial underlying factor: "Our baby is a mutant" (164). Far from being put off by this, motherly Celia says that she wants to hold him close to her. Douglas seizes the opportunity to tell her what happened when he held the baby close to him (step four): "when I picked him up, he held my fingers in his two chubby fists. . . . His little tail curled around my arm." This proves a turning point, marked by a deliciously comic interchange:

CELIA.   A tail.

DOUGLAS.   A pretty, prehensile tail.

CELIA [coldly].   That's not usual.

DOUGLAS.   He's an unusual baby.

CELIA.   I didn't want a tail. (165–66)

The play has moved closer and closer to the mode of Ionesco. When Douglas vainly cites the ways a tail could be useful while Celia whines that none of her family had tails and that now whenever they get together "they will talk about—that," we are smack in the surreal, nuttily satirical land of *Amèdèe or How to Get Rid of It* (and Albee's *The American Dream*). Celia now insists that she does not want to see the child. But Douglas remonstrates and she recants, asking him for the fifth time to call Nurse Min. He chances one more preparatory revelation (step five): the baby's eyes are

Wide, brown, and wondering. . . . Intelligent eyes.

CELIA.   I knew they would be.

DOUGLAS.   All three of them.

Long pause.

CELIA.   It's not usual.

DOUGLAS.   He's an unusual baby. (169)

Although Douglas argues that "We all have our little idiosyncrasies," Celia is too concerned about the neighbors:

CELIA.   The Jones' will talk.

DOUGLAS.   Let them.

CELIA.   And the Joneses. So will the Joneseses. (170)

Echoes of the "Bobby Watson humor" in *The Bald Prima Donna* resound. However, the vein of absurdity soon dissolves into pathos as Celia sincerely laments and Douglas tenderly consoles her.

The play's serious dimension is now in the forefront, and will stay there until the comically upbeat finale. The mutant's parents speculate on what may have caused the aberrations. Noting that the twilight has been green recently, Celia prompts the first direct allusion to the nuclear situation: "The popular press insists on radioactive dust," Douglas replies. (We note the link: green twilight, green hair.) But he scoffs at Celia's fear that they themselves may be full of radioactivity: "We don't emit fire, or glow in the dark. It has been scientifically calculated that experiments can continue at the present rate for years before there is a lethal dose in the atmosphere" (171–72). Douglas then recalls that the baby was conceived when "the rockets flew overhead" (173). He clearly implies that experiments with rockets, presumably missiles bearing nuclear warheads, caused the fallout, which in turn caused the mutation. This is either a deliberate absurdity (since the warheads would have to detonate, not merely fly overhead, to produce fallout) or a blunder on Campton's part.[61] In either case, it scrambles the connection between nuclear cause and mutative effect to a disturbing degree, and stands as a clear-cut flaw in the play's antinuclear component. The Ionescoish gimmick that resolves the pair's conflict and permits the favorable ending is also a degree beyond the pale, but it does not strike a disconcerting note because it coheres with absurdist moments which have occurred before.

Douglas has become frantic in his attempt to induce Celia to accept the baby, and even grudgingly suggests putting it up for adoption. But he suddenly gets an idea: "He makes a small distant noise like a baby crying. CELIA is startled, but says nothing. He repeats the cry, again without effect" (174). But in a moment Celia does react, and Douglas, in order to call more attention to what she heard, poo-poohs it as an illusion. He is startled to hear her say: "There it is again," and continue to hear something he cannot. This figment of her motherly imagination, sparked by Douglas's trick, overturns her decision to reject the baby. She declares that she knows why it is crying: "He is calling to me" (175). Tears flowing down her own cheeks, Celia sums up: "He is an unusual child. He has bright green hair, three eyes, and a tail, but he is my baby. I want him. Ring for Nurse Min" (176–77). Delighted, Douglas obeys. Precisely in the manner of traditional comedy, an unexpected bonus awaits to cap the heroine's newfound bliss. But in the manner of Ionescoish nuclear drama, that bonus derives from the grotesque source of the green hair, three eyes, tail, and indistinguishable sex.

CELIA.   What can we call him?

DOUGLAS.   Perhaps we should ask him.

CELIA.   But he can't ... How do you know?

DOUGLAS.   He spoke to me.

CELIA.   'Goo' or 'Gaga'?

DOUGLAS.   He said 'Hullo, Daddy. I've been waiting for you. Where's Mummy?'

CELIA.   It's not usual.

DOUGLAS.   He's an unusual baby. (177)

The door opens and, as the curtain falls, "The shadow of Nurse Min looms large on the wall." Step six was a giant step up, but a stumble may await.[62]

Little Brother: Little Sister

In *Little Brother: Little Sister*,[63] Campton again establishes a dramatic situation which deals with the possible consequences of the nuclear age for real human beings, and here he concludes on a note that is more than semi-hopeful. But in this case, as in *Then...*, improbabilities and grotesqueries are more prominent than in *Mutatis Mutandis*. Moreover, the connection with the nuclear age is superficial at best. A brother and sister in their mid-teens have lived all their lives in the family fallout shelter since most of London was "blown away" in a nuclear attack about twenty years ago. They have been nurtured, and imperiously controlled, by "an incredibly old, misshapen creature" who has served as both cook and nanny for them (7). Their parents were not around long enough for the children to remember them; fifteen years ago they apparently heard on the wireless that it was safe to leave, and tried to open the door despite Cook's warning that they would "let in the disaster" (18). When they persisted, she wielded a cleaver and ground them up in a "mincing machine" (16). The children, whom Cook named Sir and Madam just as she respectfully addressed their parents, are now verging on maturity. Putting aside childish things more and more, they have begun playing at romantic conversations and contact, and in the course of the play develop a strong urge to try life outside the shelter. When the two finally approach the door, Cook seizes them and prepares to turn Madam into a rissole. Sir, divining that she wants to keep a male around, uses his sexual appeal (and practice at romantic palaver) to overwhelm the old dragon with desire and cause a fatal heart attack. At the curtain the young man and woman walk to the door hand in hand.

The play has clear-cut ties to nuclear issues, but it is not primarily a dramatization of a hypothetical fallout-shelter situation. The main focus of the action lies securely on late adolescents confronting absurd tyranny and freeing themselves from it. The fallout shelter not only provided an especially confining prison environment for this action, but gave Campton the fringe benefit of an image that was familiar and evocative in the early 1960s. He did not choose to deal seriously with the special complications posed by his use of a shelter for the prison. He leaves us baffled (if we care) about how air, food, water, and electricity are still amply supplied after nearly twenty years—and we hear nothing about the waste disposal problem. The attack took place on December 1, 1980, far enough in the future for the nature of nuclear weapons (and civil defense) to have changed even more than it changed between 1945 and 1960, yet Campton posits the usual four-minute warning and only partial devastation that might have occurred in the earliest phase of the thermonuclear era. (The survival of a radio broadcasting system is flagrantly improbable.) The one person present who lived through the attack, the forceful but dimwitted nanny-cook, has a paranoiac terror of "letting the disaster in" that can initially be attributed to the horror she experienced, but a strictly personal aberration, her irrational distrust of what radios say, is the crucial factor in her insistence that the door stay closed. (When she made rissoles out of the parents she also tossed in the wireless [29–30].) As far as we know, fifteen years ago the children could have left the fallout shelter with their parents and survived if Cook had not been so perverse. They have had sheltered lives imposed upon them, but not by nuclear disaster.

The play's affinities to absurdist drama are also detectable but superficial. Whereas these affinities might have been enhanced, as they are in some later nuclear dramas, by conveying the claustrophobia of entrapment in a fallout shelter, with the grim alternative of radiation poisoning outside, they are instead blunted by the focus on the children's struggle to escape arbitary imprisonment, with relative normalcy beyond the door all but insured. The contrast with Beckett's *Endgame* is a case in point. Hamm and Clov exist in an enclosure which is at least a metaphorical fallout shelter,

and domineering Hamm has a grip on the younger Clov that has kept him
from leaving despite his obvious desire to. However, totally unlike Sir and
Madam, Clov craves extinction along with escape from oppression, and it
is clear that departing for the "other hell" outside would put him "under
the last dust" where he wants to be.[64] Moreover, Hamm is far from the
Ionescoish gorgon that Cook represents (her more direct ancestor is the
cook in Strindberg's *The Ghost Sonata*). Hamm is firmly in control of his
sadistic and histrionic tendencies, while Cook is an oblivious victim of hers.
Her trademark, in fact, is aggressive assertion to conceal vulnerability:
"That door's been shut for twenty years, an' it stays shut for thirty more.
I can add up. Look at this calendar. A fifty year calendar this is. Every day
marked off since we came down to this shelter. Twenty years. Leavin' thirty
to go. We're stayin' 'ere till all this calendar's used up" (29). The irrational
insistence in this speech smacks of Ionesco or Pinter characters (such as
Jean in *Rhinoceros* and Goldberg in *The Birthday Party*) much more than
Beckett's. True, early in the play Campton has Madam speak as if he were
orienting us to the best-known absurdist context: "I'm not frightened now.
Not frightened. Waiting. Something is about to happen. Something important. And we are waiting for it" (8). However, the context which has already been made clear is that they are waiting, not for some Godot, but
simply for physical and psychological maturity, which has been somewhat
frightening as it developed. That Campton is still operating partially in
"post-Ionesco" terms is borne out by most of Cook's actions, from waving
her cleaver in order to save the children from incest to letting it drop when
Sir says "Come and have a cuddle when the lights are low" (15, 42). But
center stage is dominated by the non-absurd children, whose charming and
favorable development is the core of the play.[65]

CHAPTER 7

The Private Fallout Shelter Dilemma Dramatized: Rod Serling, Elaine Morgan— and Samuel Beckett?

In both the United States and Great Britain, the period of intensified threats of nuclear war between the superpowers beginning with the conflict over Berlin in mid-1961 and ending with the resolution of the Cuban missile crisis in late 1962 saw an unparalleled heightening of public interest in home fallout shelters. In this period the Pentagon received over 100,000 letters a month requesting information on shelters and other aspects of civil defense.[1] As in the much milder surge of interest in 1950 when the Korean War broke out, the chief controversy over private shelters was whether they would turn out to be worth the trouble and expense to build. Optimists— and skilled practitioners of denial—gambled that they would not be needed. Homeowners who approached the problem logically met clear-cut paradoxes: those who would most desperately need protection for their families, citizens who lived near potential "ground zero" targets, were also those least likely to survive the initial effects of a thermonuclear attack[2]; then, if shelters did happen to save some families, the prospect of what would confront them when they finally dared to emerge was daunting. Conundrums such as these kept a great many people from investing in private fallout shelters.

If this were not enough, homeowners who decided to build them still had to face a knotty ethical dilemma that might well become a wrenching personal crisis: what does one do if an "outsider" wants to get in? The title of a 1961 *Time* article put the question bluntly: "Gun Thy Neighbor?"[3]

Presented with the immediate threat of a nuclear attack, a family or other group who had built and stocked a shelter for their exclusive use would head for the shelter. Other people in the vicinity—passersby, neighbors without shelters, visiting friends or relatives, even kindred souls who had built shelters but could not reach them in time—might plead or clamor to be added to the protected group. Even if these outsiders did not try to get in, the occupants might feel that they could—and perhaps should—offer sanctuary to an endangered few at the cost of depleting their own space, fresh air, food, water, and other requirements for survival. Rugged American individualists responded quickly to the problem: repel the intruders with whatever force is necessary. One father quoted in the *Time* article planned to mount a machine gun at his shelter door; another bought tear-gas bullets to drive out anyone who might have reached his shelter first. The same slant also emerged from unexpected sources. A Jesuit priest and sometime ethics professor condoned a civil defense coordinator's statement that "There's nothing in the Christian ethic which denies one's right to protect oneself and one's family."[4] A psychologist lecturing to shelter instructors urged them to recommend keeping a gun as standard equipment and "shooting anyone who tries to invade" (Brelis, 61). On the other hand, a healthy majority of 236 residents of a middle Western college town opposed this view. Responding to a 1962 questionnaire, half agreed that shelter owners have a "moral obligation" to take in outsiders, and only a quarter felt that owners have "a right to dispose of an intruder in any way."[5]

The fallout shelter dilemma was bound to attract a variety of creative writers. Personal life-and-death crises are at its core, and reactions to such crises would reveal the heights and depths of human character. Moreover, the dilemma contains the ingredients of both melodramatic action and impassioned debate, thus making it amenable to a wide spectrum of treatments ranging from sensational at one extreme to intellectual at the other. Many popular novels and films "featured desperate fights at shelter doors," according to Spencer Weart.[6] Philip Wylie's 1963 post-holocaust novel *Triumph*, which is set some time in the near future, takes place in a rich man's super-shelter which avoids the dilemma by having room and provisions enough for several stray outsiders. But this is clearly an exception: a character recalls that "years back, arguments flared up over whether or not people in shelters should let outsiders in, even if they overcrowded the shelters. And now the answer is plain: anyone, apparently, would kill, if it required killing to save those he had arranged for and held dear!"[7] An unlikely working television set in the shelter receives totally improbable programs that picture the widespread devastation of the United States, chaos and misrule among doomed survivors, and the horrors of people trying to enter overstuffed public shelters and well-defended private ones (135–36). The 1963 film "Ladybug, Ladybug," a melodrama whose suspense begins with a Civil Defense red alert, depicts an autocratic twelve-year-old girl inviting several school allies into her home fallout shelter but rejecting a rival. In contrast, Langston Hughes's 1962 story, "Bomb Shelters," is thoroughly comic in tone. A roomer in a Harlem tenement, Jess Simple, visualizes having a mail-order shelter only big enough for himself and his wife. He realizes that if the sirens sounded he would not be able to deny his place inside to another roomer, a poor old lady. He is caught up in a mushrooming fantasy: the lady won't go in without her three grandchildren, and they want their mother; when the father appears and insists on being included, Simple vows to keep him out because he has never bought him a beer. Luckily the all-clear sounds, but Simple's wife resolves to tear the shelter down to avoid the dilemma: "If the bomb does come, let's just *all die* neighborly."[8]

Apart from the borderline case of Samuel Beckett's *Endgame*, two very different dramatic renditions of the private fallout shelter dilemma appeared, one on American television and the other on the English stage. Rod Serling's *The Shelter* graphically depicts the dilemma unfolding in action; Elaine Morgan's *Licence to Murder* presents it retrospectively, through a court trial of a man who killed an alleged intruder. Serling's script moves from intense argument to somewhat oversensational action; Morgan's play features an intelligent courtroom debate in Act I but dissolves into crime-exposé melodrama after that. Beckett's *Endgame* is an enigmatic example. In that many-faceted and elusive drama—the richest and most widely known play treated in this book—one of several metaphorical dimensions suggests that the classic fallout shelter dilemma may have faced Hamm in the distant past. That dimension has gone largely unexplored. A careful analysis of it seems highly appropriate as a conclusion for this account of modern plays and playwrights in their nuclear-age contexts.

SERLING'S "NIGHTMARE" IMAGE OF THE DILEMMA: *THE SHELTER*

Rod Serling's *The Shelter* was presented on September 29, 1961—two months after the tensest days of the Berlin crisis.[9] This episode of the popular CBS "Twilight Zone" series, technically outside the scope of this study but published in a form adaptable to staging, offers the most focused example of the fallout shelter dilemma in the drama of the early Nuclear Age. According to Serling's biographer, the play was directly inspired not only by the "then highly topical atom bomb shelter craze," but also by the Jesuit priest's implication that "Americans would be justified in keeping their neighbors out of their shelter during an actual atomic attack."[10] In a small town about forty miles from New York City, four couples are enjoying a birthday party for Dr. William Stockton in his home. They are interrupted by a Conelrad announcement on radio that a Yellow Alert has been declared because radar has detected ominous unidentified flying objects. Only Stockton has a shelter; it measures only ten feet by ten feet; and it is minimally supplied with provisions. His neighbors begin a "mad, frenetic exodus" for their homes, but the sound of a siren pulls them up short outside. The stage is set for a grimly realistic, then eerily surrealistic portrayal of conflict over entry into the shelter. Serling's sonorous voice intones, "What you're about to watch is a nightmare" (416).

Before the series of attempted invasions, the anxiety and disorder of the Stocktons's hasty preparations for a long stay in the shelter are depicted. The main fears are an attack close to their town (unlikely) and radioactive fallout drifting from New York City (very probable). The high-strung wife, Grace, reaches a point of hysteria that leads her to ask what's the good of trying to survive only to face "rubble and the ruins and the bodies of our friends," but her stable husband points at their twelve-year-old son and says, "*That's* the reason" (421). The first person to make an appeal is Bill Stockton's closest friend, Jerry Harlowe. He implores Bill to let his family in, but meets what might be described as an anguished stone wall. Jerry gets emotional and tries to intimidate Bill, but then backs away and asks for forgiveness. Preaching half to his friend and half to the audience, Bill says gently: "I kept telling you. All of you. Build a shelter. . . . But you didn't want to listen, Jerry. None of you wanted to listen. To build a shelter was admitting the kind of age we lived in and none of you had the guts to face that" (424). The next intruder, Marty Weiss, comes with his wife and two small children. He registers heartfelt pleas outside the now-locked door of the shelter. Bill issues another firm refusal, but his face shows "the results of this massive attack on . . . his conscience, his beliefs, the habit pattern of a lifetime which he must suddenly simply turn aside" (426). Weiss caustically responds, "You probably will survive—but you're going to have blood on your hands."

The second half of the play becomes more and more like a typical episode of "Twilight Zone." Frank Henderson and his wife enter the room where the first two families have congregated. Frank is desperate and aggressive, even though Conelrad announces that the state of Yellow Alert has not yet been changed to Red. When he suggests breaking down the shelter door, all assent but Jerry Harlowe, who remonstrates that "All of us couldn't fit in there. That would be crazy to even try. . . . We'd just be killing everybody and for no reason" (429–30). When Marty Weiss suggests asking Bill to pick one family, the debate over who should be chosen ignites a fight. Jerry stops it, saying, "Just keep it up. We won't need a bomb. We can slaughter each other" (430). The siren sounds again and searchlights are perceived, raising the tension. At this point Serling quietly touches off a surreal nightmare sequence by positing that several people from the street have gathered outside and somehow know the situation. Henderson leads them to the shelter and threatens Bill to open the door, only to hear him say that he is wasting time that could be used for "figuring out how you can survive" (432). The action escalates as more men gather and a mob spirit captures everyone, even Harlowe. The now-piercing siren accompanies the efforts of the men to batter down the shelter door, and "it all reaches one vast pitch just as the door buckles and is forced open"—in effect destroying the shelter's capacity to protect anyone (435).

Suddenly the siren stops and (to borrow from Pinter's Max) you never heard such silence. Conelrad reports that the approaching objects have been identified as satellites; there is no enemy attack. Shows of exhausted relief are intermingled with absurd gestures of atonement: Weiss suggests a celebrative block party; Harlowe agrees—"Anything to get back to normal"—and tells Bill his friends will pay for the damages. Bill replies: "The damages? . . . I wonder if we realize just what those damages are? (*he looks from face to face* . . .) Maybe the worst of them was finding out just what we're like when we're normal. . . . A lot of naked animals who put such a premium on staying alive that they claw their neighbors to death just for the privilege. . . . We were spared a bomb tonight ... but I wonder if we weren't destroyed even without it" (437–38). In terms of the play's development, a group of desperate people became increasingly caught up in a struggle for mere survival. In the process, they abandoned their consideration for others and refused to accept certain inescapable facts of nuclear-age existence. Ironically, the group itself turned into a weapon potent enough to negate the efforts of the one family that had taken reasonable measures to survive. Only the coincidental absence of an actual nuclear threat prevented the fallout shelter dilemma from being resolved in the most nightmarish way possible.

THE ISSUE DEBATED IN MORGAN'S *LICENCE TO MURDER*

The other drama that treats the dilemma explicitly, Elaine Morgan's *Licence to Murder*,[11] uses the issue as the focus of a sharp courtroom debate prompted by the actual killing of an apparent intruder. The "real issue" is defined as "whether a man would be justified in the use of violence to keep an intruder out of his shelter in the event of nuclear war" (47). However, the violent event is twice removed from the dramatic reality of present action, first because it occurred in the past and is not reenacted in the play, and second because the killer (we finally learn) only pretended he thought a nuclear attack was imminent in order to commit murder with impunity. Act I, accordingly, presents an absorbing argument about a case that turns out to be a purely hypothetical example of the fallout shelter dilemma, and Act II, after the testimony of a surprise witness, approaches the case as a Perry Mason murder mystery.[12] The speciousness of the case-in-point very nearly makes the play a cop-out on the issue. Still, the argument about the dilemma is intellectually interesting as it unfolds, and the alternative course, arriving at a judgment in favor of one side or the other, is fraught with difficulties. Morgan clearly accepts the realistic premise that the question, as a character states, "can never be answered" (59).

The situation that led to the killing involves a combination of stretched probabilities. The ostensible facts are these: in early October 1960,[13] an overworked real estate executive, Brad Foster, took his wife Laura and sixteen-year-old daughter Christine on a one-month vacation as a rest cure. He rented an isolated lodge with no telephone or radio, ordered that no mail should be forwarded, and bought no newspapers. A week after the family's departure, the Civil Defense agency in his city announced that it had organized a remarkable event to take place at midnight on November 1: a full-fledged practice alert for a nuclear attack, including siren warnings and a ninety-minute power cut. Arrangements were made to utilize available public and private shelters to the fullest extent and to evacuate the remaining citizens. The Fosters took the long ride home on the crucial day and arrived at the crucial moment—just before midnight. A siren sounded the alert; people ran for their cars or for public transportation. Fearful that an actual nuclear attack was moments away, the Fosters immediately occupied their back-yard fallout shelter (4). However, their next-door neighbor, Doug McKennan, appeared on the scene and gave Brad the impression that he was trying to save himself and several other people by entering the unlocked shelter.[14] Brad told an investigating officer the next morning that he drew his gun and told Doug to leave, but he wouldn't. "So I shot him. I thought I was entitled to do it" (8). Expanding on this in court, he declares: "I thought it was him or me. I thought it was the only thing anybody could do" (20). Although most of Brad's testimony is later proven to be false, these are the presumed circumstances that form the basis of the argument in Act I.

The opposing lawyers address the audience as if it were the jury (1). Prosecution counsel Paul Ricardo approaches the issue from the standpoint of the victim: "If a man enters another man's shelter pleading for sanctuary against certain and horrible death, does that constitute a justification for killing him?" He stresses the incriminating facts that Brad Foster recognized the intruder as his neighbor and business associate Doug McKennan, killed him even though he was not behaving irrationally, and explained simply that he thought he was entitled to do it. Ricardo asks the jury to show that fifteen years after Hiroshima, decency and compassion still exist. A guilty verdict would let the world know that we are not "a nation of Brad Fosters"; acquittal would be tantamount to granting "a licence to murder" (4–5). Defense counsel James W. Murdoch keeps the focus on the decision the defendant presumably had to make in a nerve-wracking instant. Brad Foster and his family had suddenly become the first people in the country to feel that they were experiencing "the threat of the hydrogen bomb not as a remote possibility, but as a present and horrifying reality." He had the sole responsibility of insuring his family's survival. Murdoch implores the jury to view the killing as an impulsive act of self-defense in unprecedented, trying circumstances, and thus justifiable homicide (13).

One of the most interesting phases of the debate emerges from the questioning of a salesman, Edwin Baker, whose company built Foster's fallout shelter. Along with some unique points of view, Baker supplies some welcome comic relief. The soundness of his testimony is undercut early when he admits that he has not bought a shelter himself. Why? Because, even though it might be safe for the prescribed fourteen days until the outside world is habitable again, who can be sure that the Russians will not wait thirteen days "and then drop *another?*" (18). Murdoch first uses Baker to establish that a shelter built for three could not accommodate many more people during the prescribed two-week confinement without risking the survival of all. Ricardo counters by getting Baker to agree that one extra person would probably not make a crucial difference (17–18), but Murdoch later reveals that the defendant assumed McKennan meant to shepherd several neighbors in (21). Murdoch also tries to get Baker to confirm that he encouraged Foster to have a gun available. The salesman evades the question, but does confess to meeting Foster's evident qualms about using a gun with a rehearsed argument that insuring the family's survival is "a public-spirited" thing to do: "we want this country to survive the war—right? That means *people* have got to survive. Now, if you use this shelter the way it was meant to be used, that'll be three people left alive to help rebuild America" (17). Ricardo characterizes this as a salesman's gimmick to ease the customer's conscience (19), and when he confronts Foster, makes the trenchant point that if a war did start, "the possession of a shelter wouldn't depend on ownership at all, but only on who was quickest on the draw" (23).

The grilling of Brad Foster is of course the dramatic highlight of the debate. His explanations of the factors involved in his fatal act turn out to be a tissue of lies, but many of them have the ring of solid probability and therefore illuminate the problematic nature of the fallout shelter dilemma. He defends himself in social terms by claiming that everyone in his neighborhood could afford to have a shelter; "If they'd rather spend their money other ways, that's their funeral" (22). He fends off the legal impropriety with the simple argument that there wouldn't be much law left by the time he could leave the shelter. When Ricardo asks him whether other factors might have restrained him—"mercy—conscience—or common humanity"—he can only respond, "I didn't *want* to kill him! I only wanted him to go away!" He goes as far as to declare that the circumstances of the crisis would have exonerated him ethically even if his neighbor had gone away and suffered a horrible death: "*I* didn't make the war! *I* didn't send the bomb!" And he adds, "what do you think's going to happen if people get the idea they can just walk into anybody's shelter and we can't do anything to stop them?" (23) Surely Brad's retorts reflect enough logic and popular sentiment to put a sizeable proportion of the jury/audience on his side.

Act II shifts the focus entirely toward the motives he might have had for disliking Doug enough to commit an act of premeditated murder. It is revealed that Doug had recently won a vice-presidency in their firm which Brad hoped to win, and that Brad already envied him for his education, appearance, and contacts (40). To top it off, Brad knew that his wife and Doug were having an affair (50). Proof that he also knew of the practice alert all along is squeezed out in typical Perry Mason fashion, and Ricardo can sum him up as a man "who tried to exploit the fears and confusions of the last fifteen years for [his] own petty and vindictive ends," in the process subjecting his wife (and daughter) to "an ordeal of terror that would have driven most women out of their minds" (65). There is a re- deeming irony in this issue-evading plot resolution. Act I culminates in the surprise testimony of an anti-Communist student, Josef Radewski, who claims that he met Brad on the way home from his vacation and told him about the impending practice alert. This turns out to be a red herring: Radewski is later exposed as a liar who wanted to transform the case from a political one that could only result in the Communists jeering at America, whatever the judgment, into a purely personal one. By arousing suspicion, however, the lie inadvertently fulfills its purpose and, to an extent, also covers the evasive tracks of the playwright.

"ALL THOSE I MIGHT HAVE HELPED": BECKETT'S *ENDGAME*

The private fallout shelter dilemma is a surprisingly neglected context for Samuel Beckett's richly allusive drama of the mid-1950s, *Endgame*.[15] A close examination of the direct and indirect references to the nuclear situation, private fallout shelters in general, and the specific dilemma as- sociated with them proves both interesting and illuminating. Although Beckett conceived the play in the early 1950s, long before the "shelter craze," great attention had been given by the American and British gov- ernments to the desirability for shelters since late 1949, when the Soviet Union set off its first atomic explosion. A widely distributed American pa- perback issued in 1950, *How to Survive an Atomic Bomb*, suggests rein- forcing cellar walls or digging a cellar if none exists.[16] The fact that the dilemma was familiar, at least in regard to public shelters, is attested to by the comic treatment Langston Hughes gives it in a 1954 story.[17] Intention- ally or not, the situation presented in *Endgame* would have been perceived by many as a post-holocaust shelter situation, and Hamm's "story" as a tortured memoir of the way he handled the classic shelter dilemma in the distant past. His story, which he also terms a "chronicle," reaches a distinct point of anguish when he declares: "All those I might have helped. *(Pause.)*

Helped! *(Pause.)* Saved. *(Pause.)* Saved! *(Pause.)* The place was crawling with them!" (68). It is not my intention to reduce Hamm's in-process, quasi-autobiographical narrative to a concrete nuclear-age melodrama; *Endgame* is aggressively ambiguous.[18] But within the "allusive fallout" that the play generates through a myriad of suggestive devices is a perceptible metaphor of a family shelter after a nuclear holocaust, and an unobtrusive but distinct analogy to the dilemma that might have faced the person in charge.

Hamm twice refers to his constricting abode as a "shelter."[19] In his first soliloquy shortly after the play opens, he defines the endgame situation he finds himself in: "Enough, it's time it ended, in the shelter too. *(Pause.)* And yet I hesitate, I hesitate to ... to end. Yes, there it is, it's time it ended and yet I hesitate to—*(he yawns)*—to end" (3). In his second-last soliloquy, just after he bewails "All those I might have helped," he visualizes his dying moment: "It will be the end and there I'll be, wondering what can have brought it on and wondering what can have ... *(he hesitates)* ... why it was so long coming. *(Pause.)* There I'll be, in the old shelter, alone against the silence and ... *(he hesitates)* ... the stillness" (69). The text describes a setting which is fairly compatible with the idea of a fallout shelter, although in no sense does it directly evoke that image. "Bare interior. Gray light. Left and right back, high up, two small windows, curtains drawn. Front right, a door." The room contains little but an armchair on castors (Hamm's "throne"), two ashbins (for the living remains of Nagg and Nell), and a picture, "its face to wall." We eventually learn that the door leads to a smaller room ("ten feet by ten feet by ten feet") which serves as a kitchen, a bedroom/sitting room for Clov, and a storeroom (with a cupboard that has a combination lock). No hint of a bathroom emerges. The door to the outside world is in this room, unseen from the stage. Hamm once comments, "here we're down in a hole" (39), but he seems to mean simply that Clov's view is impeded by hills. The stage designer whom Beckett brought from Paris for the 1967 German revival of *Endgame*, his friend [Henrioud] Matias, apparently took as his model for the setting "the classical 'bunker' or 'shelter' in its simplest shape."[20] But if Matias, or by inference Beckett, actually meant to suggest a reinforced living area designed specifically to protect its occupants against atomic blast, firestorm, and fallout, there would be no windows—especially ones that Clov can open, as he once does (65).

A few minutes after Hamm says, "it's time it ended, *in* the shelter too" (my italics), he joins Clov in contemplating how and when their present predicament might end. Hamm 'hesitates' to end, but Clov is anxious to be "silent and still . . . under the last dust," as he later broods (57). He also knows how to manage it: by leaving. The play's plot, such as it is, revolves about Clov's threats and attempts to leave, which become more determined as time drags on (although he stands rigid by the door at the curtain). After his first weak threats, Hamm warns him: "Outside of here it's death" (9). Late in the play, when Clov is definitely preparing to leave, Hamm reiterates this with emphasis: "Gone from me you'd be dead. . . . Outside of here it's death!" (70). Clov already knows this firsthand. He has looked outside and found "There's no more nature" (11). The color of the world is gray—"Light black. From pole to pole" (32). The general impression is: "Let's see. *(He looks, moving the telescope.)* Zero ... *(he looks)* ... zero ... *(he looks)*... and zero. . . . In a word? . . . Corpsed" (29–30). Hamm later notes, "The whole place stinks of corpses," and Clov replies, "The whole universe" (46). Just before he changes his clothes for departure, Clov fully conveys his desire to meet death outside: "I open the door of the cell and go. I am so bowed I only see my feet, if I open my eyes, and between my legs a little trail of black dust. I say to myself that the earth is extinguished, though I never saw it lit. *(Pause.)* It's easy going. *(Pause.)* When I fall I'll weep for happiness" (81).

This range of allusions to a possible holocaust (with a residue of "black dust") by no means necessarily points to a nuclear attack, and Beckett objected severely to the overt post-nuclear-holocaust setting of Douglas Stein's 1984 American Repertory Theatre production.[21] However, this is almost surely the way many spectators and readers of the late 1950s, when "nuclear terror" was at a peak, would have construed these verbal allusions and scenic signs. Most would not have been put off by the incongruous windows, or prompted to reserve judgment by the spareness and openendedness of the text. They may not have noticed a number of conflicting details which are difficult to explain away: Hamm refers to a time when Clov used to inspect his paupers—"sometimes on horse" (8); Nagg says that Clov normally put sawdust in his and Nell's dustbin, but it ran out and he now fetches sand from the shore (17)[22]; Hamm orders Clov to build a raft, to which Clov replies, "I'll start straight away" (he does not, of course) (35). Clov reports in convincing fashion that "a small boy" is outside the shelter; we have no reason to doubt him until he quips to Hamm, "You don't believe me? You think I'm inventing?" (79). The two pay no more attention whatever to the phenomenon—reality, invention, or mirage, no one knows.[23] A final undercutting of whatever degree of assurance we might have reached takes place in the plot's climactic moment. Clov appears, "dressed for the road" in a tweed coat and panama hat, raincoat over his arm, bag and umbrella in hand (82). His previous image of himself gratefully merging with "the last dust" dissolves in self-contradiction. Still, this is only a logical incongruity; the metaphor of a fallout shelter after a nuclear holocaust remains intact, prompted by a wide range of indefinite but provocative allusions.[24]

The devastation which is subtly evoked seems to have been the kind generally envisioned before thermonuclear weapons were widely tested and mass-produced. Hamm's story and other details about conditions of the "other hell" outside (26) hint that bombs of the Hiroshima/Nagasaki type (fission bombs) were used. Large areas were decimated, a great many people were killed, and lingering radioactive fallout made it perilous for survivors to leave their shelters, but genocidal annihilation by anything close to a "doomsday machine" did not occur. Beckett began working on the first approximation of *Fin de partie* in 1954 and began writing the final French version in December 1955; a year or two later, he would have been more likely to suggest a vision of the gradual extermination of mankind as pictured, for example, in Nevil Shute's *On the Beach*. As it is, his images fit the pattern of those in Marghanita Laski's *The Offshore Island*. Laski depicts the long-term adaptation of family groups in two "pockets of survival" which escaped serious damage and contamination during an atomic war that obliterated most of Britain. Hamm's "family" seems to exist in a "pocket of survival," which might allow occasional forays outside the shelter (though not to inspect paupers on horseback!), and their retreat into the shelter seems to have followed a nearby catastrophe analogous to, if not modeled on, Hiroshima.

Let us assume for the moment that Hamm's story is an elaboration of recollected events. He recalls that a man came begging to him on a very distinctive day in the past. In intermittent reports, he remembers comically incongruous weather conditions: "an extra-ordinarily bitter day, . . . zero by the thermometer"; "a glorious bright day, . . . fifty by the heliometer"; "a howling wild day, . . . a hundred by the anemometer"[25]; and "an exceedingly dry day, . . . zero by the hygrometer" (51–53). Can this jumbled mix of weather reports be reconciled so that all four imply a nuclear assault? To borrow Beckett's key word, Perhaps. If we take the description of bitter cold simply as a pre-attack weather report (and not an extraordinary one at all, as Hamm notes, since it was the day before Christmas), the others can be construed, with the help of other comments from Hamm, as rapidly changing weather conditions during the successive stages of an atomic explosion. The initial (distant) bomb burst created a "glorious" brightness, even though "already the sun was sinking down into the ... down among the dead." The tremendous blast that ensued would suddenly make it "a howling wild day" on which "The wind was tearing up the dead pines and sweeping them ... away." A raging firestorm would follow the wind, eventually turning zero-degree weather into excessive heat and dryness (ideal for Hamm's lumbago). After this series of reports, Hamm says to the supplicant, "But what in God's name do you imagine? That the earth will awake in spring? That the rivers and seas will run with fish again?" (53). About himself he remarks, "I imagined already that I wasn't much longer for this world"—a thought that is compatible with anticipating the effects of radioactive fallout. Through the years Hamm's body decomposed so that he can no longer walk, and he gradually went blind. Clov became disabled so that he cannot sit down, and his eyes are now "bad" (7). Hamm predicts, "One day you'll be blind, like me," and "you'll come to a standstill, simply stop and stand still" (36–37). The deterioration of the two, and of Nagg and Nell as well, could also be attributed to malnutrition as one result of their long incarceration in the shelter; their recent diet seems to have been limited to biscuits, with an occasional bon-bon or sugar-plum.

If Hamm's account is indeed more a "chronicle" than a piece of fiction, an analogy to the classic fallout-shelter dilemma can be detected through a close examination of his confrontation with the supplicant. Hamm recalls: "The man came crawling towards me, on his belly. Pale, wonderfully pale and thin, he seemed on the point of—" (50). It is clearly conceivable that the man was a victim of a nearby nuclear explosion who is now on the verge of death. When Hamm asked him where he came from, "He named the hole" (52). This would have been a minimally protective "pocket of survival," as we learn, since the place was no longer inhabited except by the man and his young boy. A wide area in the vicinity of his "hole" seems to have been decimated; Hamm "enquired about the situation at Kov, beyond the gulf," and the man replied, "Not a sinner" (52). Hamm recalls treating the pathetic supplicant with the disdain which he would deem appropriate to one of the paupers in his alleged fiefdom: "Well, what is it *you* want?... Well, what ill wind blows you my way?" When the man "raised his face to [Hamm], black with mingled dirt and tears," Hamm tried to shunt off the doleful appeal of his eyes: "No, no, don't look at me, don't look at me"—then claimed he was "a busy man" preparing for Christmas: "Come on now, what is the object of this invasion? . . . Come on now, come on, present your petition and let me resume my labors" (51). With defensive arrogance, he characterized the man's approach first as a brash intrusion, then as a formal matter to be handled at the proper time. When the supplicant mentioned his son, Hamm responded in a way that suggests an impulsive wish not to confirm the strength of the petition: a cadaverous body and imploring eyes; now a helpless child? "And you expect me to believe you have left your little one back there, all alone, and alive into the bargain? Come now!" But all the man proceeded to request was food for his son. In response, Hamm found another route to evasion, in this case one that would even allow him to appear magnanimous: an offer of nourishment. However, he couched the offer in rhetoric designed to make the man realize the futility of accepting it if he only 'uses his head':

Corn, yes, I have corn, it's true, in my granaries. But use your head. I give you some corn, a pound, a pound and a half, you bring it back to your child and you make him—if he's still alive—a nice pot of porridge, . . . a nice pot and a half of porridge, full of nourishment.

Good. The colors come back into his little cheeks—perhaps. And then? *(Pause.)* I lost patience. *(Violently.)* Use you head, can't you, use your head, you're on earth, there's no cure for that! (52–53)

(Note the relish with which he painted an image of the reviving child even as, in effect, he retracted his offer.) Hamm topped this explosion by saying, "But what in God's name do you imagine? . . . That there's manna in heaven still for imbeciles like you?" Having "cooled down," he then accentuated how unreasonable it would be for the man to accept the corn, return to his child, and expect the food to be of any use. He inquired how long the journey took, no doubt anticipating the reply (he knew how far it was); "Three whole days." He then asked in what condition he had left the boy; "Deep in sleep." His forcible retort: "But deep in what sleep, deep in what sleep already?" Perhaps secretly appalled at his brutal behavior toward the wretched man, Hamm showed a touch of genuine sympathy (with a hidden loophole): "I finally offered to take him into my service. He had touched a chord." The words he added to this offer suggest its hidden underside: "Here if you were careful you might die a nice natural death, in peace and comfort." Hamm has just recalled imagining that he himself "wasn't much longer for this world"; surely he expected the man to die very soon and be off his hands. Nevertheless, he had nobly offered him succor. Outrageously in Hamm's eyes, the man was then audacious enough to ask him if he would "take in the child as well—if he were still alive" (53). Reporting this to Clov later, Hamm clarifies his reaction: "Before accepting with gratitude he asks if he may have his little boy with him" (60). "It was the moment I was waiting for," Hamm recalls, and paints a picture of the man poised intensely for his reply: "I can see him still, down on his knees, his hands flat on the ground, glaring at me with his mad eyes . . ." (53–54). What happened then Hamm does not say; he pauses to speculate how he will finish the story. In one of Beckett's favorite artistic ploys, suspense is left spinning its wheels.

Remarkably, however, Hamm returns to the scene of the action later, and does so not by 'getting on with his story' but by involuntarily re-experiencing his mental state at the time. Just after he vainly asks Clov for a sign of affection and Clov crisply exits, Hamm is moved to his highest level of despairing emotion in the play.[26] This soliloquy remains sheerly expressive, without the histrionics and oratory that he normally indulges in. At its core is the anguish of guilt.

You weep, and weep, for nothing, so as not to laugh, and little by little ... you begin to grieve. . . . All those I might have helped. *(Pause.)* Helped! *(Pause.)* Saved. *(Pause.)* Saved! *(Pause.)* The place was crawling with them! *(Pause. Violently.)* Use your head, can't you, use your head, you're on earth, there's no cure for that! *(Pause.)* Get

out of here and love one another! Lick your neighbor as yourself!
(Pause. Calmer.) When it wasn't bread they wanted it was crumpets.
(Pause. Violently.) Out of my sight and back to your petting parties!
(68–69)

It is not until after these effusions that he contemplates going on with his
story, and then he does not. In fact, this tortured confessional (with the
ghost of a troubling moral imperative, "Love thy neighbor," hovering over
it) seems to be the true continuation and expansion of what Hamm calls
his story, but which now is perhaps exposed as defensively fictionalized
truth. The single supplicant was most probably followed by several more
"crawling" beings; he responded to each one as he responded to his fictional antagonist, "Use your head, can't you, use your head, you're on
earth, there's no cure for that!" In his final soliloquy, after he believes Clov
has left, Hamm considers modifying his story in one highly significant respect: "If he could have his child with him ..." (83). This may further align
the story with the truth of what really happened. On this occasion the
fictional guise is applied not to cover up the enormity of his many rejec-
tions, but to open the door for the one element that redeemed him: the
man *did* have his son with him; Hamm *did* take him in. The earlier version
hung in suspension when the statement, "It was the moment I was waiting
for," led to nothing. Hamm repeats it just after voicing his new inspiration,
and continues (my italics throughout): "You don't want to *abandon* him?
You want him to bloom while you are withering? Be there to solace your
last million last moments? . . . *He* doesn't realize, all he knows is hunger,
and cold, and death to crown it all. But you! *You* ought to know what the
earth is like, nowadays. Oh I put *him* before his responsibilities!" (83). (My
reading of the last sentence is admittedly conjectural, but given the context
I have developed, its most likely meaning is, *I* [Hamm] would first think
of what's best for the boy [i.e. death], not of what duties you want him to
fulfill as you wither and die.[27]) Again the story is suspended, but this time
it satisfies Hamm: "Well, there we are, there I am, that's enough." How
could it satisfy him? Because he knows that he relented and took in the
boy; he did save one of the many he might have saved. (Conceivably two.[28])
The "story" has been Hamm's all along, even though he has recited most
of it to Nagg and outlined some to Clov. Especially now, when he assumes
Clov has left the shelter forever, Nell is dead, and Nagg is very near death,
the story can only be a means of therapeutic self-expression, two parts self-
excoriation and one part self-congratulation. He does not need to have the
story say explicitly what his redeeming act was; besides, it would open a
new can of worms, since his interaction with Clov over the years can hardly
be described simply as "solace" for his own "last million last moments."
It would lead to "More complications!" (78) suspiciously like those that

might ensue if Clov's sighting of a small boy outside is accurate ("If he exists he'll die there or he'll come here," Hamm says).

The evidence that Clov 'didn't die there but came here' has been examined at length by critics. The key exchange seems quite sufficient:

HAMM: Do you remember when you came here?

CLOV: No. Too small, you told me.

HAMM: Do you remember your father?[29]

CLOV (wearily):   Same answer. . . .

HAMM: It was I was a father to you.

CLOV: Yes. . . . You were that to me.

HAMM: My house a home for you.

CLOV: Yes. . . . This was that for me.

HAMM (proudly):   But for me, (gesture towards himself) no father. But for Hamm, (gesture towards surroundings) no home. (38)

Beckett himself has apparently expressed no opinion as to whether the boy in Hamm's story is based directly on Clov. Asked by Rick Cluchey, who was playing Hamm at the time, he responded: "Don't know if it's the story of the young Clov or not. . . . Simply don't know."[30] Nevertheless, actors playing Clov in productions monitored by Beckett have gone on the assumption that this is his actual identity.[31] Hamm's later reference to Clov as "my son" should not have the effect of disrupting this assumption because Clov easily qualifies as an adoptive son. No doubt Clov has come to wish strongly that he had been left outside to die, but Hamm unfortunately did not follow his own advice to Clov's father. Of all those he might have saved, Clov alone was chosen. The four occupants of Hamm's "pocket of survival" have been generally miserable, but his anguished decision to allow only one (small) human to enter cannot be ascribed solely to natural venomousness—surely one of his qualities. If this ultra-focused reading of one important thread that runs through *Endgame* has some validity, Hamm's decision not to over-burden his shelter was prudent and his acceptance of Clov as a future servant was benevolent, if also a touch selfish.

It is generally agreed that *Endgame* is "one of a spate of works of art directly promoted by the existence of first the atomic and then the hydrogen bomb," as Vivian Mercier puts it.[32] S. E. Gontarski adds that both *Endgame* and *Happy Days* are "permeated with the suggestion of nuclear devastation" (80). I hope I have shown that one dimension of this many-layered drama is an extended analogy to the insoluble family fallout-shelter dilemma which, as the world gradually recovered from the numbing fatalism of the era that nurtured Beckett's postwar plays, has luckily been allowed to fade from our consciousness.

Notes

INTRODUCTION

1. Cambridge: Harvard University Press, 1988; New York: Pantheon Books, 1985.

2. The two most useful books on the fiction are Paul Brians's *Nuclear Holocausts: Atomic War in Fiction, 1895–1984* (Kent, OH: Kent State University Press, 1987), and David Dowling's *Fictions of Nuclear Disaster* (Iowa City: University of Iowa Press, 1987). The only book on the poetry is John Gery's *Nuclear Annihilation and Contemporary American Poetry: Ways of Nothingness* (Gainesville: University Press of Florida, 1996).

3. The 1985 Northwestern dissertation of Robert Hostetter, "The American Nuclear Theatre, 1946–1984," is the only extended study I have come across. It stresses theatricalist works of 1980–84 and does not attempt thorough coverage of previous drama. The title of John Elsom's *Cold War Theatre* (London: Routledge, 1992) describes its period, not its subject.

4. Telegram of October 18, 1945 printed in *A Southern Life: Letters of Paul Green, 1916–1981*, ed. Laurence G. Avery (Chapel Hill: University of North Carolina Press, 1994), 418.

5. Lifton's landmark studies are *Death in Life: Survivors of Hiroshima* (New York: Random House, 1967) and, with Richard Falk, *Indefensible Weapons: The Political and Psychological Case Against Nuclearism* (New York: Basic Books, 1982). In *Missile Envy: The Arms Race and Nuclear War* (New York: William Morrow, 1984), Helen Caldicott sums up the phenomenon in direct relation to the situation in 1964:

Out of sight is out of mind, and rapidly people's fears of a nuclear war disappeared. The superpowers quietly and efficiently continued testing and increasing their arsenals without any interference from the public or world opinion. The people of the world lapsed into a state of psychic numbing and pushed the fear of nuclear annihilation into their collective subconscious. (330)

6. New York: Samuel French, 1990, 47.

7. London: Samuel French, 1985, 16.

8. In his *Early Warnings* (New York: Dramatists Play Service, 1983), 16.

9. New York: Knopf, 1985, 9.

10. "Edward Albee Interviewed by Digby Diehl," *Transatlantic Review*, 13 (Summer 1963): 72 (reprinted in *Conversations with Edward Albee*, ed. Philip C. Kolin [Jackson: University Press of Mississippi, 1988], 36).

11. *The Theatre of the Absurd*, 3rd. ed. (Harmondsworth: Penguin Books, 1980), 430–31.

12. "The State of the Theater: Interview by Henry Brandon," *Harper's*, 221 (November 1960): 69; reprinted in *The Theater Essays of Arthur Miller*, ed. Robert A. Martin (Harmondsworth: Penguin Books, 1978), 235–36.

13. Letter to Louis Kronenberger responding to his article, "The Decline of the Theater," *Commentary*, 1 (November 1945): 47–51, printed in *Dramatist in America: Letters of Maxwell Anderson, 1912–1958*, ed. Laurence G. Avery (Chapel Hill: University of North Carolina Press, 1977), 203–4.

14. *Three Plays* (London: Heinemann, 1963), 306.

15. "Theatre and Living," in *Declaration*, ed. Tom Maschler (London: MacGibbon and Kee, 1957), 111–12.

16. The play was performed in London in 1963 but not published until 1970 (Walton-on-Thames: Margaret and Jack Hobbs).

17. St. Lucia: Australasian Drama Studies, 1991; reprinted from *Theatregoer*, 3 (March 1963): 19–36. In an introduction, Vic Lloyd states that Cusack "was disturbed by the fact that 'the Great' writers of the time were silent about 'the apocalyptic doom facing the human race, unless ...' and by the question 'how can we make the apathetic and the hostile understand?' "(3).

18. I have examined only a few of these, the three printed in *After Apocalypse: Four Japanese Plays of Hiroshima and Nagasaki*, edited and translated by David G. Goodman (New York: Columbia University Press, 1986), and the De Filippo play, which Thornton Wilder mentions in relation to his unfinished nuclear drama. Three sources have been valuable: Carlos Buján, *La figura del físico atómico en el teatro alemán contemporáneo: la responsabilidad del científico como tema literario* (Salamanca: Ediciones Universidad de Salamanca, 1979); S. Beynon John, "The Ultimate Infernal Machine: The Atomic Bomb and Contemporary French Avant-garde Theatre," *Romance Studies*, 6 (1985): 110–27; and Sandra Messinger Cypess, "Women Dramatists of Puerto Rico," *Revista/Review Interamericana*, 9 (Spring 1979): 24–41.

19. Norman Moss led me to this distinction in *Men Who Play God: The Story of the Hydrogen Bomb*, rev. ed. (Harmondsworth: Penguin Books, 1972), 13.

CHAPTER 1

1. Anne O'Hare McCormick, "The Promethean Role of the United States," *New York Times*, August 8, 1945, 22.

2. Kurt Vonnegut, who witnessed the destruction of Dresden firsthand, says in the autobiographical first chapter of *Slaughterhouse-Five*, "Not many Americans knew how much worse it had been than Hiroshima," and later cites an authority who says the same thing about Tokyo. This attests to the fact that casualty figures make little impact upon the imagination; Vonnegut had *seen* Dresden, while millions were affected by Hiroshima without seeing more than dramatic photographs. *Slaughterhouse-Five, or The Children's Crusade: A Duty-Dance with Death* (New York: Dell, 1968), 10, 188.

3. Quoted in Spencer R. Weart, *Nuclear Fear: A History of Images* (Cambridge: Harvard University Press, 1988), 103 (and in *Slaughterhouse-Five*, 185!).

4. From his editorial in *Saturday Review of Literature*, August 18, 1945; expanded and printed in October as *Modern Man Is Obsolete* (New York: Viking Press, 1945), 8.

5. Interview with Michael Amrine, " 'The Real Problem Is in the Hearts of Men,' " *New York Times Magazine*, June 23, 1946, 7.

6. New York: Pantheon Books, 1985, xix.

7. I am referring to two volumes of poetry: Mark Kaminsky's *The Road from Hiroshima* (New York: Simon and Schuster, 1984) and Brown Miller's *Hiroshima Flows Through Us* (Cherry Valley: Cherry Valley Editions, 1977).

8. "Atomic Scientists Have Two Responsibilities," *Bulletin of the Atomic Scientists*, 3 (December 1947): 356.

9. Editorial by Eugene Rabinowitch, *BAS*, 3 (July 1947): 169.

10. Rabinowitch, "Forewarned—but Not Forearmed," *BAS*, 5 (October 1949): 275, 292.

11. "Arms Can Bring No Security," *BAS*, 6 (March 1950): 71.

12. By William L. Lawrence in *The Hell Bomb* (New York: Knopf, 1951).

13. Indianapolis: Bobbs-Merrill, 1955, chapter title on p. 15.

14. Norman Moss, *Men Who Play God: The Story of the Hydrogen Bomb*, rev. ed. (Harmonsworth: Penguin Books, 1972), 91.

15. Bernard A. Weisberger, *Cold War, Cold Peace: The United States and Russia Since 1945* (New York: American Heritage, 1984), 103.

16. *Parliamentary Debates (Hansard): House of Commons*, 537 (1955): 1899.

17. "The Dawn of a New Decade," *BAS*, 16 (January 1960): 3, 5.

18. "New Year's Thoughts 1963," *BAS*, 19 (January 1963): 2. Curiously, the clock was not changed in this period.

19. Chapter title for the period 1960–63, p. 200.

20. President Kennedy's words in his speech during the Berlin crisis, which is printed in Steven R. Goldzwig and George N. Dionisopoulos, *"In a Perilous Hour": The Public Address of John F. Kennedy* (Westport, CT: Greenwood Press, 1995), 163–70 (quotation from p. 164).

21. As reported in Helen Fuller, *Year of Trial: Kennedy's Crucial Decisions* (New York: Harcourt, Brace and World, 1962), 235.

22. *"In a Perilous Hour"*, 167.

23. "Fallout Shelters," *Life*, September 15, 1961, 95–108. The issue included detailed building plans for different income levels. For an interesting context, see F. K. Berrien, Carol Schulman, and Marianne Amarel, "The Fallout-Shelter Owners: A Study of Attitude Formation," *Public Opinion Quarterly*, 27 (1963): 206–16.

24. "A Matter of Survival," *Economist*, 201 (October 21, 1961): 223–24.

25. Spencer Weart points out that after Kennedy's Berlin crisis speech in which he urged families to take measures to protect themselves, "The federal civil defense agency got more than 6,000 letters a day asking for information," and "for two months newspapers got more letters to the editor on shelters than on any other issue." A poll carried out by a Kennedy aide found that "shelters had become the chief domestic concern, a fad verging on hysteria" (255).

26. An English journalist reported that "the boom in private shelters . . . has collapsed almost without trace" ("Shelters out of Style," *Economist*, 207 [June 22, 1963]: 1256). Weart notes that "only about one in fifty [Americans] built any sort of fallout shelter" in this period (263). Among the abstainers were a twenty-man committee that took eighteen months to study the issue (Moss, 223).

27. "To Build or Not to Build?" *BAS*, 17 (November 1961): 355.

28. An authoritative recent source is Raymond L. Garthoff, *Reflections on the Cuban Missile Crisis*, rev. ed. (Washington: Brookings Institution, 1989). See also Richard Rhodes, *Dark Sun: The Making of the Hydrogen Bomb* (New York: Simon and Schuster, 1995) 170–76.

29. This event followed a new Kremlin demand for removing its missiles, and incited hard-liners around Kennedy to urge him to get tougher. The United States had already (secretly) guaranteed not to invade Cuba, but now would also have to respond in kind by removing its missiles from Turkey. Kennedy chose to comply (partly because he already intended to remove those missiles, obsolete "Jupiters"). See Garthoff, 97–129 passim, and Weisberger, 223–25.

30. France and China did not sign the treaty, basically because they wanted to "catch up." France had conducted a series of tests since the first one in February 1960; China was preparing for its initial test, which occurred in October 1964.

31. Eugene Rabinowitch, "First Step—to Where?" *BAS*, 19 (October 1963): 2.

32. Rabinowitch, "New Year's Thoughts 1964," *BAS*, 20 (January 1964): 2.

CHAPTER 2

1. See the chronological checklist, "Timeline," in Paul Brians's *Nuclear Holocausts: Atomic War in Fiction, 1895–1984* (Kent, OH: Kent State University Press, 1987), 351–52, and David Dowling's *Fictions of Nuclear Disaster* (Iowa City: University of Iowa Press, 1987), especially Chapters 2–5.

2. I have found only scattered comments about the play.

3. Printed in *Dramas of Modernism and Their Forerunners*, ed. Montrose J. Moses (Boston: Little, Brown, 1931), 501–47. This edition is preferable to the one published by Covici-Friede in 1929 (New York) or the acting edition published by Samuel French in 1935 (New York), since Moses includes both the original ending of Act III and the Theatre Guild's variant version (545–47), while the others print only the Theatre Guild's ending.

4. Nichols wrote the original draft of the play, but because his agent told him he "did not know the first thing about dramatic structure," he enlisted Browne to help him. Browne describes the process of collaboration amusingly in *Too Late to Lament: An Autobiography* (London: Victor Gollancz, 1955), 298–300.

5. According to Browne, the performances "set New York intellectually ablaze" (*Too Late to Lament*, 299). *The Oxford Companion to the Theatre*, 4th ed., edited by Phyllis Hartnoll (Oxford: Oxford University Press, 1983), mistakenly gives 1932 as the year of first production.

6. In *Nuclear Fear: A History of Images* (Cambridge: Harvard University Press, 1988), Spencer Weart traces this tendency to the Christian apocalyptic tradition and to aspects of alchemy (13–16).

7. In his *The World Set Free and Other War Papers* (New York: Scribner's, 1926), 1–249.

8. Quoted by Weart, 6, who points out similar ideas in the early writings of Soddy's colleague, Ernest Rutherford, and the best-selling books on radioactivity by the French scientist Gustave Le Bon (10). I am especially indebted to part one of Weart's book: "Years of Fantasy, 1902–1938."

9. The authors describe the Prime Minister as a Conservative (508), and note that he "reminds us a little" of Stanley Baldwin, Conservative P.M. when the play was written. But he is also meant to remind us of two prominent Liberal P.M.s, Henry Campbell-Bannerman and Herbert Henry Asquith. On the other hand, Foreign Affairs Secretary Evelyn Arthur is linked to three Conservatives: Robert Arthur Salisbury, Arthur James Balfour, and Joseph Austin Chamberlain (Foreign Affairs minister when the play was written) (513). Topical allusions to political figures were a trademark of Extravaganza.

10. Lightfoot is paraphrasing Whitehead's *Science and the Modern World* (1925): "If Shelley had been born a hundred years later, the twentieth century would have seen a Newton among chemists." The passage that includes this is the epigraph of the play.

11. *The Bodley Head Bernard Shaw: Collected Plays with Their Prefaces*, 7 vols., edited by Dan H. Laurence (London: Reinhardt, 1970–74), I, 535. Marchbanks also resembles Shelley, critics have noted.

12. Weart, 22–24. Weart says that this stereotype "was most convincingly portrayed" in *Wings Over Europe* (23).

13. Significantly, he intends to spend some of that time reading Shelley—a mirror of his mind—and looking at "the narcissi in the Park" (535).

14. In the Samuel French acting edition, the Minister of War shoots him. The Theatre Guild had asked Nichols and Browne for permission to alter the last act; they consented. Browne judged the new finale "incomparably better than ours" (*Too Late to Lament*, 300).

15. The Theatre Guild changed this to "the League of United Scientists of the World"—removing the allusion to "Workers of the world, unite!"

16. The best sources on this subject are Michael R. Booth's introduction to *English Plays of the Nineteenth Century, V: Pantomimes, Extravaganzas and Burlesques*, edited by Booth (Oxford: Oxford University Press, 1976), 1–63, and Martin Meisel's chapter on Extravaganza in his *Shaw and the Nineteenth-Century Theater* (Princeton: Princeton University Press, 1963), 380–428.

17. *The Bodley Head Bernard Shaw*, V, 430.

18. For example, Lightfoot seems to think that mankind must be destroyed before evolution can begin elsewhere. Shaw's characters are quite willing to let mankind dwindle into obsolescence.

19. Quoted in *The Best Plays of 1928–29*, edited by Burns Mantle (New York: Dodd, Mead, 1929), 88.

20. Shaw quoted by Meisel, 383.

CHAPTER 3

1. Quoted in *The Atomic Age Opens*, edited by Gerald Wendt and Donald Porter Geddes (Cleveland: World, 1945), 42.

2. "The Atomic Age," *Life*, 19 (August 20, 1945): 32.

3. New York: Pantheon Books, 1985, 10. Boyer ranges far beyond imaginative literature in his attempt to describe and assess the American cultural response to nuclear events from late 1945 through 1950. His section on literary responses, "Words Fail: The Bomb and the Literary Imagination" (243–56), limits itself to the difficulties writers found in treating the new conditions artistically, and as a result touches upon only a few poems, short stories, and statements by well-known authors. In Richard G. Scharine's book, *From Class to Caste in American Drama: Political and Social Themes Since the 1930s* (Westport, CT: Greenwood, 1991), a chapter entitled "The Cold War—Onstage Sublimated Protest and the Marx of Satan" (67–97) is disappointingly thin on nuclear dramas, but is useful for background.

4. "What Hath Man Wrought!" *U.S. News* (August 17, 1945): 38.

5. From a 1990 lecture Vonnegut quotes in *Fates Worse Than Death: An Autobiographical Collage* (New York: Berkley Books, 1992), 103.

6. Styron, "The Enduring Metaphors of Auschwitz and Hiroshima," *Newsweek*, 121 (January 11, 1993): 28; Ciardi quoted in Studs Terkel, *"The Good War": An Oral History of World War Two* (New York: Pantheon Books, 1984), 201.

7. "The Peace," *Time*, 46 (August 20, 1945): 19.

8. "Foreword," in *Treasury for the Free World*, edited by Ben Raeburn (New York: Arco, 1946), xiii–xiv. The reaction of the novelist and doctrinaire Objectivist Ayn Rand is somewhat peripheral but interesting. Asked to do a screenplay about the development of the atomic bomb for Hal Wallis's production studio, she responded with a long rationalist "Analysis of the Proper Approach to a Picture on the Atomic Bomb," based on interviews with prominent atomic scientists and administrators of the project, including Oppenheimer, and information about corporations and industries involved. (The document is printed with her detailed synopsis of the screenplay in the volume *Journals of Ayn Rand*, edited by David Harriman [New York: Dutton, 1997], 311–44). She shows confidently that the Bomb was *"not a creation of government—but of the free cooperation of free men"* (324). Her scenario concludes with a young boy exulting over Hiroshima: "his face is shining with pride, courage, self-confidence" (344). In letters of February 13 and 15, 1946 she refers to her extensive research and hard work on the project, which never reached the filming stage (*Letters of Ayn Rand*, edited by Michael S. Berliner [New York: Dutton, 1995], 254).

9. "Address upon Receiving the Nobel Prize for Literature, Stockholm, December 10, 1950," in Faulkner, *Essays, Speeches & Public Letters*, edited by James B. Meriwether (New York: Random House, 1965), 119.

10. Quoted in Jackson J. Benson, *The True Adventures of John Steinbeck, Writer* (New York: Viking, 1984), 819.

11. From an interview with Hersey quoted in Jay Parini, *John Steinbeck: A Biography* (London: Heinemann, 1994), 488.

12. Quoted in *The Atomic Age Opens*, 48.

13. *Timebends: A Life* (New York: Grove, 1987), 167, 516.

14. "Most Terrible Drama of All Time," *Saturday Review of Literature*, 33 (October 21, 1950): 22–23. Sherwood was also one of the few dramatists to comment on the 1946 Bikini tests. Taking issue with military leaders who argued that the atomic bomb is simply another "piece of ordnance" and thus should not provoke "unreasoning psychological fears," he cites Dr. David Bradley's *No Place to Hide* (Boston: Little, Brown, 1948), the best-selling chronicle of a member of the radiological monitoring team at Bikini, which stresses that "the real atomic menace" the tests revealed is "the lingering poison of radioactivity" (" 'Please Don't Frighten Us,' " *Atlantic Monthly*, 183 [February 1949]: 77–79).

15. *A Southern Life: Letters of Paul Green, 1916–1981*, edited by Laurence G. Avery (Chapel Hill: University of North Carolina Press, 1994), 431.

16. From an interview with Meredith quoted in Benson, 588.

17. Letter of April 1947 quoted in Benson, 597.

18. Earlier in his memoir Miller acknowledges having felt a

> hole in my heart regarding my response to the first report of Hiroshima. How could I have felt such wonder? Such relief, too, that the war was over at last? How could I have dared study the first descriptions of the workings of the bomb and feel some pride in man's intellect?
>
> Whence this detachment? One day it would seem the very soul of the matter: a failure to imagine will make us die. (167)

19. Miller records that its theme, "the dynamics of denial," led him to conceive *After the Fall* (520). He informed me that he wants the script to remain unpublished.

20. Donald Ogden Stewart's *How I Wonder* (unpublished; performed 1947) features an astronomy professor who ruminates on a range of current issues, among them atomic power. The best source of information is Brooks Atkinson's review, *New York Times*, October 10, 1947, 34. Fred Eastman's *The Great Choice (An Incident of the Next War): A Play in One Act Modeled After Sophocles'* Antigone (New York: French, 1949; never performed?) is a revision of a 1932 one-act antiwar play which simply inserts the new argument that "war is obsolete" now that atomic weapons have been developed (14). Eastman hoped that the play would "make its contribution, however small, to human survival in this Atomic Age" (6). The most interesting borderline play is Theodore Apstein's *Paradise Inn* (published in *The Best One-Act Plays, 1951–1952*, edited by Margaret Mayorga [New York: Dodd, Mead, 1952], 23–46). It depicts a married couple who decided over a year ago to leave New York City for fear of being "bombed off the face of the earth," but who come to realize that their escapist life at the Paradise Inn in a tranquil

Mexican town has bred disruption between them. Both are on the verge of returning separately to New York when they discover each other's plans, discuss their motives, and set off together, reconciled. The play reflects the kind of exaggerated but understandable Atomic Age terror in the lives of ordinary citizens that, for instance, Judith Merril's 1950 novel, *Shadow on the Hearth*, exhibits in greater depth. The fact that the Soviet Union had shown in September 1949 that it too had atomic weapons is surely relevant. Jack Kirkland also adapted Pat Frank's novel *Mr. Adam*; it was performed but not published (Hostetter, 107).

21. I have used the text (without citing pages) in *Fortune*, 33 (January 1946): 116–17, 219. The play is reprinted in *The Atomic Age: Scientists in National and World Affairs*, edited by Morton Grodzins and Eugene Rabinowitch (New York: Basic Books, 1963), 47–52. Ridenour's skit was actually preempted by a brief radio drama written on request for CBS on the eve of the Japanese surrender and performed three hours after the event: Norman Corwin's prose poem, "14 August" (*"Untitled" and Other Radio Dramas* [New York: Holt, 1945), 499–504). Later expanded as "God and Uranium," the poem reads like a faintly ironic sermonette:

> God and uranium were on our side.
> The wrath of the atom fell like a commandment,
> And the very planet quivered with implications.
> . . . .
>
> Sound the gun for Achilles the Atom and the war workers: Newton and
>   Galileo, Curie and Einstein, the Archangel Gabriel, and the community
>   of Oak Ridge, Tennessee. (499)

Another prose poem by Corwin, "Set Your Clock at U235" (*"Untitled"*, 511–15), was read by Paul Robeson on a forum program broadcast October 29. It warns of a possible atomic holocaust, but stresses the promising capacities of the discoveries: "The chemicking that could destroy us . . . can also do as bidden by us: outperform whole teams of genii: be servile to the meek: reform our wayward systems peacefully. / The choice rests in the trusteeship of victory . . ." (514).

22. This is one of Ridenour's main points in an earlier *Fortune* piece, "Military Security and the Atomic Bomb," *Fortune*, 32 (November 1945): 170–71, 216–23.

23. Printed in *The Best One-Act Plays 1946–1947*, edited by Margaret Mayorga (New York: Dodd, Mead, 1947), 181–202, the text I have used. An acting edition was published by Samuel French in 1947. The play was written for a group called Stage for Action and produced at the Cherry Lane Theatre, New York, in December 1946.

24. The most sophisticated study of the Living Newspaper is C. W. E. Bigsby's "The Federal Theatre and the Living Newspaper" in his *A Critical Introduction to Twentieth-Century American Drama, 1: 1900–1940* (Cambridge: Cambridge University Press, 1982), 211–36; see also Joanne Bentley, *Hallie Flanagan: A Life in the American Theatre* (New York: Knopf, 1988), 386–89, and Stuart Cosgrove's "Introduction" to Liberty Deferred *and Other Living Newspapers of the 1930s Federal Theatre Project*, edited by Lorraine Brown (Fairfax, VA: George Mason University Press, 1989), ix–xxv. A bibliographical warning: $E=mc^2$ (New York: French, 1948) lists its author as Hallie Flanagan *Davis* and is alphabetized under Davis in most catalogs and bibliographies, but her earlier book *Arena* uses Flanagan.

25. Hallie Flanagan, *Arena: The History of the Federal Theatre* (New York: Blom, 1965 [c.1940]), 71.

26. Ed. Dexter Masters and Katharine Way (New York: McGraw-Hill, 1946).

27. *The Autobiography of Upton Sinclair* (New York: Harcourt, 1962), 297.

28. Girard, KA: Haldeman-Julius, 1948.

29. The Valley Community Theatre of Claremont, California performed it in June 1948, London's tiny Torch Theatre in December, and Erwin Piscator's Dramatic Workshop of the New School for Social Research in January 1949. On the last, see Gerhard Probst, "Erwin Piscator and Upton Sinclair," in *Upton Sinclair: Literature and Social Reform*, edited by Dieter Herms (Frankfurt: Lang, 1990), 240.

30. Bentley, *In Search of Theater* (New York: Atheneum, 1975), 40. Somewhat in contrast, Maxwell Anderson told Sinclair in a letter of June 4, 1947 (he had received a pre-publication script), that the play is "well-built and well-written, and in parts moving and fascinating." However, he was disappointed that "in the end all the lad can say is: Stop killing each other. Well, that's been said . . . and the wars get bigger and more final" (*Dramatist in America: Letters of Maxwell Anderson, 1912–1958*, edited by Laurence G. Avery [Chapel Hill: University of North Carolina Press, 1977], 216–17).

31. The fullest study of the play is in André Muraire's published dissertation, *Polémique et littéraire chez Upton Sinclair après 1939* (Lille: Université de Lille III, 1981), 622–41. He compares it to Sinclair's 1950 sci-fi drama *The Enemy Had It Too*, in which a poisonous virus-weapon, "the Bio," all but decimates the earth's population before Martians intervene.

32. *Doctor Fist: A Drama in Three Acts* (c. 1955), a 124-page typescript. The original manuscript is housed in the Doheny Library at the University of Southern California. Its existence was brought to my attention by John Ahouse, Assistant Head of Special Collections and author of *Upton Sinclair: A Descriptive, Annotated Bibliography* (Los Angeles: Mercer & Aitchison, 1994). I am greatly indebted to him for this service.

33. *The Traitor: A Play in Two Acts* (New York: French, 1949). The play was first performed on March 31, 1949; it opened in New York at the Forty-Eighth Street Theatre on April 4.

34. *New York Times*, April 10, 1949, section 2, 1.

35. *New Republic*, 120 (April 18, 1949): 30–31.

36. *New Yorker*, 25 (April 9, 1949): 52. In *Herman Wouk: The Novelist as Social Historian* (New Brunswick, NJ: Transaction, 1984), Arnold Beichman discusses the play briefly and links it to *The "Lomokome" Papers* (1949), a sci-fi novella set on the moon which Wouk called "a mirror satire of nuclear confrontation" (69).

37. The radioactive metal thorium (atomic weight 232.12) was considered a feasible alternate for uranium. It is mentioned in $E=mc^2$.

38. *Saturday Review*, 31 (May 21, 1949): 34.

39. *The Cold War: A Study in U.S. Foreign Policy* (New York: Harper, 1947).

40. Carr has named four notable extremists: the reactionaries John E. Rankin and J. Parnell Thomas, the ultraradical Vito Marcantonio, and the diehard isolationist Robert A. Taft. Note the revealing redundancy in the last part of Emanuel's statement: he calls America the "strongest, most powerful" nation.

41. David Caute, *The Great Fear: The Anti-Communist Purge Under Truman and Eisenhower* (New York: Simon and Schuster, 1978), 413.

42. Kappo Phelan in *Commonweal*, 50 (April 22, 1949): 45.

43. Los Angeles: Fantasy, 1951. Cornel (Adam) Lengyel now goes by the name of Cornel Adam. In 1997 he published a volume of poetry, *A Lookout's Letter* (Gliwice, Poland: Mandrake Press), which includes a sonnet recording that from his "perch on Bald Mountain" he saw "the flash from the first secret test" of the atom bomb at Yucca Flat, Nevada, but "could not understand the strange signs of the time." The poem concludes with an allusion to *The Atom Clock*: man has learned too much, "yet too little for wisdom. / Too early, too soon, our lad's not yet ripe for it" (12). I am indebted to Mr. Adam for sending me material about his career.

44. The play was not published until 1951, but an acting edition dated 1950 is recorded in the National Union Catalogue and a publisher's blurb says that the play won the Maxwell Anderson Award for 1950. The first performance seems to have been at the University of Dubuque in 1953. My study is based on the much-revised edition which appeared in *Poet Lore*, 64 (1969), 435–57; it is superior in dramatic coherence and poetic quality, yet does not differ significantly in substance as an early dramatic reaction to the Atomic Age. A brief, unsigned review of the early edition appeared in *Players Magazine*, 27 (May 1951): 189; it calls the play "original, eloquent and angry." Thomas Mann complimented it in a 1950 note to Lengyel.

45. In the early edition the characters are named and described. The Young Miner, Martin Crale, is said to be "confused by the world and his part in it—groping for answers—not quite sure there are any answers" (9).

46. The early edition lacks the "mutual annihilation" passage.

47. I see no evidence that Lengyel is alluding to the "clock of doom" which began appearing on the cover of the *Bulletin of the Atomic Scientists* in 1947. The first edition of the play equates the atom clock with the "infernal machine that's bound to blow up in our faces" (7).

48. This bears some resemblance to the plutonium bomb used in the Trinity test (Fat Man). Two identical hemispheres of plutonium, covered by nickel plating, were moved together with a sheet of gold foil positioned between them so that they almost "went critical." "One wrong move would have brought slow radiation death to all," but not the huge explosion that the characters envision (Wyden, 206).

49. In 1951–52 Lengyel wrote a short science-fiction play, *The Master Plan* (published in 1978: Georgetown, CA: Dragon's Teeth Press), in which the only non-defective survivors of a nuclear war pursue a Master Plan designed by one of the scientists most responsible for the holocaust. The Plan fails despite the availability of "all the gadgets of science" in the super-shelter, but a band of degenerated humans led by the scientist's brother leave the possibility that a modified human race will rise from the ashes.

CHAPTER 4

1. *The Noël Coward Diaries*, edited by Graham Payn and Sheridan Morley (Boston: Little, Brown, 1982), 37. Coward also chided the media hype about atomic

power after the Bikini tests in mid-1946, noting his belief that the extravagant claims for the Bomb's destructiveness are overblown: "I am convinced that all it will really do is destroy human beings in large numbers" (entry of July 1, 1946, *Diaries*, 59).

2. Letter of November 20, 1945, quoted in Ted Morgan, *Maugham* (New York: Simon and Schuster, 1980), 493.

3. "Preface: On Power Over Nature," *The Burning Glass* (London: Macmillan, 1953), xv. This play incorporates a rather distant analogy to the atom bomb (a "burning glass" capable of burning down targeted areas and melting lakes). Its theme, Morgan says, "is the long-prevalent fashion of believing, uncritically, that each development of man's power over Nature, unless it happens to threaten his body with injury or death, is necessarily beneficent" (viii). The focus of its plot, however, is the protagonist-inventor's decision whether or not to give the secret of his discovery to the British government.

4. From his memoir, *The World Is a Wedding* (New York: Coward-McCann, 1963), 130.

5. Preface to *Geneva, The Bodley Head Bernard Shaw: Collected Plays with Their Prefaces*, 7 vols., edited by Dan H. Laurence (London: Reinhardt, 1970–74), VII, 23. Doris Lessing sums up how she felt about Hiroshima as a Southern Rhodesian: "When the atom bombs were dropped on Hiroshima and Nagasaki they did not seem to us so much worse than the pulverizing of Tokyo and Osaka and Dresden and Coventry. What we felt was, Thank God the war is over." She adds: "Only later did we learn the war would have ended anyway, and very soon" (*Under My Skin: Volume One of My Autobiography, to 1949* [New York: HarperCollins, 1994], 346).

6. Christopher Driver, *The Disarmers: A Study in Protest* (London: Hodder and Stoughton, 1964), 17.

7. In June 1945 Prime Minister Churchill was secretly asked for tacit approval to use the atom bomb and he concurred (Peter Hennessy, *Never Again: Britain 1945–51* [London: Jonathan Cape, 1992], 265). However, he was not asked his opinion under the specific circumstances of late July, when Japan was suing for peace with the sole condition that the emperor be retained in power. In any event, virtually no one knew he had given any kind of consent.

8. Leonard Bertin, *Atom Harvest* (London: Secker and Warburg, 1955), 18, 20.

9. "The Atomic Bomb and the Prevention of War," *Bulletin of the Atomic Scientists*, 2 (October 1946): 19. It is interesting to note that Upton Sinclair worked this idea into his picture of the post-holocaust world in *A Giant's Strength* (Girard, KA: Haldeman-Julius, 1948); a radio announcer states in Act III: "There appears to be no longer the least possibility that Britain can wage war, and the problem is how to keep any portion of her homeless and destitute population alive" (36).

10. Kingsley Martin, *New Statesman*, quoted in Driver, 18. Solly Zuckerman reports that when the British agreed in 1946 to "adapt a few RAF stations for the reception of B49 bombers and for the storage and handling of atom bombs," this new arrangement "helped turn Britain into what some call America's 'unsinkable aircraft carrier' " (*Monkeys, Men, and Missiles: An Autobiography 1946–88* [New York: Norton, 1988], 270).

11. Huxley, *Chrome Yellow; The Gioconda Smile; Ape and Essence; The Genius and the Goddess* (New York: Harper Colophon Books, 1983), 169.

12. Orwell stated this idea as early as two months after Hiroshima in a letter to the London *Tribune* later entitled "You and the Atom Bomb" (in a volume of his reprinted journalism, *In Front of Your Nose, 1945–1950,* edited by Sonia Orwell and Ian Angus [New York: Harcourt, Brace, and World, 1968], 6–10). He imagines "a permanent state of 'cold war' " (9) evolving from an international nuclear stalemate (incidentally using a key term that Bernard Baruch is sometimes credited with coining in 1948, although Walter Lippmann used it as the *title* of a book in 1947).

13. *Lord of the Flies*, Casebook Edition, edited by James R. Baker and Arthur P. Ziegler (New York: Putnam's, 1964), 11.

14. Golding stated this in a 1962 interview. He goes on to say that in spite of rudimentary common sense "there is a large chance that [atomic bombs] will be used and we'll be done for." (James Keating, "Interview with William Golding," *Lord of the Flies*, Casebook Edition, 190–91.)

15. The first British theatrical production of the nuclear age seems to have been *The Atomic Bomb* by Bridget Boland. My only source for this is Andrew Sinclair's *War Like a Wasp: The Lost Decade of the 'Forties* (London: Hamish Hamilton, 1989), which describes it as "one of the last productions which ENSA [Entertainments National Service Association] sent out to inform the armies before their demobilization" (188).

16. Nickson's "Shaw on Nuclear War" (*Independent Shavian*, 22, ii–iii [1984]: 30–33) quotes Shaw's journalism on the subject but does not discuss the plays or the preface to *Geneva*. The third volume of Holroyd's biography, *Bernard Shaw, 1918–1950: The Lure of Fantasy* (New York: Random House, 1991), quotes a few statements. The previously unpublished article, printed under the heading "Bernard Shaw on Peace (1950)," appears in *Unpublished Shaw* (SHAW 16), edited by Dan H. Laurence and Margot Peters (University Park: Pennsylvania State University Press, 1996), 185–93. It is noteworthy for showing that Shaw had kept up on the very latest development in the nuclear arms race, the American decision to build a hydrogen bomb.

17. *The Bodley Head Bernard Shaw*, VII, 313–75. The play was substantially finished in 1947 but amended several times before its first English performance at the Malvern Festival on August 13, 1949.

18. "First Fable." *The Bodley Head Bernard Shaw*, VII, 429–33.

19. One of the most widely read early essays prompted by the atomic bomb, Norman Cousins's *Modern Man Is Obsolete* (New York: Viking, 1945), gives the gist of this idea well before Shaw: "The trend during the last fifty years toward shorter work weeks and shorter hours will not only be continued but sharply accelerated" (18).

20. In *Transformations and Texts: G. B. Shaw's* Buoyant Billions (Columbia, SC: Camden House, 1992), Steven Joyce reveals that at one point in Shaw's process of composition the atom bomb was discussed in Act III by members of the Buoyant family. (He does not say so explicitly, but I think we can deduce that Mr Smith and his son Junius do not bring up the subject in Act I.) The Son—Ben in this version—claims to be a "professional revolutionist" who, as a scientist, is well equipped for the job since science "is the only sphere in which we can still hope for miracles" (50–51). It is The Youth, Fiffy, whom others recognize as the budding

world-betterer and who declares he will make beneficial use of the bomb: "Let me get hold of it, and I'll start a war on the tsetse fly and make the deadly African bush habitable. . . . I will sweep away impenetrable jungles, irrigate barren deserts, and move mountains. Tigers and cobras, locusts and white ants, will become as legendary as dragons and unicorns" (55).

21. In the London *Times* on the day before Christmas, 1949 (shortly after the Soviet Union exploded an atomic device), Shaw urged a shift in attention from atomic warfare to "the far more vital and pressing subject of atomic welfare." ("Atomic Welfare," reprinted in Shaw, *Agitations: Letters to the Press 1875–1950*, edited by Dan H. Laurence and James Rambeau [New York: Ungar, 1985], 352.)

22. Writing soon after Hiroshima, Shaw states: "From all over the world I have been asked what I have to say about the atomic bomb, about which H. G. Wells said all there is to say, and more, thirty years ago." ("The Atom Bomb," *New York Journal-American*, August 19, 1945, reprinted in condensed form by Richard Nickson in *Independent Shavian*, 20, ii-iii [1982]: 27.)

23. Paul Boyer in *By the Bomb's Early Light: American Thought and Culture at the Dawn of the Atomic Age* (New York: Pantheon Books, 1985) details what he calls "the search for a silver lining" in the immediate aftermath of Hiroshima (Chapter 10, 109–21).

24. A 1947 rehearsal edition of *Buoyant Billions* includes a passage, later omitted, in which a female member of the Buoyant family ("She") reminds the others that atomic bombs "kill women and children as well as men. Killing men didnt matter so long as women were left: we could keep the earth populated with five per cent of men or less; but wipe us out, and where are you?" (Joyce, 55).

25. "The Atom Bomb," 28. Interestingly, at this early date Shaw anticipates Orwell when he says that the wars that threaten us in the future are "civil wars" of many possible kinds, including one in which Communists may drop atomic bombs on capitalists, capitalists on Communists, "and both of them on Fascists."

26. "The Atomic Bomb," London *Times*, August 20, 1945, reprinted in *Agitations*, 337.

27. Here as in *Farfetched Fables*, Shaw is probably echoing speculations dating from World War I on possible new forms of poison gas. But he might possibly have seen or heard of the Finletter Report, *Survival in the Air Age*, published in January 1948. This apparently contained the substance of comments made in the September 16, 1949, *Peace News* by Brock Chisholm, Director General of the World Health Organization, quoted by Driver (18): "The atomic bomb is obsolete. It is child's play compared to biological weapons. There is a product in existence which if spread extensively can kill on contact or if breathed in. It can kill all living beings within six hours and leave the area safe for troops to occupy within the twelve hours it takes to disappear." Contemporary readers might relate Shaw's speculation to the neutron bomb, an atomic weapon that destroys mainly through radiation rather than blast and firestorm and thus approximates the effects he describes. The first successful test was held in 1962; the bomb became a center of controversy in the late 1970s when President Carter proposed to deploy it in European bases.

28. *Summer Day's Dream: A Play in Two Acts*, in *The Plays of J. B. Priestley*, 3 vols. (London: Heinemann, 1950), III, 405–76, the text I have used. An acting edition was published by Samuel French in 1950. The play was produced at St.

Martin's Theatre in London and ran for fifty performances in September and October, 1949.

29. London *Times*, September 9, 1949, 2; review by R. D. Smith in *New Statesman and Nation*, 38 (September 17, 1949): 353. In an attempt to counteract negative reactions such as Smith's, David Hughes attempts a critical renovation of what he calls "this beautiful, humorous and unsentimental play" (in *J. B. Priestley: An Informal Study of His Work* [London: Rupert Hart-Davis, 1958], 213).

30. *Spectator*, 183 (September 16, 1949): 353. Fleming calls this "a thoroughly bogus picture."

31. *The Offshore Island: A Play in Three Acts* (London: Cresset Press, 1959).

32. For instance by J. B. Priestley in "Off-Shore Island Man," *Essays of Five Decades*, edited by Susan Cooper (Boston: Little, Brown, 1968), 304–8.

33. Since 1946 the U.S. government, while maintaining air bases and storage facilities in Britain, continued to resist making Britain a full partner in the development of nuclear weapons. Reluctance to share atomic secrets with a leak-prone administration was the crucial factor, but suspicion about the red tinge of English welfare-state politics was also involved (in the play, an American soldier remarks, "These Europeans, they're all of them commies at heart" [39]). When in early 1950 President Truman sanctioned the production of a hydrogen bomb, and later that year a known-Communist atomic scientist long employed by the British, Klaus Fuchs, confessed to giving Russia atomic secrets from 1943 to 1947, resistance hardened. Meanwhile, Britain had begun an independent program to develop its own nuclear weapons.

34. Charles explains that "the level of world radiation is already too high for us to let off any but very little bombs" (81).

35. Communist China emerged as a monolithic, if not nuclear-armed, world power in 1949 with the defeat of Chiang Kai-shek's armies and the establishment of the People's Republic of China. In late 1950 their massive intervention into North Korea to repel United Nations forces (led by General MacArthur and dominated by Americans) focused world attention on their potency. They did not explode their first nuclear device until 1964, but Laski no doubt postulated that they would have developed an atomic arsenal and that it would be intact since they had not been involved in the war.

36. A graphic contemporary description of the "military mind" as a manifestation of contingencies inherent in the profession appears in Samuel P. Huntington's *The Soldier and the State: The Theory and Politics of Civil-Military Relations* (Cambridge: Harvard University Press, 1957), 59–79.

37. During a political crisis her husband had sent her and the children to their country cottage, well-stocked "just in case," when the bombs fell (50).

38. Sergeant Bayford asks Mary if her brother believes in God. Mary replies, "No, of course not. *(She sees his shocked face, and asks puzzled)* Why, do you?" A private breaks in, "Have a heart, Serge. Why the hell should they believe in God? None of the C.P.'s have" (35–36).

39. The quotation is from Thomas Browne's "Urn Burial." Baltinsky alludes to Odysseus's having to seal his sailors' ears with wax to protect them from the enticing sound of the sirens.

40. The 1959 BBC television production in mid-April was derided by the anonymous London *Times* critic but heralded in the *Daily Express* as "A magnificent

Some great power will capture the moon and hold it as a military base. Another will very likely and very soon set an artificial satellite revolving about our planet and be able to drop hydrogen bombs from it to targets on the earth, aiming them with astronomical accuracy. And lest these prognostications sound fantastic let me assure you that the scientists and the war departments of every great nation are studying plans for exactly these projects. (*Dramatist in America*, 299)

One wonders (idly) if Arch Oboler might have attended the affair.

18. "Foreword," *Night of the Auk*, [16]. Ironically, the few favorable comments the play received after the New York opening were directed at the setting and acting. The only retrospective study I have found states that the "evocative setting was the only successful feature of Arch Oboler's *Night of the Auk*, a Broadway play that suffered from pretentious verse-like prose mouthed by stereotyped characters" (Ralph Willingham, *Science Fiction and the Theatre* [Westport, CT: Greenwood, 1994], 51). Oboler would have agreed with Ray Bradbury's comment about designing the scenery for a futuristic play: "the harder you try to create the world of the future, the worse your failure" ("Introduction," in his *The Wonderful Ice Cream Suit and Other Plays* [New York: Bantam, 1972], xi).

19. For example, Brooks Atkinson: "Stirring up scientific jargon with portentous ideas, [Oboler] writes dialogue that is streaked with purple patches and sounds a good deal like gibberish" (*New York Times*, December 4, 1956, 50); and the *Time* critic: "the play mingled one or two thrills with an appalling number of frills, one or two philosophic truths with a succession of Polonius-like truisms, an occasional feeling for language with pretentious and barbarous misuse of it" (*Time*, 68 [December 17, 1956]: 65).

20. Produced in an amateur competition in April 1956, the play was published in *The Best Short Plays of 1955–56*, edited by Margaret Mayorga (Boston: Beacon Press, 1956), 155–74.

21. Could Clifford Odets's *The Flowering Peach* (1954) have provoked this idea? The play begins with Noah learning in a dream that God intends to destroy the world, an allusion to an atomic holocaust. Purkey's playwright refers to himself as "an old man with a dream" just before he mentions the Noah pattern of his play (174).

22. Purkey also wrote a much more improbable nuclear one-act, *The Eden Echo: A Comedy Fantasy in One Act* (Boston: Baker's Plays, 1976). In this post-holocaust play, an atomic war prompted God to rid the earth of men; however, an "Eve" discovers an "Adam" in a cave.

23. *The Highest Tree: A Play* (New York: Random House, 1960). The play was first presented by the Theatre Guild at the Longacre Theatre in New York on November 4, 1959.

24. Another important factor was the propaganda triumph the Soviet Union had gained by unilaterally suspending tests on March 31, 1958. (They recommenced them when the United States and Great Britain did not respond in kind.) The background information in this paragraph derives from Robert A. Divine, *Blowing on the Wind: The Nuclear Test Ban Debate 1954–1960* (New York: Oxford University Press, 1978) and Richard L. Miller, *Under the Cloud: The Decades of Nuclear Testing* (New York: Free Press, 1986).

25. Adlai Stevenson, a prominent advocate of a test ban who ran for president in 1956, recognized Schary's play as a contribution to the cause by writing a brief laudatory foreword to the text.

26. All six reviews I have seen would strongly discourage prospective playgoers, even those sympathetic to Schary's cause. The one with the most potential impact, Brooks Atkinson's in the *New York Times*, November 5, 1959, 41, is lukewarm compared to the diatribes by Kenneth Tynan (*New Yorker*, 35 [November 14]: 114, 116), Henry Hewes (*Saturday Review*, 42 [November 21]: 34), and the drama critic of *Time* (74 [November 16]: 57).

27. The action of the play begins two days before Thanksgiving in 1959 and ends on the holiday. Schary almost surely visualized the atmospheric conditions that prevailed much earlier that year, however. The protagonist's son says he "read a story in the paper this morning about some commercial jet that was examined for radioactive fallout" (20). He is referring to a real event that was reported on February 25, 1959, when "a Pan American 707 jetliner, which had been flying above 30,000 feet, was found to be coated with fallout" (Divine, 262; see "Jet Is Radioactive," *New York Times*, February 25, 1959, 62). Schary says he "really went to work" on the play in February ("*The Highest Tree* and How It Grew," *Theatre Arts*, 43 [November 1959]: 11).

28. Caleb prefaces this statement by saying, "Father, those damn fruit flies depress me." He is almost surely referring to the work of Hermann J. Muller and his successors demonstrating that X-rays can produce mutations in fruit flies (see Muller's "Changing Genes: Their Effects on Evolution," *Bulletin of the Atomic Scientists*, 3 [September 1947]: 267–72, 274). Caleb's focus on strontium 90 reflects scientists' concerns at the time: "In early 1959 reports of disturbingly high measurements of strontium 90 in the soil, milk, and wheat in some parts of the United States generated widespread uneasiness," according to George T. Mazuzan and J. Samuel Walker in *Controlling the Atom: The Beginnings of Nuclear Regulation 1946–1962* (Berkeley: University of California Press, 1984), 247.

29. I have found no evidence which the two men could be relying upon to support this claim, but I have little doubt that Schary found it somewhere (perhaps in the two-volume report of the 1957 hearings of the Special Subcommittee on Radiation of the Joint Committee on Atomic Energy, *The Nature of Radioactive Fallout and Its Effects on Man*).

30. In his *Theatre Arts* piece (cited above), Schary reveals that for him the play revolves around Aaron's prospect of dying soon, not around an argument. Aaron interacts with his family and his lover without telling them this, and he reexamines his life's work in the light of it, concluding that up to now he (with Devereaux) has climbed the nearest tree, not the highest one (12).

31. Ardrey's *Sing Me No Lullaby* (1954) portrays a leftish intellectual hounded by the FBI for his Communist past; Denker/Berkey's *Time Limit!* (1956) was the first notable play about the Korean War.

32. As I have noted, tests were stopped voluntarily on November 4, 1958, a year before the play was performed. Schary was probably responding to the controversy in the Geneva conference over a *permanent* test ban.

33. Drawing on Gallup polls in the period, A. Costandina Titus reports that in late 1956 "56 percent disagreed with the proposal that the U.S. halt H-bomb tests. Likewise, in May 1958, 60 percent said the U.S. should not stop testing, and as

late as March 1962, 66 percent said the U.S. should resume atmospheric testing, compared to 25 percent who responded negatively." (*Bombs in the Backyard: Atomic Testing and American Politics* [Reno: University of Nevada Press, 1986], 87).

34. *Reporter* (New York), 21 (December 10, 1959): 39.

35. Response to questionnaire in *Contemporary Dramatists*, edited by James Vinson (London: St. James Press, 1973), 674.

36. *Contemporary Dramatists*, 675. Meserve directs this comment at the body of Schary's drama, not just *The Highest Tree*.

37. The play was first performed at a festival in Italy on June 27, 1961, then in London on February 27, 1965. It was published in *Feiffer's Album* (New York: Random House, 1963), and reprinted in *Best Short Plays of the World Theatre 1958–1967*, edited by Stanley Richards (New York: Crown, 1968), 75–83, the text I have used. An acting edition was published by Samuel French in 1963.

38. Interestingly, Langston Hughes treated the same general theme even more facetiously in a 1954 story, "Radioactive Red Caps" (reprinted in *The Best of Simple* [New York: Hill and Wang, 1961], 210–13). His narrator fantasizes that southern whites will allow Negroes in bomb shelters because they won't want their red caps radioactive ("Atoms, they tell me, is catching" [212]).

39. *To Be Young, Gifted and Black: Lorraine Hansberry in Her Own Words*, adapted by Robert Nemiroff (New York: Signet, 1970), 41.

40. *A Raisin in the Sun: [The Complete Original Version]*, with a new introduction by Robert Nemiroff (New York: Signet, 1988), 26, 82. Incidentally, the play was not performed until nuclear tests had been suspended for three months.

41. Robert Nemiroff notes in his introduction to the play that Hansberry conceived it for television in late 1961, then "recast it tentatively for the stage." But, unsatisfied with the revision, "early in 1962, she set it temporarily aside" (*The Collected Last Plays*, edited by Nemiroff [New York: New American Library, 1983], 223, 225). Hansberry died in 1965 at the age of 34; the play was first published in *Les Blancs: The Collected Last Plays* (1972). I have cited the more recent printing.

42. Nemiroff quotes the letter in his introduction to *The Collected Last Plays*, 223.

43. Hansberry treats this "as if we are experiencing the learning process in microcosm" (247), a cogent example of employing nonrealistic dramatic compression to remind the audience of the occasional thrill that education can bring.

44. In *Hansberry's Drama: Commitment and Complexity* (Urbana: University of Illinois Press, 1991, 141–54), Steven R. Carter analyzes the play from the point of view that it engages *Waiting for Godot* "on the most profound level, posing image against image, feeling against feeling, vision against vision" (141–42). See also Anne Cheney's analysis in *Lorraine Hansberry* (Boston: Twayne, 1984), 123–30.

45. There *is* one female among the band of survivors, but we must forgive male-privileging pronouns and collective nouns in this era, especially those of an early feminist.

46. *To Be Young, Gifted and Black*, 116.

47. Ibid., 260.

48. *The Collected Last Plays*, 150–51.

49. In his *The Wonderful Ice Cream Suit and Other Plays* (New York: Bantam, 1972), 129–61, the text I have used. An acting edition was published in 1988 (Woodstock, IL: Dramatic Publishing Co.). The play was staged with two of his other short plays at the Coronet Theater, Hollywood, from October 1964 to February 1965, then for three nights at the Orpheus Theater, New York, in October 1965. See John J. McLaughlin's review, "Science Fiction Theatre," in *Nation*, 200 (January 25, 1965): 92–94.

50. "To the Chicago Abyss," *Magazine of Fantasy and Science Fiction*, May 1963; reprinted in *Beyond Armageddon: Twenty-One Sermons to the Dead*, edited by Walter M. Miller and Martin H. Greenberg (New York: Primus, 1985), 261–71. The story is explicit about a few things that are left vague in the play; the most notable is that the event which "ruined cities" in 1970 (about twenty years before time present) is called "A.D., Annihilation Day" (266).

51. The man's evocation of coffee at the start of the story is a fair example: "The scent, the odor, the smell. Rich, dark, wondrous Brazilian beans, fresh ground!" becomes "The odor, the scent, the smell, / the aroma of rich dark wondrous / Brazilian beans, fresh ground!"

CHAPTER 6

1. *Parliamentary Debates (Hansard): House of Commons*, 537 (1955): 1903.

2. "Britain and the Nuclear Bomb," *New Statesman*, 54 (November 2, 1957): 555.

3. Wesker, *As Much as I Dare: An Autobiography (1932–1959)* (London: Century, 1994), 508–9.

4. From an unpublished memoir begun in 1951, *The Queen of all the Fairies*, quoted by Michael Billington in *The Life and Work of Harold Pinter* (London: Faber and Faber, 1996), 44.

5. The excised passages are quoted in S. E. Gontarski's *The Intent of Undoing in Samuel Beckett's Dramatic Texts* (Bloomington: Indiana University Press, 1985), 80, and the marginal note in James Knowlson's bilingual edition of *Happy Days/ Oh les beaux jours* (London: Faber and Faber, 1978), 135. For steering me toward this reference I am greatly indebted to Professor Knowlson, author of the distinguished biography *Damned to Fame: The Life of Samuel Beckett* (New York: Simon and Schuster, 1996). He could recall no other explicit allusion to the Nuclear Age in Beckett's works, letters, or conversations.

6. *Diaries, Volume One: 1939–1960*, edited by Katherine Bucknell (London: Methuen, 1996), 424.

7. Osborne, *Look Back in Anger* (London: Faber and Faber, 1957), 84–85. Osborne also satirizes public sentiment when he has Cliff describe a newspaper piece by the Bishop of Bromley: "he makes a very moving appeal to all Christians to do all they can to assist in the manufacture of the H-bomb" (13).

8. *Walking in the Shade: Volume Two of My Autobiography, 1949–1962* (New York: HarperCollins, 1997), 369. Lessing adds that in her novel *Shikasta* the Bomb falls and devastates the Northern hemisphere, but readers "talked as if I had described the ruination of the whole world. . . . [I]t was taken absolutely for granted that if a Bomb fell, then it had to be totally destructive. *The* Bomb—and *the* end" (370).

9. Eugene Rabinowitch, "The First Year of Deterrence," *BAS*, 13 (January 1957): 3.

10. *On the Beach* (New York: Ballantine Books, 1957), 239.

11. Campton, *Laughter and Fear: Nine One-Act Plays* (London: Blackie, 1969), 32, 231.

12. Gene A. Plunka reports that this play, performed on BBC television in November 1957 and on CBS in January 1958, is no longer available because the tapes have been erased (*Peter Shaffer: Roles, Rites, and Rituals in the Theater* [Rutherford, NJ: Fairleigh Dickinson University Press, 1988], 67). The unsigned review in the London *Times* (November 22, 1957, 8) deplores "the entertainment industry cashing in on current affairs" through a play that involves "a gross distortion of Anglo-Russian relations. . . . 90 minutes' suspense is being purchased at too high a price."

13. "People Kill People," in *Voices from the Crowd: Against the H-Bomb*, edited by David Boulton (Philadelphia: Dufour, 1964), 181.

14. Frank Parkin, *Middle Class Radicalism: The Social Bases of the British Campaign for Nuclear Disarmament* (New York: Praeger, 1968), 100. I have gleaned the names largely from Christopher Driver, *The Disarmers: A Study in Protest* (London: Hodder and Stoughton, 1964), which includes a chapter on the dramas of protest ("Art in a Cold Climate," 217–27). For larger contexts applied to British literature and theatre, see Alan Sinfield, *Literature, Politics and Culture in Postwar Britain* (Oxford: Basil Blackwell, 1989), 238–41: "CND and a New-Left Intelligentsia," and Stephen Lacey, *British Realist Theatre: The New Wave in Its Context 1956–1965* (London: Routledge, 1995), 32–39: "Contesting Hegemony: Theatre and Anti-Consensual Politics."

15. I am relying on the unsigned review in the London *Times*, March 11, 1958, 3, which calls the drama "a straightforward attempt to sway public opinion on the use of nuclear weapons." The use of a tribunal to convict a "lethargic Everyman" of passive complicity in a nuclear holocaust, with witnesses for the prosecution drawn from the people whom one would normally blame (here, a pilot, commanding officer, and careless technician who triggered the attack), directly anticipates a long sequence in a minor comic masterpiece of nuclear fiction, James Morrow's *This Is the Way the World Ends* (New York: Henry Holt, 1986).

16. "The Small Personal Voice," in *Declaration*, edited by Tom Maschler (London: MacGibbon and Kee, 1957), reprinted in her *A Small Personal Voice: Essays, Reviews, Interviews*, edited by Paul Schlueter (New York: Knopf, 1974), 7, 10.

17. "Britain and the Nuclear Bomb," 555.

18. Letter of July 4, 1959, *The Letters of Sean O'Casey*, 4 vols., edited by David Krause (vols. I and II: New York: Macmillan, 1975–80; vols. III and IV: Washington, DC: Catholic University of America Press, 1989–92), IV, 56.

19. Letter of April 17, 1961, *Letters*, IV, 214–15.

20. Letter of February 5, 1955, *Letters*, III, 588.

21. Letter of July 1, 1963, *Letters*, IV, 422.

22. *As Much as I Dare*, 506.

23. *The Wesker Trilogy: Chicken Soup with Barley; Roots; I'm Talking About Jerusalem* (Baltimore: Penguin Books, 1964 [c. 1960]). The other two plays refer briefly to atom bombs; see pp. 62, 214.

24. *Almost a Gentleman: An Autobiography. Volume II: 1955–1966* (London: Faber and Faber, 1991), 149.

25. Osborne voiced extreme indignation over Britain's first hydrogen bomb explosion, with added venom for the government misleading everyone about the timing to forestall protest, in "They Call It Cricket," in *Declaration*, edited by Tom Maschler (London: MacGibbon and Kee, 1957), 63–84. In contrast, his 1959 play *The World of Paul Slickey* makes five incidental references to the nuclear situation, each in a context of fun or light satire. Back to normal, he manifested his bent for slashing invective in response to the Berlin crisis of August 1961 when he published a "letter of hate" to "those men of my country who have defiled it. The men with manic fingers leading the sightless, feeble, betrayed body of my country to its death. . . . Till then, damn you England. You're rotting now, and quite soon you'll disappear" ("A Letter to My Fellow Countrymen," reprinted in his *Damn You, England: Collected Prose* [London: Faber and Faber, 1994], 193).

26. First printed in *New English Dramatists* [I], edited by E. Martin Browne (Harmondsworth: Penguin Books, 1959), 11–95; I have cited the recent reprint in Lessing, *Play with a Tiger and Other Plays* (London: Flamingo, 1996), 101–86. First performed on March 23, 1958, as one of the Sunday Night performances of the Royal Court Theatre. Lessing recalls that she received a virtual promise of a run at the Court from Tony Richardson, but after he left for America others who considered it "unfashionable not only in subject but also in form" decided against one (*Walking in the Shade*, 226).

27. Review entitled "The Do-Gooders," *New Statesman*, 55 (March 29, 1958): 405.

28. Perhaps overreacting to the latest in literary fads, both Worsley in *New Statesman* and Alan Brien in *Spectator*, 200 (March 28, 1958): 389, jumped to the conclusion that Tony is portrayed as an "angry young man." Brien complains that he is "too obviously a catalogue of mannerisms and postures chosen from the works of Osborne, Amis and Braine"; Worsley calls him "another specimen of the furiously articulate young men of today," adding that his attack on do-gooders, "carried out with a virtuoso brilliance, cannot have left many left-wing withers unwrung." But Worsley himself shows that Tony is no Jimmy Porter by saying that what he wants is "a private life that can be led with a little quiet and dignity." Lessing views the phenomenon of the angry young man critically in her autobiography (*Walking in the Shade*, 228–35), and says that the play evolved from her disdain for "languid" youths who have "no time for politics," especially those who harass their activist mothers (225–26).

29. The play's critical reception was generally favorable. Worsley heralded it as "the most exciting new play to turn up in London since *Look Back in Anger*"; Brien called it "a bawdy, brawling, confused eavesdropping of a play" (which does graphically convey its texture). The London *Times* critic damned with faint praise, concluding that the main characters "are so clear-sighted, rational, and articulate . . . that the lack of any development in the situation baffles us and destroys our belief in the thing itself" (*Times*, March 24, 1958, 3).

30. Published in his *Three Plays* (London: Heinemann, 1963), 209–307; first presented in London at the Queen's Theatre on August 24, 1960, eight weeks after the debut of his best-known play, *A Man for All Seasons*.

31. The play later implies that Bolt is thinking of *unilateral* disarmament; it is

directed at the Prime Minister (Harold Macmillan at the time). Bolt quite cogently argued the case for unilateral nuclear disarmament in "Do You Speak Nuclear?," *New Statesman*, 60 (December 24, 1960): 1000–1001.

32. They are by no means latter-day versions of Wilde's earnest Jack and frivolous Gwendolen.

33. Patton is quoted in Helen Caldicott, *Missile Envy: The Arms Race and Nuclear War* (New York: Bantam Books, 1984), 321.

34. The finale of Arthur Kopit's *End of the World* (1984) makes the most conspicuous use of the concept.

35. Jeremy Brooks puts it gracefully in his review of the play: Gwen's despair at Jack's avoidance of commitment "drives her to a seeming-mad act of destruction in order to draw him into her orbit of feeling" (*New Statesman*, 60 [September 3, 1960]: 304).

36. In a 1961 interview with Tom Milne and Clive Goodwin (reprinted in *Theatre at Work: Playwrights and Productions in the Modern British Theatre* [New York: Hill and Wang, 1967], 63), Bolt says that the subject of nuclear weapons is "absolutely central" to the view of life reflected in *The Tiger and the Horse* and his 1955 radio play *The Last of the Wine*: "the atomic bomb, . . . quite apart from its overriding importance in itself, . . . willy-nilly drives home the fact that the individual and his society are of equal importance, and cannot sensibly be considered apart from each other."

37. "Second Interview" in Ronald Hayman, *Robert Bolt* (London: Heinemann, 1969), 79.

38. Gene A. Barnett, in "The Theatre of Robert Bolt," *Dalhousie Review*, 48 (Spring 1968): 19, says that "This climactic act of commitment . . . shows the rebirth of selfhood in Jack Dean. Further, since he is more realistic and intelligent than the others, he insists, though signing the petition, that in spite of every hindrance, the bomb will be put to use." I am inclined to think, with Jeremy Brooks in his *New Statesman* review, that "intellectually" this turn of plot "can just be made to hold water. Emotionally, it cannot" (304).

39. Bolt's 1955 radio play *The Last of the Wine* uses the threat of a hydrogen bomb attack on London to display a wide range of responses among a close-knit group, including a grandmother who can accept death because her generation knew the joy of living, "the last of the wine." The plot focuses on a young woman involved in two trying relationships who welcomes destruction and waits to see which man loves her enough to face annihilation with her; while waiting, an unidentified aircraft approaching London is reported. See the London *Times* reviews of December 13, 1955, 5, and February 8, 1960, 13. *The Last of the Wine* was broadcast in December 1955 and again in February 1960. A stage adaptation was presented at the Theatre in the Round, London, in 1956; I find no evidence that it was published.

40. Printed in *The Generations: A Trilogy of Plays* (London: John Calder, 1964), 84–157; performed on BBC television on June 22, 1962.

41. For the latter event, Mercer used a BBC newsreel film of a Committee of 100 demonstration, including a striking excerpt from a Bertrand Russell address. The play makes it clear that protesters are not jailed simply because they "obstruct thoroughfares" by sitting down; if Colin had consented to being "bound over to keep the peace for one year," he would not have gone to jail (85–86).

42. *The Birth of a Private Man*, in *The Generations*, 224–25. This play was presented on BBC television on February 1, 1963. Frieda's humanism manifests itself early in *A Climate of Fear* when she tells Frances, "I can assure you having no political beliefs is an absolutely painless sacrifice. I keep my respect for people who are human beings first and idealists second" (92). She presumably comes to feel that her children fill this bill, and are thus worthy of more respect than her husband gives them.

43. Colin evolves into a state of disillusionment with all reform movements and total despair over the nuclear situation. Like Myra in Lessing's play and Gwen in Bolt's, he has moments when he feels he is "always waiting for that last hemisphere of blinding light" (226).

44. By far the fullest study of *The Generations* is Don Taylor's "David Mercer and Television Drama," appended to the volume on pp. 236–82.

45. Harmondsworth: Penguin Books, 1960.

46. *The World Is a Wedding* (New York: Coward-McCann, 1963), 199.

47. Critics' reactions to the play have been mixed, with the negatives largely directed at Kops's problematic articulation of his general but qualified *carpe diem* theme. John Russell Taylor says that "unfortunately the 'philosophy' weighs a little heavy on the piece and the author does not seem to have quite the intellectual flexibility necessary to put over such a bald message about human values without making his drama naïve in the least acceptable sense" (*Anger and After: A Guide to the New British Drama*, 2nd ed. [London: Methuen, 1969], 176). Benedict Nightingale comments acutely that "The Bomb is . . . simplistically seen as the last throw of a society already destroying itself in numerous small ways," and adds that the play "suffers at times from Kops's weakness for emotional exaggeration and dramatic overstatement" (*Contemporary Dramatists*, 446–47). Philip Klass notes that "East End barrel-thumping does not mix at all well with philosophy" in the play, but concedes that "there is much power in several scenes," especially those that feature "material dealing with life in the kinds of streets in which [Kops] grew up" ("Bernard Kops," in *British Dramatists Since World War II*, edited by Stanley Weintraub [Detroit: Gale Research, 1982], 281). See also the unsigned review in the London *Times*, September 6, 1960, 13, and Alan Brien's brief diatribe in *Spectator*, 205 (September 9, 1960): 372.

48. From an interview with Michael Bath: " 'Why Do You Write Plays, Mr. Campton?' " in *New Theatre Magazine*, 10, iii (1970): 19. Four of Ionesco's early plays were produced in London from November 1956 to June 1958. English translations became readily available from 1958 on.

49. John Russell Taylor, in *Anger and After*, differentiates Campton's "comedies of menace" from the absurdist ones of Pinter on the basis that in Pinter's "the menace is the more pervasive and potent precisely because it is undefined," while in Campton's "the menace is clear enough: it is the Bomb" (184). Michael Anderson makes another distinction in his entry on Campton in *Crowell's Handbook of Contemporary Drama* (New York: Crowell, 1971): the political and intellectual content of the nuclear-age plays "reveals itself as humane and commendable," but "lacking in the darker and deeper exploration of the human psyche characteristic of other writers in the school of the absurd" (82). Largely echoing Taylor, Arnold P. Hinchliffe in *British Theatre 1950–70* (Oxford: Basil Blackwell, 1974) generalizes that unlike Absurd dramatists, "Campton has a prominent social conscience" (125).

50. In "Personal Progress," an essay appended to his *Laughter and Fear: Nine One-Act Plays* (London: Blackie, 1969), Campton says that his early works "may be absurd plays, but they have a positive outlook." He also states that they "are not naturalistic, but they do not express that chaos which is essential to The Absurd" (233). Curiously, two or three years after making the latter statement, he explains the generic title of his collection by declaring (with echoes of Friedrich Dürrenmatt as well as Beckett): "It seems to me that the chaos affecting everyone today—political, technical, sociological, religious, etc. etc.—is so all-pervading that it cannot be ignored, yet so shattering that it can only be approached through comedy. Tragedy demands firm foundations: today we are dancing among the ruins" (printed in *Contemporary Dramatists*, 134).

51. I have used the text in *Laughter and Fear*, 29–44. The playlet was originally performed in 1957 as the fourth part of a Campton production entitled *The Lunatic View*.

52. Taylor in *Anger and After*, perhaps relying upon a flawed performance rather than the text, seriously errs when he states that in the end the two "decide to make together a gesture in favour of life, whatever it may cost, and as the curtain falls they take off the bags" (183).

53. Letter of December 16, 1997 to the author.

54. Webster's unabridged dictionary defines the adjective "heterodyne" in a manner reminiscent of Ionesco's *The Lesson*: "having to do with the combination of radio oscillations of somewhat different frequencies coupled in such a way as to produce beats whose frequency is the difference or sum of the frequencies of the combined oscillations."

55. In 1951 Sean O'Casey jeered at the idea that brown paper can act as a shield against atomic flash (*The Letters of Sean O'Casey*, II, 776–77), which suggests that the recommendation was current then. In the segment "Civil War" of the 1961 theatrical satire *Beyond the Fringe* with Alan Bennett, Peter Cook, Jonathan Miller, and Dudley Moore (New York: Random House, 1963), Peter Cook says (ironically), "there is a lot you can do about radiation as soon as the dust has settled—jump into a brown paper bag. Draw it on rather like a shroud [cf. Kops' *The Dream of Peter Mann*]. . . . You can do anything you want to inside your bag! So there you have it. The bomb drops, the dust settles, jump into your brown paper bag, and hop along to your local civil defense leader" (54–55). Campton recalls reading a government leaflet "issued at the beginning of World War II recommending brown paper bags as a shield against blast" (letter to the author).

56. When the Smiths first sit down with the Martins to talk in *The Bald Prima Donna* (*The Bald Soprano* in the American translation), silences, hesitations, and the attentive striking of a clock punctuate the awkward conversation. A sample:

MR SMITH: Oh dear, oh dear, oh dear! [*Silence.*]

MR MARTIN: Is there anything wrong? [*Silence.*]

MRS SMITH: He can't control himself when he's bored stiff. [*Silence.*]

MRS MARTIN: Oh really, Sir, you shouldn't at your age. [*Silence.*]

MR SMITH: Age doesn't count where the heart's concerned. [*Silence.*]

MR MARTIN: Is that true? [*Silence.*]

MRS SMITH: That's what they say. [*Silence.*]

MRS MARTIN: They say the contrary's true, too. [*Silence.*]

MR SMITH: The truth lies between the two. [*Silence.*]

MR MARTIN: That's true, too. [*Silence.*]

(Ionesco, *Plays, Volume I*: The Lesson; The Chairs; The Bald Prima Donna; Jacques or Obedience, translated by Donald Watson [London: John Calder, 1958], 98.)

57. Printed in *Little Brother: Little Sister; Out of the Flying Pan* (London: Methuen, 1966), 47–61. The tiny play was originally performed on February 1, 1960, as part of a Campton production entitled *A View from the Brink*.

58. The most notable examples occur at the end of the Smiths' discussion of the Bobby Watson clan (90–91), after the Martins' "discovery" scene (when the maid refutes the Martins' deductive reasoning [96–97]), and when the Fire-Chief sparks horrified silence by mentioning the bald prima donna (115).

59. Ionesco called the play a "tragedy of language" because his faithful transcription of conventional English statements transformed the words surrealistically into "sounding shells devoid of meaning" and "emptied" the characters of "psychology" ("The Tragedy of Language," in his *Notes and Counter Notes: Writings on the Theatre* [New York: Grove Press, 1964], 179).

60. In *Laughter and Fear*, 155–77. The play was published under Campton's own imprint in 1960, and was first performed in that year.

61. Campton comments, "If I had thought more precisely when writing *Mutatis*, I would have taken care to indicate that the rockets were merely signs of the times and not in themselves responsible for the mutations" (letter to the author).

62. Campton says of *Mutatis Mutandis* that he "wanted to write a play that had, if not a happy, at least a hopeful ending," and explains that the ending "was meant to suggest that the future may be terrifying, but it is still in our hands" ("Personal Progress," 232–33).

63. The long one-act was first published under Campton's imprint in 1960 and first performed on January 31, 1961. I have used the 1966 text, cited above, that includes *Out of the Flying Pan*.

64. *Endgame: A Play in One Act* . . . (New York: Grove Press, 1958), 26, 57.

65. Christopher Driver in *The Disarmers* sums up cogently: "Campton has contributed in purely theatrical terms a parable of freedom, authority, and sanctions" (227). He goes on to speculate on the play's possible implication that our world "is like a shelterful of childish or adolescent nation-states, kept in control only by the fact of the meat-cleaver in the hands of the super-powers." It seems to me that if a political analogy is to be drawn, it would view the meat-cleaver as the same kind of paradoxical deterrent as nuclear weapons: Cook kills people in order to save them. As she tells the children, "Thank your lucky stars you've got a Cook. She'll keep you from savagery if she 'as to mince you first" (15).

CHAPTER 7

1. Dean Brelis, *Run, Dig or Stay? A Search for an Answer to the Shelter Question* (Boston: Beacon Press, 1962), 67.

2. This became more and more obvious through the years as nuclear arsenals

grew in potency. It is not surprising that government agencies and businesses promoting shelters gradually dropped the term "bomb shelter" and replaced it with "fallout shelter"—tacit acknowledgement that shelters could offer little protection against anything but secondary radiation effects.

3. *Time*, 78 (August 11, 1961), 58.

4. L. C. McHugh, "Ethics at the Shelter Doorway," *America*, 105 (September 30, 1961): 826. I hasten to add that the "partial code of essential shelter morality" that McHugh offers is broadminded and thoughtful.

5. Sidney Kraus, Reuben Mehling, and Elaine El-Assal, "Mass Media and the Fallout Controversy," *Public Opinion Quarterly*, 27 (1963): 197, 199.

6. *Nuclear Fear: A History of Images* (Cambridge: Harvard University Press, 1988), 256.

7. *Triumph* (Garden City, NY: Doubleday, 1963), 95.

8. In Hughes, *Simple's Uncle Sam* (New York: Hill and Wang, 1965), 36.

9. Printed in *A Variety of Short Plays*, edited by John C. Schweitzer (New York: Scribner's, 1966), 410–38.

10. Gordon F. Sander, *Serling: The Rise and Twilight of Television's Last Angry Man* (New York: Dutton, 1992), 181. Nuclear paranoia also figures in another episode of the early 1960s, *One More Pallbearer*. To gain revenge for humiliations, a man carries out an elaborate plan which includes faking a nuclear holocaust (Sander, 181).

11. *Licence to Murder: A Play in Two Acts* (London: Samuel French, 1963). The play, Morgan's first, had its debut on March 26, 1963 at the Vaudeville Theatre, London. Since the text was published in England, it uses English spellings of such terms as "licence," "defence," and "neighbour." I have used these variant forms only when quoting.

12. At one point in Act II, a friend of the prosecuting attorney tells him, "I'd say you've been watching too much Perry Mason!" (33)—which may apply to the playwright. Compressed, her play would have made an intelligent, suspense-filled episode of that popular series.

13. Morgan locates the action of the play "near the southeast coast" of America; the defense attorney notes the possibility that "long-range bombing planes" might come from Cuba (25). Her choice of late 1960 for the central event is therefore curious. Castro had taken power in Cuba a year before this, but the Bay of Pigs invasion did not occur until a half-year later. Since she presumably wrote the play after the Cuban missile crisis in late 1962, she may be "borrowing" the anxiety of later events to enhance the interest of the plot.

14. Civil Defense had advised against locking shelters from the inside so that rescue teams could gain access to them after an attack (6). Brad later notes that he assumed Doug thought the Fosters were still away so that their shelter would be empty. It is somewhat appalling to note that the London *Times* reviewer, in a generally vacuous squib, gathered that Brad claimed he mistook Doug for "a contaminated intruder from a nuclear explosion" (*Times* [March 27, 1963], 15).

15. New York: Grove Press, 1958.

16. By a consultant to the National Security Resources Board, Richard Gerstell (New York: Bantam Books, 1950), 36, 38.

17. "Radioactive Red Caps," in his *The Best of Simple* (New York: Hill and Wang, 1961), 210–13. Simple worries that he might be "Jim Crowed out of bomb

shelters," but the narrator assures him that white folks wouldn't let that happen: "Just suppose all the Negroes down South got atomized, charged up like hot garbage, who would serve the white folks' tables, nurse their children, Red Cap their bags, and make up their Pullman berths?" (211).

18. Estelle Manette Thaler describes the absence of a limited frame of reference as follows: "*Endgame* deliberately de-emphasizes the specificity that usually characterizes apocalypticism, so that the general deterioration may exist anywhere at any time" ("Apocalyptic Vision in *Heartbreak House* and *Endgame*: The Metaphor of Change," *Zeitschrift für Anglistik und Amerikanistik*, 34 [1986]: 347). James E. Robinson stresses the multiplicity of reference, calling *Endgame* "Beckett's most intricate exercise in presenting figurations of an eschatology of infinity" ("Samuel Beckett's Doomsday Play: The Space of Infinity," in *Theatrical Space*, Themes in Drama, 9 [Cambridge: Cambridge University Press, 1987], 218). Theodor W. Adorno's well-known 1961 essay on the play acknowledges its postwar context, but credits Beckett for avoiding the implicit "mockery of itself" that any "alleged drama of the atomic age" would constitute, "solely because its plot would comfortingly falsify the historical horror of anonymity by displacing it into human characters and actions" ("Trying to Understand *Endgame*," translated by Shierry Weber Nicholsen in Adorno, *Notes to Literature, Volume One* [New York: Columbia University Press, 1991], 245). Jonathan Kalb sums up Adorno's general point as follows: "*Endgame*, in other words, is not about life after nuclear holocaust, which neither Beckett nor anyone else could possibly depict; it is about *our* lives, which are lived under the threat of disaster, nuclear and otherwise" (*Beckett in Performance* [Cambridge: Cambridge University Press, 1989], 81).

19. "Refuge" replaces "shelter" in the English edition. The two terms seem to have been interchangeable in England as shorthand for bomb shelter or fallout shelter. For example, in the popular English comic book/play/film "When the Wind Blows" by Raymond Briggs (I quote from the 1986 book published by Penguin), James Bloggs tells his wife, "We'd better commence the construction of the Fall Out Shelter immediately," and he reads in a County Council pamphlet about how to build an "Inner Core or Refuge" (2, 3).

20. Dougald McMillan and Martha Fehsenfeld, *Beckett in the Theatre: The Author as Practical Playwright and Director, Volume 1: From* Waiting for Godot *to* Krapp's Last Tape (London: John Calder, 1988), 204. Cited hereafter as "McMillan."

21. See Kalb, *Beckett in Performance*, 81. Jack MacGowran claims that Beckett would never discuss what has caused the devastation, and adds, "It's some vision. . . . The seeds of *Endgame* were in fact in Lucky's speech . . . referring to the return of the world to its former state of a ball of fire, or the glacial age" (McMillan, 174). The only image in Lucky's speech that might be construed as a nuclear explosion is one of people "plunged in fire whose fire flames if that continues and who can doubt it will fire the firmament that is to say blast hell to heaven . . ." (*Waiting for Godot: Tragicomedy in 2 Acts* [New York: Grove Press, 1954], 28b).

22. For the 1967 Schiller-Theater production in Berlin, Beckett cut this passage. Michael Haerdter stated (inaccurately) in his notebook, "With this cut vanishes the last allusion to Clov's ever having left the shelter, ever being able to leave it" (McMillan, 232).

23. It is possible to interpret Hamm's ensuing line—"It's the end, Clov, we've

come to the end. I don't need you any more" (79)—as implying a decision to replace Clov with the boy. Clov was a satisfactory servant until recent years (or days); the child might restart the cycle.

24. Alan Astro is the only critic I have noticed who goes as far as to say that *Endgame* "shows us a day in the lives of the last survivors of a giant catastrophe, presumably a nuclear war"; even he later admits, "We never learn the exact nature of the catastrophe" (*Understanding Samuel Beckett* [Columbia: University of South Carolina Press, 1990], 131, 133). If Roy Walker is right, among early reviewers of the play "only J. W. Lambert [London *Times*] mentioned nuclear fission as the nucleus of Beckett's characters" ("Love, Chess and Death," *Twentieth Century*, 164 [1958], 542).

25. The Grove Press edition has "ane*n*ometer," an obvious misprint.

26. On playing the role of Hamm after consulting with Beckett, Patrick Magee said in an interview: "Hamm's assurance is a front. He's a jelly underneath all that" (McMillan, 178).

27. The French version is "Oh je l'ai mis devant ses responsabilités."

28. Hamm may have taken in Clov's father and kept him until he died; there is no evidence pro or con. S. E. Gontarski records that Beckett, when contemplating the French two-act version, wrote a note which "suggests that [Hamm's] father and son are adopted; that is, Nagg too may have been someone taken into the shelter as a servant: 'A un père adoptif / un fils adoptif' " (*The Intent of Undoing in Samuel Beckett's Dramatic Texts* [Bloomington: Indiana University Press, 1985], 52). The only way of reconciling this idea with the play as it stands is to twist it to mean that Hamm adopted a son and *Clov* a father.

29. The Grove Press edition omits the question mark, which appears in the French version.

30. *The Theatrical Notebooks of Samuel Beckett, Volume II*: Endgame, *with a Revised Text*, edited by S. E. Gontarski (New York: Grove Press, 1992), 61.

31. In a 1964 performance that Beckett directed, Jack MacGowran played Clov "as if Clov was the person who was brought there by the man, so that the story is not really fiction at all. It's a retelling of those early years, which Clov may or may not remember because he has been there so long" (McMillan, 174).

32. Mercier adds: "What makes it unique is that it never mentions these agents of devastation" (*Beckett/Beckett* [New York: Oxford University Press, 1977], 174.

Selective Bibliography of Background Works

Agar, Herbert. *The Unquiet Years: U.S.A. 1945–1955*. London: Rupert Hart-Davis, 1957.

The Atomic Age Opens. Ed. Gerald Wendt and Donald Porter Geddes. Cleveland: World, 1945.

The Atomic Age: Scientists in National and World Affairs. Ed. Martin Grodzins and Eugene Rabinowitch. New York: Basic Books, 1963.

Baylis, John. *Ambiguity and Deterrence: British Nuclear Strategy, 1945–1964*. Oxford: Clarendon Press, 1995.

Bottome, Edgar. *The Balance of Terror: Nuclear Weapons and the Illusion of Security, 1945–1985*. Rev. and updated ed. Boston: Beacon Press, 1986.

Boyer, Paul. *By the Bomb's Early Light: American Thought and Culture at the Dawn of the Atomic Age*. New York: Pantheon Books, 1985.

Brelis, Dean. *Run, Dig or Stay? A Search for an Answer to the Shelter Question*. Boston: Beacon Press, 1962.

Brians, Paul. *Nuclear Holocausts: Atomic War in Fiction, 1895–1984*. Kent, OH: Kent State University Press, 1987.

Buján, Carlos. *La figura del físico atómico en el teatro alemán contemporáneo: la responsabilidad del científico como tema literario*. Salamanca: Ediciones Universidad de Salamanca, 1979.

Bulletin of the Atomic Scientists, 1–20 (1945–1964).

Caute, David. *The Great Fear: The Anti-Communist Purge Under Truman and Eisenhower*. New York: Simon and Schuster, 1978.

Contemporary Dramatists. Ed. James Vinson. London: St. James, 1973.

Cousins, Norman. *Modern Man Is Obsolete*. New York: Viking Press, 1945.

Declaration. Ed. Tom Maschler. London: MacGibbon and Kee, 1957.

Divine, Robert A. *Blowing on the Wind: The Nuclear Test Ban Debate 1954–1960.* New York: Oxford University Press, 1978.

Dowling, David. *Fictions of Nuclear Disaster.* Iowa City: University of Iowa Press, 1987.

Driver, Christopher. *The Disarmers: A Study in Protest.* London: Hodder and Stoughton, 1964.

Fuller, Helen. *Year of Trial: Kennedy's Crucial Decisions.* New York: Harcourt, Brace & World, 1962.

Garthoff, Raymond L. *Reflections on the Cuban Missile Crisis.* Rev. ed. Washington: Brookings Institution, 1989.

Gowing, Margaret, assisted by Lorna Arnold. *Independence and Deterrence: Britain and Atomic Energy, 1945–1952.* 2 vols. New York: St. Martin's Press, 1974.

Hostetter, Robert. "The American Nuclear Theatre, 1946–1984." Diss., Northwestern University, 1985.

Lacey, Stephen. *British Realist Theatre: The New Wave in Its Context 1956–1965.* London: Routledge, 1995.

Lifton, Robert Jay. *Death in Life: Survivors of Hiroshima.* New York: Random House, 1967.

Lifton, Robert Jay, and Greg Mitchell. *Hiroshima in America: Fifty Years of Denial.* New York: G. P. Putnam's, 1995.

May, Elaine Tyler. *Homeward Bound: American Families in the Cold War Era.* New York: Basic Books, 1988.

Mazuzan, George T., and J. Samuel Walker. *Controlling the Atom: The Beginnings of Nuclear Regulation 1946–1962.* Berkeley: University of California Press, 1984.

McNamara, Robert S. *Blundering into Disaster: Surviving the First Century of the Nuclear Age.* New York: Pantheon Books, 1987.

Miller, Richard L. *Under the Cloud: The Decades of Nuclear Testing.* New York: Free Press, 1986.

Moss, Norman. *Men Who Play God: The Story of the Hydrogen Bomb.* Rev. ed. Harmondsworth: Penguin Books, 1972.

Oakes, Guy. *The Imaginary War: Civil Defense and American Cold War Culture.* New York: Oxford University Press, 1994.

One World or None: A Report to the Public on the Full Meaning of the Atomic Bomb. Ed. Dexter Masters and Katharine Way. New York: McGraw-Hill, 1946.

Parrish, Thomas. *The Cold War Encyclopedia.* New York: Holt, 1996.

Paterson, Robert H. *Britain's Strategic Nuclear Deterrent: From Before the V-Bomber to Beyond Trident.* London: Frank Cass, 1997.

Rhodes, Richard. *Dark Sun: The Making of the Hydrogen Bomb.* New York: Simon and Schuster, 1995.

Scharine, Richard G. *From Class to Caste in American Drama: Political and Social Themes Since the 1930s.* New York: Greenwood, 1991.

Sherwin, Martin J. *A World Destroyed: Hiroshima and the Origins of the Arms Race. With a New Introduction by the Author.* New York: Vintage Books, 1987 [c. 1975].

Sinclair, Andrew. *War Like a Wasp: The Lost Decade of the 'Forties*. London: Hamish Hamilton, 1989.

Taylor, John Russell. *Anger and After: A Guide to the New British Drama*. 2nd ed. London: Methuen, 1969.

Taylor, R.K.S. *Against the Bomb: The British Peace Movement, 1958–1965*. Oxford: Clarendon Press, 1988.

Titus, A. Constandina. *Bombs in the Backyard: Atomic Testing and American Politics*. Reno: University of Nevada Press, 1986.

Ungar, Sheldon. *The Rise and Fall of Nuclearism: Fear and Faith as Determinants of the Arms Race*. University Park: Pennsylvania State University Press, 1992.

Weart, Spencer R. *Nuclear Fear: A History of Images*. Cambridge: Harvard University Press, 1988.

Weisberger, Bernard A. *Cold War, Cold Peace: The United States and Russia Since 1945*. New York: American Heritage, 1984.

Wenger, Andreas. *Living with Peril: Eisenhower, Kennedy, and Nuclear Weapons*. Lanham, MD: Rowman and Littlefield, 1997.

Willingham, Ralph. *Science Fiction and the Theatre*. Westport, CT: Greenwood, 1994.

Winkler, Allan M. *Life Under a Cloud: American Anxiety About the Atom*. New York: Oxford University Press, 1993.

Wittner, Lawrence S. *Rebels Against War: The American Peace Movement, 1933–1983*. Philadelphia: Temple University Press, 1984.

Wyden, Peter. *Day One: Before Hiroshima and After*. New York: Simon and Schuster, 1984.

Zuckerman, Solly. *Monkeys, Men, and Missiles: An Autobiography 1946–88*. New York: Norton, 1988.

Index

About the Author

CHARLES A. CARPENTER is Professor Emeritus of English at Binghamton University. He has published a book on Shaw's early plays and has contributed many articles to scholarly journals. His works include the two-volume work *Modern Drama Scholarship and Criticism 1966–1990: An International Bibliography.*